Organized Labor in
Postcommunist States

Pitt Series in Russian and East European Studies

Jonathan Harris, Editor

Organized Labor in Postcommunist States

FROM SOLIDARITY TO INFIRMITY

Paul J. Kubicek

UNIVERSITY OF PITTSBURGH PRESS

Published by the University of Pittsburgh Press, Pittsburgh, Pa. 15260
Copyright © 2004, University of Pittsburgh Press
Manufactured in the United States of America
Printed on acid-free paper
10 9 8 7 6 5 4 3 2 1

Library of Congress Cataloging-in-Publication Data
Kubicek, Paul.
  Organized labor in postcommunist states : from solidarity to infirmity / Paul J. Kubicek.
    p. cm. — (Pitt series in Russian and East European studies)
  Includes bibliographical references and index.
  ISBN 0-8229-5856-2 (pbk. : alk. paper)
  1. Labor unions—Europe, Eastern—Case studies. 2. Post-communism—Europe,
Eastern—Case studies. I. Title. II. Series.
  HD6660.7.K8 2004
  331.88'0947—dc22

                                              2004013596

CONTENTS

TABLES

PREFACE

Civil society is one of the primary terms invoked in discussions of democratization and postcommunist transformation. The ever expanding literature on civil society rests upon a number of assumptions, including the notion that the demise of communism meant a rebirth of civil society and that, in turn, civil society would be instrumental in creating democratic polities in postcommunist states. While these claims may be valid in some circumstances, they do not hold up that well when applied to trade unions, which are the largest organizations in civil society in all postcommunist states. Not only have unions not experienced a rebirth—on the contrary, they have seen a drop in membership—but they have been largely unable to create for themselves a pronounced political role to allow them to shape the postcommunist transformation. It is this disjuncture between what might loosely be called a "theory" of civil society and the reality of organized labor that was the impetus for this work.

As my work progressed, however, I became more interested in how organized labor is being shaped by the reform processes in the region. In other words, rather than viewing these actors in civil society as "independent variables" affecting the course of transition, my concern is how the transition itself is affecting them. The answer, in short, is that structural economic changes, including privatization and nascent globalization, have largely weakened unions in the region, just as they have also undermined the position of unions in a number of Western countries.

This work, however, would not have been possible without the assistance of numerous individuals. The first words of thanks must go to the numerous Polish, Russian, Ukrainian, and Hungarian trade unionists and scholars who were willing to take time out of their schedules to assist me. I know that many remained uncertain or even dubious about what I was planning to do with my information, but they indulged my curiosity with their experiences and impressions. I hope that I have faithfully represented their positions. Many of these individuals are mentioned by name in the notes section, but I would like to give special thanks to those activists, academics, and activists/academics who provided me with special assistance in my travels in the region. This list includes Laszlo Neumann, Sven Sterner, Vadim Borisov, Irene Stevenson, Vasyl Kostrytsia, Juliusz Gardawski, Wlodzimierz Pankow, David Ost, and Ardrii Mrost. Anna Wilanowski provided research assistance and help with some of the Polish language sources. I must also thank the reviewers for University of Pittsburgh Press, whose comments, I hope, resulted in a much stronger work. Nathan MacBrien of the Press worked closely with me through the publication process. By keeping me informed of how work on his end was progressing and offering assistance on where to focus my editing efforts, he made the usual lengthy and occasionally trying review process run quite smoothly. For that I am most grateful. Of course, these helpful souls are not responsible for my interpretations and conclusions, with which many might disagree.

I should also acknowledge some of my own guiding principles and biases that creep into this work. I sympathize with the industrial workers and trade union activists attempting to defend workers' positions in the postcommunist environment. I imagine that most who study this topic feel the same way, as one would be less likely to study a group that one thinks is hopelessly retrograde or a barrier to positive economic and political change. Without debating all the merits of the transition to capitalism in this region, there is little doubt that certain groups rank as "losers" in this process. Chief among them are industrial workers, the heart of the trade union establishment and a group that was, rhetorically at least, celebrated under communism. In those days, glory was given to socialist labor, whereas today the "hero" is the businessman and the capitalist reformer. However, reformers such as Leszek Balcerowicz in Poland, Vaclav Klaus in the Czech Republic, and Anatolii Chubais in Russia, although often praised in the West, are reviled by large segments of the population in their own countries, and still worse words are reserved for the "oligarchs" or "new Poles" ("Czechs," "Bulgarians," "Ukrainians," any nationality can be used with this adjective in this way). Their stories are rather well known. Those of the workers, however, are not, barely creeping into both popular accounts and academic analyses. This work is an effort to fill an important gap in our thinking about postcommunist political change by both accounting for organized labor's weakness and making clear how the twin aims of democratization and marketization can conflict with each other in actual practice. Unfortunately, most of the time market orthodoxy has prevailed, and, to criticize the unions a bit, few have been able to come up with a credible alternative reform model.

I do hope that these biases do not undermine my analysis of the situation, and (without giving away the whole story) the reader who stays to the end will realize that this book is not a virulent anticapitalist tract. In part, this is so because unionists in the region themselves do not feel that way. The whole story is thus rather complex, rarely a matter of either/or and black/white. Few things are rejected wholesale. The task instead is to interpret shades of gray, look for nuance, and press for policies that can satisfy multiple demands. If this task is hard for an academic analyst, imagine what it must be for government officials and trade union activists in the region, who must cope with far greater difficulties than I.

Fortunately, one significant obstacle standing in my way while pursuing this study—money—was removed thanks to the generous help of several organizations who funded my research in Russia and Ukraine in 2001 and in Poland in 2002. Grants were provided by the International Research Exchange Board (IREX) with funds provided by the United States Department of State through the Title VIII Program and the National Endowment for the Humanities, The American Political Science Association Small Research Grant Award, American Councils for International Education Research Grant with funds through the Title VIII Program for Eastern Europe and the former Soviet Union, and Oakland University. Of course, their financial sponsorship in no way implicates them in my conclusions.

I should note as well that parts of my arguments and research have appeared in two previously published articles. An early version of my argument on the role of structural economic change—"Organized Labor in Postcommunist States: Will the Western Sun Set on It, Too?" —appeared in *Comparative Politics* (October 1999, pp. 83–102). Some of my arguments in chapter 5 and chapter 7 appeared as "Civil Society, Trade Unions and Post-Soviet Democratisation: Evidence from Russia and Ukraine," in *Europe-Asia Studies* (June 2002, pp. 603–24, accessible at www.tandf.co.uk/journals/carfax/09668136.html). I thank the publishers of both journals for permission to reprint some of my contentions here.

Following tradition, I put my thanks to my family in the last paragraph. By no means, however, should this be construed that their assistance—mainly in patience and understanding—was inconsequential. The years 2001–2002 brought us many blessings on the home front, and for a good stretch of time I was overseas working on this project instead of playing with Jonah and helping Alyce with all the work of having a little one in the house and another on the way. Thanks for giving me a long "leash" to pursue this work, and I hope to make it up in the future.

ABBREVIATIONS

ASZSZ	Federation of Autonomous Unions (Hungary)
AWS	Solidarity Electoral Action (Poland)
CBOS	Public Opinion Research Center (Warsaw)
CMKOS	Czech and Moravian Confederation of Trade Unions
EBRD	European Bank for Reconstruction and Development
ESZT	Academic Employees Union (Hungary)
ETUC	European Trade Union Confederation
EU	European Union
EWC	European Work Councils
FDI	foreign direct investment
FNPR	Federation of Independent Russian Trade Unions
FPU	Federation of Ukrainian Trade Unions
GAZ	Gorky Automotive Plant (Russia)
ICFTU	International Confederation of Free Trade Unions
IFI	international financial institution
ILO	International Labour Organization
ILO-CEET	International Labour Organisation Central and East European Team
IMF	International Monetary Fund
KAMAZ	Kamsky Automotive Plant (Russia)
KNSB	Confederation of Independent Bulgarian Trade Unions
KOR	Workers' Self-Defense Committee (Poland)
KOZ	Slovak Confederation of Trade Unions
KRP	Congress of Russian Trade Unions

KTR	Confederation of Labor of Russia
KVPU	Confederation of Ukrainian Free Trade Unions
LIGA	Democratic League of Independent Trade Unions
MDF	Hungarian Democratic Forum
MNC	multinational corporation
MOSZ	Hungarian Work Councils Association
MSZOSZ	National Confederation of Hungarian Trade Unions
NCRI	National Council for the Reconciliation of Interests (Hungary)
NPG	Independent Miners' Union (Soviet Union/Russia)
NPGU	Independent Miners' Union of Ukraine
OECD	Organization for Economic Cooperation and Development
OPZZ	All-Polish Trade Union Alliance
RSPP	Russian Union of Industrialists and Entrepreneurs
RTK	Russian Tripartite Commission
SLD	Democratic Left Alliance (Poland)
SPA	State Property Agency (Hungary)
SZDSZ	Alliance of Free Democrats (Hungary)
SZEF	Trade Union Cooperative Forum (Hungary)
SZOT	National Council of Trade Unions (Hungary)
UDF	Union of Democratic Forces (Bulgaria)
VKT	All-Russian Confederation of Labor
VOST	All-Ukrainian Union of Workers' Solidarity
VPU	Free Trade Unions of Ukraine
VTsSPS	All-Union Central Committee of Trade Unions (Soviet Union)

Organized Labor in
Postcommunist States

Civil Society, Trade Unions, and the Political Economy of Postcommunist Transformation

THE COLLAPSE OF COMMUNISM was marked in many ways, not the least of which was its ironic character. A system of rule ostensibly built on the Great Truth of Marxist-Leninist doctrine was openly exposed as politically and morally wanting. Nationalism, far from withering away as communists supposed, returned with a vengeance, helping to bring down communist states and emerging as a potent force in the postcommunist era. The progressive ideology of socialism also proved incapable of competing against its historically retrograde rival, and the socialist experiment is now derided as a long and painful detour from capitalism to capitalism.

The most poignant touch of irony, perhaps, was that workers living in communist "workers' paradises" organized themselves outside the confines of the party-state and played a prominent role in bringing about an end to communism. The workers' role was most obvious in Poland, but independent trade unions were players in the burgeoning, anticommunist civil society in all countries in the region. Workers allied themselves with political movements demanding change, and their activities had a great deal of political importance, revealing how the authorities had lost legitimacy even in the eyes of the one class in whose interest they purported to rule. For all the focus on the role of dissident intellectuals in the fall of communism, it was only when workers mobilized that all the contradictions and shortcomings of communism were fully exposed. Unable to address these issues and satisfy the demands from below, the regimes collapsed.

In most academic parlance, of course, the defeat of communism was not hailed as a triumph of the workers, but as a victory for "civil society," a term that has become a mantra for activists and academics alike.[1] Beyond this label, however, in the class and organizational structure of civil society, workers played a prominent, if not leading, role in many anticommunist movements. Workers, of course, made up the majority of the adult population in all Eastern European communist countries, and workers' associations, meaning both the communist-dominated and newer, "independent" trade unions, were by far the largest groups in civil society. Both of these groups survived the collapse of the party-state, and thus workers, it seemed, would have an immense organizational advantage over other groups in the fledgling civil societies in the region. Moreover, organized labor had a lot of economic muscle as well, and thus it seemed likely that organized labor would play a central role in both the political and economic transformation of formerly communist countries. Indeed, Adam Przeworski, theorizing about how governments could and should proceed with reforms in the immediate postcommunist period, put labor unions center stage, arguing that governments would have to either win their support or completely subdue them to push through marketizing reforms.[2]

Rosy (and alarmist) assessments of union power, however, turned out to be exaggerated, and in general unions have been paper tigers, lacking real claws and easily tamed by postcommunist governments.[3] Indeed, the postcommunist period has been remarkable for the lack of organized workers' activity, despite the fact that all states have witnessed a precipitous economic decline, real wages for workers have shrunk (and in many cases are not paid on time), and the communist-era social safety net has vanished. In states such as Russia and Ukraine, privatization has turned into a *prikhvatizatsiia* (grabbing) in which management has gobbled up state assets and left the workers with crumbs. A former Russian finance minister summed up the situation nicely: "You are witnessing the greatest plundering of the century, and perhaps in all human history; protests are not heard. People bow their heads and complain, as though things could not get worse; as if everything is as it should be."[4] This is not exclusively a post-Soviet phenomenon, or a result of a political victory by a rapacious new *nomenklatura*/oligarchy. As then–finance minister of Poland Leszek Balcerowicz confessed, Solidarity the union was run roughshod by Solidarity the government while "shock therapy" was pushed through as a means to strip workers of their power to distort markets and to empower employers against them.[5] Elsewhere, unions in the Czech Republic stood by while Vaclav Klaus promoted a Central European version of Thatcherism, Hungarian unions are still fractured and weak, and Bulgaria's once-influential *Podkrepa* union has been hamstrung trying to find a balance between competing claims of workers' rights and the economic reforms mandated by the IMF.

Throughout the region, unions have been unable to coalesce either as a political or an economic force. They have failed to obtain an effective voice in developing and shaping economic reforms, and they have been unable to use their muscle to push for the social-democratic, corporatist institutions and policies that they generally favor. If democratization and economic liberalization were expected to produce winners and losers, organized labor certainly would rank among the losers. For many, the victories of 1989–1991 have turned out to be hollow. Ironically, despite working in a democratic system, labor cannot find its voice and force politicians to take notice of its demands. David Ost and Stephen Crowley, the editors of the most comprehensive study of unions across the region, conclude that "Far from being recognized as guarantors of broad citizenship . . . they [trade unions] are more usually seen as relics of an obsolete past not really relevant for a capitalist future."[6]

Postcommunist trade unions are indeed, in Sherlock Holmes's phrase, "dogs that don't bark." The point, of course, is that by many measures they *should*, and thus labor quiescence is a mystery to be solved. This work will document labor's general weakness and offer explanations as to why this is the case. However, it is also important to consider whether this is a passing phase or something more permanent, and if the latter what the consequences will be in terms of democratic consolidation and economic performance. Many union leaders and some academic observers tend to assume that unions are "Sleeping Beauties," victimized by a temporary spell but able to reawake and rise to prominence again. At the same time, however, the basic political and economic playing field has been reshaped, and unions have had little role in writing the rules for the new game. In particular, property has been redistributed, new systems of industrial relations have been established, and the region's economies are being integrated into the global market. All of these changes could seriously compromise organized labor's ability to act as a powerful force, and thus whether and under what condition it will reemerge are interesting questions, both from the standpoint of "transitions theory," and concrete assessments and projections about individual cases. These questions address the relative effects of old legacies and the new environment, ask how reforms shape the arena for social actors, and compel us to examine whose benefit various reforms have actually served.

This work therefore fits into the burgeoning literature on democratic transitions, civil society, and reforms in postcommunist countries, but it is distinctive on several grounds. First, it is less a celebration of democratic reform and a triumphant civil society than an effort to show how and why key actors in society can be harmed by processes of transition and become excluded from shaping a new political order. Moreover, it does not exclusively take actors in civil society as the primary "independent variable," the one that produces effects on political institutions and policies. Rather, it argues that labor has been unable to act in this manner and instead has been decisively affected by actions and actors from above. In other words, the causal arrow has been reversed; instead of looking at how social actors affect reforms, this work is more concerned with how reforms affect social actors, especially which actors become privileged and which actors lose status and power. The end result is more a focus on the political economy of reform—the interaction between market, state, and social actors in the reform process—than on civil society as a force pushing for change or deeply involved in processes of democratic consolidation. Of course, to the extent that key social actors are excluded or politically marginalized, I will assess what effect this has had on the transition and prospects for the consolidation of a new political and economic order.

Additionally, this study's focus is on organized labor, the largest group in postcommunist civil societies but nonetheless rarely the subject of concentrated attention. This is unfortunate, because economic interest associations, of which organized labor is one of the most important, should be crucial players in both political and economic transformations. As Philippe Schmitter observes, in a modification of sorts to the classic transitions literature, democracy is more than about holding elections, and the most important political actors may in fact not be political parties, especially—he claims—in states making the first steps to democracy. Instead, he argues that democratic consolidation heavily depends upon the role of interest associations, which aggregate and articulate interests. The development of interest associations and their relations with the state constitute a crucial "partial regime" within the broader context of democratization that decisively affects the quality of democracy and the ability of the state to provide tangible material benefits to its citizens.[7] Nancy Bermeo echoes this notion, basing her claims upon several historical studies of civil society's role in democratization. She notes that a sense of "connectedness" between civil society and parliaments is crucial, since these ties link the populace to the government and give legitimacy to state policies.[8]

Weak interest associations, however, may facilitate the aggrandizement of state power and authoritarian tendencies. David Ost, in an early examination of interest group activity in postcommunist states, maintains that a "gaping hole" exists where economic interest associations should be organized, the result of which is state domination over society.[9] Society-centered models of politics, which would have been the most logical expectation, now, he claims, are particularly "inappropriate," as the state has gained a strong degree of autonomy from society and pressure "from below" is either muted or ineffectual. If, as Ost suggests, what we see is a state that is still strong and a civil society that has little influence in political life, then the question might be how far the democratic transition has gone or is likely to go in states across the region. Put another way, the formal institutions of democracy may be in place, but the processes that are associated with democracy, such as public input, openness, feeling of political efficacy, and government accountability, may be lacking. For example, Richard Rose, in New Europe Barometer surveys (1998–2000) conducted in sixteen postcommunist countries, finds that 46 percent of people report no difference in their feelings of political influence, and 23 percent believe that they have less influence today than under communist regimes.[10] This lack of political efficacy should be disturbing for those who believe that notions of citizenship have a prime place in any discussion of democratization.

This work will look in detail at the plight of trade unions in four countries: Poland, Russia, Hungary, and Ukraine. The choice of these four cases is based on the fact that they provide variance on both independent and dependent variables (market reforms and labor weakness, respectively), as outlined in table 1.1. There are variations in speed and the scope of reforms in all four countries. Poland and Hungary are clearly reform leaders, although the former implemented "shock therapy" and the latter chose a more gradual approach to reform. Russia has implemented more reforms than Ukraine and by the end of the 1990s had a large marketized sector, but Russia and Ukraine clearly lagged and still lag behind states in East-Central Europe. Additionally, labor activism is a *relative* term (meaning strength of labor compared among these four countries), and here I am primarily taking into account the position of labor at the beginning of the postcommunist transformation. Obviously, Poland witnessed a large amount of labor activism, particularly under the last years of communism, and its labor organizations have been more active and do appear to be stronger than those in Hungary or, for that matter, in any other postcommunist country.[11] This does not mean that in any absolute sense that Polish, much less Russian, trade unions are strong, but only that for the most part they have been better organized and played a larger role in political and economic life than Hungarian or Ukrainian unions. The goal of this study, however, by comparing cases having different stimuli (market reforms) and some variance on outcomes, is to assess the impact of postcommunist change on trade unions. In addition, within each country study there will be some focus on branch and enterprise variation, and similarities of these dimensions are tracked across countries.

These mini–case studies nested in the country studies will be important to understand the relationship between structural economic change, including marketization, privatization, and globalization, and the development of actors in civil society, particularly trade unions. Several authors, writing about the experience of organized labor in the West, have noted that these trends have often had negative effects on unions and the corporatist institutions that give an institutionalized role to unions in making government policies.[12] Together, they largely define the new political economy of advanced industrialized states. To the extent that politicians and union leaders in postcommu-

Table 1.1 **Reform Pace and Labor Activism**		
Economic Reforms	*More Active Labor Movements*	*Less Active Labor Movements*
Sustained Market Reforms	Poland	Hungary
Sporadic or Minimal Market Reform	Russia	Ukraine

nist countries would like to see their countries look like social-democratic Germany or Austria, how ironic it is that the social-democratic corporatist features of these states that helped empower labor are now under assault from market forces. As the East begins to look more like the West, the plight of organized labor may become worse, not better.

This is not to say that globalization or free markets are wholly bad, that all was better under communism, or that postcommunist states are all merely "bourgeoise" democracies that completely disenfranchise the working class. Certainly, most people, including workers, at least in East-Central Europe, believe their lives are getting better, and they have faith in most principles of democracy and the market.[13] However, as mentioned, both democratization and marketization can produce losers, groups that, for a variety of reasons, lack the political and economic resources to have their voices heard and demands taken into account. And since they lack a voice because trade unions have been emasculated, people are still angry. Indeed, Crowley and Ost assert that labor weakness in the initial stages of democratization may have "profound political implications" because it means that the frustrations traditionally channeled by unions into class-based claims end up being expressed in "nationalist, fundamentalist, and other illiberal directions."[14] This is most clear in the case of Russia, given the past appeal of Zhirinovsky and the more current support given to Putin and his "dictatorship of law," but there is also evidence for this throughout postcommunist Europe, including Poland, Romania, Slovakia, and the former Yugoslavia. Although it is difficult to produce a direct cause-and-effect relationship, there is perhaps a link between labor weakness and illiberal politics that threatens democratic consolidation.

Labor weakness is not the only way in which democracy is under assault in postcommunist states. Globalization also needs to be examined with a skeptical eye. It can be a menace to democracy because governments (and, by extension, citizens) lose sovereignty and now must consider international political and economic influences that may run counter to the interests and concerns of their domestic constituencies. Bormeo notes that globalization now means that there is "severe crowding on the captain's bridge [of the state]," since "powerful international actors were invited to take a role in decision making just as hordes of citizens expected a meaningful role in shaping the direction of their new democracy after years of authoritarian exclusion."[15] There is evidence of this foreign influence at the national level in postcommunist Europe in cases where IMF directives either determine policy for the state (arguably this has occurred in Russia) or so tie the hands of state leaders that there is little option but to pursue austerity measures, despite promising to do something different (as in Hungary and Poland). These actions do compromise democracy insofar as governments are expected to reflect the will of the people and elections are supposed to offer voters a real choice. If elections do not matter, then a basic component of democracy is lost. This study attempts to look at these problems at the macro level of various political actors, as well as the more subtle influence of global and market forces that specifically affect trade unions at the national and enterprise levels. Economic forces are undermining organized labor's capacity to act as a unified political and economic force. I will examine several environments to determine the validity of this claim, as well as spell out what the real consequences are of organized labor's weakness.

It may first be useful to provide more context as to how organized labor fits—or does not fit—into existing theories and paradigms of civil society, democratization, and transitology.

Fitting Unions in the Civil Society Literature

One of the foremost themes surrounding democratization in postcommunist countries is civil society. This term—which initially emerged in some of the dissident literature as a normative idea, the antithesis of communism, a "parallel polis" where people could live "as if they were free," in Vaclav Havel's words—is now ubiquitous in the study of democratization. For many, civil society has become the sine qua non of democracy.[16] Thomas Carothers notes, "Civil society is the connective tissue that transitional countries need to join the forms of democracy with their intended substance, to ensure that new democratic institutions and processes do not remain hollow boxes and empty rituals."[17] Evidence from postcommunist Europe, at first glance, appears to bear these claims out. Where civil society has stronger roots—as in countries like Poland, the former Czechoslovakia, Hungary—democratization has been largely successful and can now be said to be consolidated as evidenced by their accession to the European Union in 2004. In other cases —such as the Balkan states, Russia, Ukraine, Belarus, and Central Asian countries—the relative weakness of civil society is invoked to explain the lingering, or in some cases growing, authoritarianism in the state, even when the basics of "electoral democracy" may have been established.[18] For many, this correlation is sufficient proof of the power of civil society.

The argument linking civil society to democracy is longstanding in democratic theory and is most frequently attributed to Alexis de Tocqueville, who is also experiencing a bit of a renaissance.[19] For Tocqueville, the "art of association" was the "mother of all science," which is generally interpreted to mean that free associations of citizens—in other words, civil society—is necessary to mitigate antidemocratic forces of individualism and allow citizens to check the power of the state. In his view, these associations would also function as "schools of democracy" by instilling democratic values in citizens.[20] Dissidents in Eastern Europe picked up this language, and the notion that civil society provides both a structural and cultural support to democracy accounts for why it is lauded in the democratization literature today.

Despite its popularity (or, perhaps, because of it), there are several debates surrounding the concept of civil society. One question revolves around the definition of the term. Most definitions share a common base: civil society is a network of citizens and organizations, largely autonomous from the state, that articulate values, act collectively to accomplish their goals, and are capable of checking state power. It tends to be defined broadly, as a space between the individual and the state, resting upon *civic* bonds rather than those of family. Implicitly, an individual joins civil society as a matter of choice; it is not purely ascriptive. However, many fault this notion as being too broad, since it can include anything from chess clubs, student groups, environmental societies, women's leagues, trade unions, business lobbies, and political parties. Many distinguish between civil society and political society, the latter including those explicitly political groups such as parties or lobbying organizations that are directly involved in politics and policy formulation.[21]

Another problem considers the link between civil society and democracy. For many, this link is not a given. Carothers notes that there is a certain "romanticization of civil society" by many in the West, insofar as it is viewed simply as "town hall politics writ large" and composed of "legions of well-mannered activists who play by the rules, settle conflicts peacefully, and do not break any windows."[22] In part, this is attributable to a mythologized Tocquevillian conception of American civil society, but also a reflection of the fact that the visible face of civil society in Eastern Europe—in the leaders of Solidarity, Civic Forum, Sajudis, and other liberally oriented, anticommunist groups—was democratic. These examples, however, miss the point that in certain cases—in which political participation precedes political institution-alization, to use Samuel Huntington's terminology—a vibrant civil society can undermine democracy. The classic case is Weimar Germany, and in com-paring Weimar to present-day Russia one set of scholars notes that democ-racy in Russia survives in part because civil society is so weak.[23] Others might note that groups in civil society need not be "civil" and can include radical nationalists, fascists, communists, or others who do "break windows" or do not wholly embrace democratic or liberal values.[24] The *quality*, not *quantity*, of civil society therefore is central to any debate. This problem has led some to define civil society in such a way that it must be open, inclusive, tolerant, and moderate.[25] These amendments, I would argue, go too far, and by so lim-iting the definition of civil society, the alleged links between civic involvement and democracy cannot be investigated.

Another problem, one perhaps less immediately obvious, revolves around the arguments of James Madison that creep into the civil society literature. Madison famously maintains in "Federalist X" that pluralism is beneficial because it mitigates the pernicious effects of factions, since a multiplicity of groups prevent any one faction from becoming a majority and create (in modern political science lexicon) "cross-cutting cleavages."[26] In addition, it can be argued that by belonging to many groups, a citizen's interests diver-sify and become more tolerant of outside views. Competition among several groups—with no single group constituting a majority—safeguards democ-racy and the rights of minorities. This pluralist assumption is implicit in the civil society literature, as the focus is on the benefits of general popular activism and organization and not on the democratic credentials (or lack thereof) of any particular group. Put another way, much of the literature on civil society tends to make it an abstract notion and assume that its activities, *en toto* at least, are directed to the common good. Rarely is there concerted attention given to the different components that comprise it, or the various and often antagonistic interests that they espouse.

This digression into debates surrounding civil society is important, be-cause after moving beyond the abstract idea of civil society and discussing trade unions themselves, it becomes apparent they do not fit neatly into many of the claims made about civil society. This is not to say, of course, that trade unions are not part of civil society. Almost all observers would agree that unions form a large and important element of almost any state's civil society. Of course, it is possible that unions can often play an explicit political role, and thereby they should also be understood as part of "political society." In postcommunist Europe, trade unions lobby parliaments and executives, make alliances with political parties, and in many cases run candidates for office, occasionally as a separate political party. This dual nature is most obvious in the case of Solidarity, but this is also the case among unions in Russia, Ukraine, and Hungary. In part, whether unions are placed in "civil" or "political" society may be a matter of semantics, but I contend that this consideration leads to another, more important conclusion. Unions (and for that matter many other groups) are not entirely "civic" if, as is often the case, "civic" is taken to mean "civic-minded" or seeking to benefit the polity or the citizenry *as a whole*. Civil society in its totality *may* generate these outcomes (deriving from Madison or from Mill's notion that competition among ideas will allow better ones to prevail), but its individual parts are oriented toward their own interests, and it is this notion of "interest" that is lacking or is downplayed in much of the discussion surrounding civil society.[27]

Unions are not universal organizations; they are particularistic. They must, first and foremost, serve the interests of their members, which may or may not coincide with the greater good.[28] Moreover, it should also be noted that not all unions, even unions in the same country, have similar interests. These differences may be especially marked during a transition to democracy or a launch of market reforms, or both, during which time pluralism is allowed and the worker's prospects as a winner or loser in market condition may be conditioned by industry, region, age, or skill level.[29] In most postcommunist countries, there has been a splintering of the labor movement, with some unions (usually the communist successor unions) taking a more skeptical view of free market reforms and newer, independent unions embracing some aspects of change and aligning with more liberal political parties. Thus, treating unions as an undifferentiated whole would be as mistaken as analyzing civil society without paying attention to the particular features of its major components.

This discussion provides a segue into another issue: the relationship between trade unions and democracy. Although unions have, of late, fallen into disrepute (especially in the United States and the United Kingdom) and are commonly criticized for running themselves in an undemocratic manner, most analysts, taking a longer view, would suggest a positive correlation between working-class mobilization and democratization.[30] Workers, being the plurality, if not the majority, in most countries, see democracy as a means of empowering themselves, and working-class organizations and parties have pushed for democratization in many countries and have been willing to play by democratic rules once democracy has been established. Of course, there are exceptions. The Bolshevik Party would certainly rank as one (*if* considered a movement of the working class), but today's organizations include the Mussolini-inspired Confederation of Free Trade Unions in Russia, orthodox communist movements like Working Russia, and stodgy, bureaucratic behemoths like the Federation of Ukrainian Trade Unions, all of whose commitment to democracy can be questioned. While in some cases (Russia and Ukraine most notably) unions' democratic credentials may be dubious, most unions in the region espouse democracy in rhetoric and play by the rules of the game.

However, as the comment above from Balcerowicz suggests, unions are still viewed with suspicion by politicians, insofar as unions might, albeit democratically, undermine market reform. The contrast is all too evident. Civil society as a whole, with all its normative assumptions included, is lauded. Unions are, to put it mildly, another matter—groups that need to be beaten or subdued if democratic consolidation and marketization are to have a chance.[31] Of course, this discussion points to a central tension between democracy and the market, one that can be overblown (e.g., several countries have weathered the storm of the "dual transition"), but one that nonetheless merits attention, especially considering (as this study will) how markets affect democracy, not only the dangers of democracy (and trade unions) to the market.

Unions are not the only groups in civil society that may undermine democracy and marketization. Even the once sacrosanct Catholic Church in Poland has been derided as a potential threat to consolidating democracy there.

The point, however, is that civil society must be distinguished from the parts that compose it. Moreover, I suggest that the parts are more important (and more interesting) than the whole. Using civil society in a normative or Madisonian sense may obscure more than it reveals and arguably may be a chimera. It is necessary to take a closer look at "civil society" as it is, which means looking underneath labels and moral claims and examining the workings and *interests* of its parts. These parts will differ markedly from each other, and unions are but one element, and not even a homogeneous one at that. However, they do purport to represent the largest number of citizens, but they can get lost in the shuffle if the focus is only on "civil society." Given the demands of democracy and the market, the tension between them, and the saliency of making the dual transition to both, I submit that political economy —by which I mean the interplay of the state, the market, the groups with particular interests—needs to be brought to the forefront when examining postcommunist politics. This study aims to do just that and thus move beyond general discussions of civil society.

Searching for Trade Unions in Transitology

Many of the arguments made in the previous section are even more appropriate as a critique of the transitology literature, which subsumes some of the arguments made in the civil society literature and has become a veritable paradigm in the study of postcommunist political change as well as democratization more generally. The genesis for much of this literature was the multivolume *Transitions from Authoritarian Rule,* which attempted to improve upon theories of democratic "prerequisites" and offer a model of democratization based upon strategic choices made by human agency.[32] This work spawned numerous other volumes stressing how democracy could be "crafted" or designed by elites, and much attention in this genre is given to institutional design and the bargains that make democracy possible.[33]

The bases of transitology are rather well known. In brief, liberalization is precipitated by splits within the elite of the authoritarian regime. These fissures are caused by socioeconomic crises, demands for change from below, and external pressure or events. In other words, the *status quo* becomes untenable, and liberalization becomes an option for elites hoping to defuse popular opposition, bolster the position of reformers within the elite, or provide legitimacy for new policy initiatives. Reformers within the regime then try to court moderates within society, and this coalition must fend off assaults from hard-liners in the regimes and radical groups in society. Liberalization, however, is rarely sufficient, and thus democracy emerges as an option. However, it must be made palatable to elements from the old guard, so a "pacted" transition based upon bargains between reformers and moderates is the preferred course to ensure a peaceful transition and one more likely to be consolidated. These pacts often encompass such items as immunity for the old elite, guaranteed seats in parliament for certain groups, preservation of special prerogatives for the military, and protection of private property for the bourgeoisie.

This model, based primarily on the experience of Southern Europe and Latin America, became the standard by which most transitions, including postcommunist ones, were evaluated. In part, this is understandable. Previous ways of understanding communist systems were tossed aside when the regimes collapsed in 1989–1991, and scholars looking to make sense of these events latched on to this ready-made, apparently exportable model. There are also, prima facie, enough similarities between the earlier transitions and postcommunist cases to make comparisons. Gorbachev's Soviet Union, for example, seems to fit the description of a system in crisis that opted for liberalization. The same could be said for Poland and Hungary in the 1980s. The differences among the regions and countries were downplayed, as Schmitter maintains that the postcommunist cases could be treated "conceptually and theoretically equivalent to those that preceded them."[34] Moreover, by using these models, postcommunist studies find a means to reintegrate into comparative politics more generally, which was often assumed to be clearly desirable.

While many embraced this new approach (and the influx of Latin Americanists suddenly writing on postcommunist transitions), others were far more skeptical. Ken Jowitt observes a "fetishlike repetition of the phrase 'transition to democracy,' as if saying it often enough, and inviting enough Latin American scholars from the United States to enough conferences in Eastern Europe (and the Soviet Union), will magically guarantee a new democratic capitalist telos in place of the ethnic, economic and territorial maelstrom that is the reality today."[35] While Jowitt was not the only one uncomfortable with this development, transitology was clearly, at least in the initial years following communism's collapse, ascendant, and defenders of area studies were on the defensive even in the pages of the leading journal devoted to Slavic studies.[36]

Since rising to prominence, however, transitology has been attacked on several fronts, many of which are quite relevant for my discussion of trade unions. Among more generic criticisms is the observation that the outcome of democracy cannot be determined by applying formal reasoning to the general model of transitology, unless the actors rely upon mistaken assumptions.[37] Indeed, despite its pretense to be a general model, transitology is, according to Barbara Geddes, so handicapped by its own possibilistic and voluntaristic structure that few testable hypotheses can be produced. She maintains that very few of the arguments advanced in the transitions literature appear to be true.[38]

More problems emerge once the transitions literature is "stretched" to postcommunist Europe. It is on this front that fierce debate is encountered between self-described "comparativists" such as Philippe Schmitter and advocates of "area studies" such as Valerie Bunce. Charles King states the matter very clearly with respect to studying democratization in Russia.

> There are two ways to speculate about the future of Russia's ongoing transition. One is to know a great deal about the behavior of over powerful executives and divided legislatures in environments where credible commitment is low, huge incentives for free riding exist, institutional anarchy encourages self-serving political and economic behavior, rent seeking and patronage networks among central and peripheral entrepreneurs prevent broad cooperation, and social cleavages along ascriptive lines such as ethnicity overshadow both ideology and class as a basis for political mobilization. The other is to know a lot about Russia.[39]

Stephen Cohen likewise laments "Russian studies without Russia," meaning that categories derived from the experience of others and with a certain ideological agenda have been used to describe the Russian transition. The result, however, is Orwellian, when "transition," a word with a generally positive connotation, is used to describe something that should be described as a tragedy, disaster, or collapse. For Cohen, this is nothing less than an intellectual and moral outrage.[40]

When the lines of battle are drawn so clearly, it is hard to remain neutral. Although I would posit that it is not simply an either/or choice as some would have it, I will not conceal my allegiance. This study is based upon in-depth empirical examination and as such shares much in common with the best of the area studies tradition. It does not aspire to lump postcommunist countries into predesigned conceptual boxes. However, as should be perfectly clear, it is not oblivious to theory and in fact will borrow extensively from theorists on globalization and labor relations. At the same time though, I fundamentally believe that transitology has severe (although perhaps not fatal) flaws. These, however, need to be made explicit so that it is apparent how the study of organized labor contributes to the understanding of postcommunist transformations.

One shortcoming of transitology is that its implicit optimism and use of particular categories may present a "teleology which would hinder adequate conceptualization of the varied types of democracies that have been emerging."[41] In other words, transitology, with its normative assumptions and linear structure, has problems accounting for the reasons that transitions might get stuck, as they arguably have in Russia and Ukraine. Another problem is the lack of attention to history or local particularities. Once the transition is in place, the general dynamic is largely the same, and the calculations of actors are future based, not rooted in the past. As Adam Przeworski argues, the obstacles to reform are "determined by a common destination [the requirements of democracy], not by the different points of departure."[42] This argument seems quite myopic, given the fact that those postcommunist states that started out with particular advantages (Poland, Hungary, the Czech Republic, Slovenia) have performed far better than their neighbors both in terms of democratic consolidation and marketization. This ahistoricism is almost inevitable in any general model, but it may mean that in an effort to be parsimonious and generalizable, the model misses the most interesting parts. "Path dependency," the notion that history matters, has thus been taken up by many as an important factor.[43] While it might be conceded to the transitologists that some of the dynamics that led to the initial decisions to liberalize might be comparable, the subsequent challenges of consolidating democracies appear to be far more dependent upon history and structural, country-specific factors. This has been the approach in the most comprehensive accounts of democratic transitions to date, where the type of previous authoritarian regime is given great importance in explaining the challenges and outcomes of consolidation.[44] In the case of postcommunist countries, the points of departure were different when compared to Latin America by virtue of the presence of totalitarian and posttotalitarian regimes. These regimes aspired to squash all independent organizations and control all property, and thus the playing field for the transitions in these countries (Poland and Hungary, being partially liberalized, may rank as exceptions) was markedly different. The result was a lack of social structure or an incipient "political society" of parties and interest organizations that would be seen in bureaucratic-authoritarian regimes of Latin America. Pacts therefore became less likely (Poland and Hungary again the exceptions that demonstrate this rule), because the totalitarian "syndrome" meant that once liberalization proceeded, the ideological trappings of the regime would begin to unravel, leading to its collapse.[45]

Notions that "history matters" may be rather unobjectionable (and unremarkable), but what does this mean for trade unions? The answer is—plenty. The historical baggage of postcommunist unions will be more fully explored, but for now it should simply be noted that these unions (and postcommunist societies more generally) did not enter the postcommunist period with a tabula rasa. The largest trade unions in all postcommunist countries are the successors to those that existed under communist rule and were subservient to the interests of the communist parties. These unions suffer today in part to a credibility gap engendered by this inheritance. Since they did not truly represent workers in the past, they may be tarnished today in the eyes of many. In some cases, their leadership may still be dependent on the state through residual corporatist arrangements, and thus the union is incapable of really challenging the political elite. At the same time, however, the unions are fighting to defend some aspects of the past system: job security, institutions for workers' input, and union control over property and social services. Thus, unions have an ambiguous relationship with the communist past, which in part can explain their relationship with marketization and democratic reformers. This legacy therefore cannot be overlooked in any discussion of trade unions today.

The most serious myopia in transitology, however, is the assumption that the challenges confronting the postcommunist states are similar to earlier transitions. Postcommunist states are in such different circumstances they cannot be easily compared with those in Latin America or Southern Europe.[46] Transitology is so preoccupied with finding similarities that it glosses over differences. The result, as Valerie Bunce maintains, is comparing apples not with oranges, but with kangaroos![47] The reason for this claim is that postcommunist states were confronted with two challenges that did not exist in Latin America: creating a market-oriented economy and constructing new state institutions and structures.[48] Latin American transitions were privileged over those in postcommunist Europe because Latin American states already had market systems and a well-institutionalized state. In contrast, postcommunist regimes must build markets from a system that was based nearly exclusively on state ownership and that denied markets any role (Hungary being a limited exception). In addition, many states are new or were seriously handicapped by a power vacuum as the party-state disintegrated, and therefore creating effective authority (let alone a democratic one) was a priority that was not confronted in Latin America. I will not focus much on the state building or nation building aspects of postcommunist transitions, as they are somewhat peripheral to the examination of trade unions. However, the dual transition to both the market and democracy is central to our analysis. At the risk of invoking a bit of Marxism, it is difficult to understand the pathologies of democratic transition in several states (notably Russia and Ukraine, less so perhaps in Poland, the Czech Republic, and Hungary) without taking into account how marketization and the resulting economic dislocation has affected political processes. The economic project in postcommunist states has been far more ambitious than simply imposing austerity measures, which was the main thrust of policy during democratic transitions in Latin America. Bunce notes that "in Southern Europe and Latin America, *the* issue was democratization; that is, a change in political regime . . . By contrast, what is at stake in eastern Europe is nothing less than the creation of the very building blocks of the social order."[49] Because of the perceived need for this dual transition, therefore, economic questions—and economic actors such as trade unions—should play a prominent role in the study of postcommunist transformation. In other words, democratization hinges upon political economy.

This argument points to a related shortcoming in the transitions approach: a narrow definition of democracy.[50] Democracy is defined exclusively in terms of institutions and procedures, not power relations within the broader society. While there is some variation, democracy is generally defined as the existence of free and fair elections and respect for basic human and civil rights—that is, freedom of speech and assembly—that make democratic contestation possible. Questions of political economy are absent, and Schmitter et al. in their initial formulation even take them off the table, noting that the transition must not involve any kind of redistribution of wealth, property, or privilege.[51] Other writers agree: Adam Przeworski and Guiseppe Di Palma clearly define democracy based upon elections and rules, and Andreas Schedler maintains that regime stability and continuity is the key component of democratic consolidation, not deepening democracy.[52] Other scholars generally concur on a minimalist definition (defined as between Joseph Schumpeter's electoral democracy and the enumeration of certain rights as spelled out in Robert Dahl's *Polyarchy*[53]), suggesting that the main task of consolidation of democracy is simply coopting potential counterelites, so that all elites will be players in the democratic game.[54] As Paul Christensen notes in his critique of this literature, democracy is "about rules, not *who* rules."[55]

The shortcomings of this approach should be obvious. The result approximates the "fallacy of electoralism"; that is, equating democracy with the holding of elections.[56] This is clearly a narrow view of democracy, one that does not give much purchase on understanding or classifying regimes. For example, by these conventional definitions, Russia is a democracy. Elections are held, there is choice, and people do—for the most part—have the right to express their opinion. The fact that voters do not have good choices, the fact that economic resources are concentrated in the hands of a tiny elite, the fact that patronage matters more than elections, and the fact that the state-owned media favor certain candidates over others are all outside of this conception of democracy. Questions of property—central to any understanding of postcommunist states—are artificially separated from consideration of democracy. This is clearly a misplaced notion. If, for example, the existence of a middle class is taken as a prerequisite of democracy, then property relations must be examined to have any understanding about how the democratic system functions. In many postcommunist cases, "democracy" has arisen with nothing less than the mass theft of state enterprises and the economic disenfranchisement of millions of workers, whose stake in their enterprises was taken from them. Even in an apparently successful case such as Poland, unions were pushed aside when the business of economic reform was addressed by technocrats in the government, despite the fact that it was the unions and their workers that created the democratic opening to put the new elite in power. Christensen, arguing for a broader definition of democracy, suggests, "The problem of disjuncture between the formal rules of democracy and the actual power relations within a state is no more evident than in Russia, precisely because the struggles over property, control of resources, social (dis)empowerment, and state (non)responsiveness are so acute."[57] This is not unique to Russia, of course. Looking deeper into the political economy of democratization, while often messy and not easily amenable to formal models, is therefore necessary in order to get a better and more accurate rendering of what democracy means in actual practice.

Trade unions play a central role here, and including them enriches the study of democratization. They, along with business groups, are located at the nexus of political and civil society, and at the intersection of politics and the economy. They are crucial in any understanding of political economy, for their actions reveal the interplay and tension between democracy and the market. Their empowerment or lack of power cuts to the question of *who* rules, which is arguably at least as important as the institutional rules of the democratic system. Of course, this terrain is less value neutral. However, it is certainly legitimate to ask who benefits from the rules of new political and economic arrangements. The chapters that follow document not only organized labor's weakness in the postcommunist period but also assess the causes for labor's decline and, most important, examine what impact this has on the democratization project in the region.

2

The Postcommunist Inheritance

AN UNDERSTANDING OF THE HISTORY of organized labor under communism is crucial because today's trade unions are not built from scratch; their experience under communist rule shapes them today and arguably helps account for many of their current problems. The mobilization of labor in the late communist period, especially in Poland and the Soviet Union, was in retrospect the apogee of labor activism. Even though labor probably will be unable to recreate this historical moment, this period is important because it offers a glimpse of what labor might have become *if* it could have seized opportunities offered by communism's collapse. Labor's present infirmities, of course, should be obvious to even the most casual observer, but it would nonetheless be useful to demonstrate *how* to conceptualize and understand labor's weakness. Many arguments have been put forward to explain labor's predicament. While several of these arguments may have validity, they do not devote concerted attention to the lasting effects of structural economic change on organized labor. This study aims to fill this gap, and in so doing look beyond the political economy of the transition to how the transition itself will shape a new landscape for unions and other actors.

Organized Labor under Communism

Communism, of course, aspired to be a "dictatorship of the proletariat," a system in which workers would have ultimate political authority. Workers were central to Marxist-Leninist doctrine and state institutions. The Communist Party was the party of the working class, and in communist cant and culture workers were privileged.[1] Trade unions were based upon universal membership and thus were the largest organizations in communist states (even larger than the Party itself).

The communist reality, however, did little to empower workers. The party-state, despite its pretensions to the contrary, was not "by, for, and of" the workers. As early as 1921, the Bolshevik Party acted, in Karl Radek's words, to "impose its will" on the "reactionary" (read: anti-Bolshevik) workers.[2] Over time, the Party became, in Milan Djilas's term, a "New Class," an exploiter of the workers.[3] Its bureaucratic machinery stifled initiatives from below, offered no democratic choice, and subjugated the trade unions, making them, in Lenin's formulation, "schools of communism" and "transmission belts" from the Party to the masses. Unions were organized in both territorial and branch principles, but all bodies were subject to the rules of democratic centralism, thus ensuring that directives from above would be carried out. This Soviet model, with some amendments (e.g., the creation of workers' councils in Poland and Hungary) was imposed upon Eastern Europe after World War II.

This position of the trade unions can be viewed as paradoxical, given the abyss between the communist doctrine of workers' empowerment and the reality that took power from the workers and gave it to the ruling Party. As a result, trade unions were put in an awkward position and served, according to many analysts, a "dual role."[4] Unions were little more than adjuncts of the party-state. In this role, their primary loyalty was to the Party, not the workers, and their responsibility was to ensure workers' discipline and fulfillment of the plan. Even outside the enterprise, the unions' various cultural activities (lectures, libraries, clubs, etc.) were arms of the propaganda machine of the state, designed to educate the "new man" to be able to "work in the Communist manner."[5] In this vein, workers were atomized, manipulated by the bureaucracy of the ruling elite.[6] Workers' solidarity against the state or management was virtually impossible to achieve. All workers' organization was to be through party-approved channels, and any independent activity, as seen in the Novocherkassk strike in 1962 in the Soviet Union, the miners' strikes in the Jiu Valley of Romania in 1977, and in numerous strikes in Poland in 1970, 1976, and ultimately 1980–1981, would be crushed.

Some analysts, while conceding that there were repressive elements, nonetheless find that unions also played a representative role and thus made efforts to defend workers. According to this line of argument, unions were charged with protecting workers from possible abuses of power by individual managers, including unjust dismissals and failure to ensure safe working conditions. Other observers suggest that beyond the enterprise unions were integrated into policy making through corporatist institutions.[7] Some go even further, suggesting that an "institutional pluralism" had developed in the Soviet Union, through which "The trade unions frequently [spoke] out in defense of the immediate interests of the urban poor and industrial workers.... Policy [was] an outcome of puzzling, bargaining, and brokering among interests, probably somewhat responsive to public opinion."[8] According to several analysts, the results of a mellowing post-Stalinist system was the "Soviet social contract," according to which workers received job security, rising wages, and a host of benefits in return for their political passivity.[9] Workers were thus incorporated into the system, albeit in such a manner that they forfeited the right to engage in independent political or social activity.

In the past, debates would rage over which explanation of workers' politics and subsequent workers' quiescence was most convincing. Were workers fundamentally repressed by the state, or were they more or less content, willing to abide by this "contract" imposed upon them? Most, however, would concede that in the end repression was a crucial factor, recognizing à la Hobbes that when all else fails, clubs are trump. Violent suppression of workers' protests and other independent political activity seemed to confirm this assessment. David Mandel, aware of both sides of the argument, notes that union defense of workers' interests against the state or management was the exception, and as a rule the unions were part of a system that "rested upon repression and the threat of repression."[10] Survey evidence from Poland confirmed that workers themselves "harbor no illusions about the unions' production bias, nor do they exhibit much confidence in unions' capacity to get things done, ranking them well below party and management in the enterprise power hierarchy." In Hungary also, surveys revealed low levels of confidence in both unions and workers' councils.[11]

Focus on either of the "dual roles," however, may miss a fundamental element of trade unions and industrial relations under communism. As recent scholarship by Vadim Borisov et al. and Sarah Ashwin has shown,[12] if the system had rested fundamentally upon repression alone, then the lifting of repression should have led to a widespread workers' movement and an abandonment of the communist-dominated unions. Neither has happened. On the other hand, if workers had been "bought off," then economic collapse and the state's inability or unwillingness to live up to the contract today should lead to workers' mobilization. Again, this has not been the case. The reason is that unions also served a "third role" that continues in many cases until today: an arm of management within the enterprise.[13] The unions were given responsibility for doling out various social benefits (e.g., housing, day care, vacation lodging, pension) nominally under control of either the state or the enterprise. Unions thus reinforced a paternalistic mode of economic relations and did nothing to encourage workers' autonomy. On the contrary, their control over various fringe benefits helped ensure that workers would stay in line and follow union (in effect management) directives. Lacking any real independence, they were "paper trade unions,"[14] and workers did not look to them to handle any grievances they may have had, relying instead upon personalized contacts and relationships. Directors of enterprises were also members of the unions (as they were deemed to be "workers"), and on the local level managers either led the unions outright or exercised effective control over them. Given the peculiarities of the communist system, workers and managers could even find a genuine basis for alliance based upon the desire to obtain more resources for their enterprise from the state. Workers were thus integrated into the system not at the macrolevel (e.g., loyalty to the Soviet state or the Party), but they and their unions were integrated into the enterprise, the *kollektiv*. Andras Tóth makes a similar argument with respect to Hungarian workers, and J. E. M. Thirkell et al. acknowledge the same pattern throughout Eastern Europe.[15] Control over unions was thus "dual": by the party-state and by managers. Under communism, this largely looked like the same thing. However, in the postcommunist period, as the party-state has disintegrated, the past links between management and unions have become much more clear and perhaps constitute the most important holdover from the communist period.

It is worth mentioning that there were some variations on Soviet-style industrial relations under communism. The most significant innovation was workers' councils, which were designed to be an organ of participation and self-management for workers at the enterprise level. These emerged at various times in Poland, Romania, Yugoslavia, and Hungary, and workers were given powers for self-management in the Soviet Union as a result of the 1987 Law on State Enterprises. Their very creation was in part an admission by the regime that the unions were not effective in giving voice to the workers. However, these structures did not lead to real workers' empowerment. In Romania, the majority of the council members was not elected, and the council was usually comprised of representatives from management. In Poland, the autonomy and prerogatives of these bodies were severely limited, as they were placed within a common decision-making body together with the unions and local party organization. Their failures, together with that of the unions, were underscored by strikes in 1970, 1976, and eventually with the emergence of Solidarity. In general, throughout the region, there was a concerted effort by the regime to foster a *sense* of workers' involvement without jeopardizing the implementation of predecided policies. Again, the rhetoric of workers' rule did not correspond with the reality, and symbolic meetings of workers' councils did little to strengthen workers' power over the enterprise, let alone national policy.[16]

One could add much more about how unions and other workers' organizations functioned under communism, but I think the general point is clear. They never became centers of real power or authority. They were subjugated to both the party-state and to management. Even though this system has changed in the last decade, the legacy still matters. Most postcommunist unions are the successors of these emasculated unions, and even though the state has largely been taken out of the troika of state-management-union, the links between the latter two are still often in place, even when enterprises have been privatized. The *kollektiv* remains an important entity, both in reform laggards such as Russia and Ukraine, but also in certain sectors of the economy in Eastern Europe.[17] Workers were bound to this unit in basic economic (as well as psychological and cultural) ways and thus have been unable to break free of ties to management, particularly as economic conditions deteriorate and management's continued benevolence is necessary in order to keep jobs and precious benefits. Mandel notes that most workers have a "hard time seeing themselves as autonomous social and political actors. The temptation is still strong to look to management or to the state authorities (the 'good tsar' syndrome)."[18] This corresponds with what Ashwin calls "alienated collectivism" among miners, where even at a privatized mine workers still yearn for a *khoziain* (boss) to take care of things.[19] In Eastern Europe, the unions have arguably done a better job of breaking with some aspects of the communist past, but there too, as we shall see, they remain in a subordinate position vis-à-vis management.

Trade Unions and the Collapse of Communism

An examination of unions under communism would not be complete without a recognition that the system of labor relations did eventually break down. The causes for this breakdown are numerous: economic stagnation; insensitivity of the elites to workers' interests; the ineffectiveness of the token participatory organs created for workers; increasing education for workers and creation of a "pure" working class (not former peasants); and the failures of communist revisionism. As workers' dissatisfaction increased, labor passivity gave way to activism in several countries. Labor protest would ultimately contribute to the collapse of communism itself.

While there were efforts to reform communism in Hungary in 1956 and in Czechoslovakia in 1968, the most significant event was the emergence of the Solidarity movement in Poland in 1980. Of course, Solidarity did not appear out of thin air. It could trace its heritage to strikes in Gdansk and other Baltic ports in 1970–1971 and 1976. Much has been written about Solidarity, although there remains a debate about whether Solidarity is best understood as a workers' movement, or whether the ideals of Solidarity were spawned by intellectuals and a discourse on civil society and "anticipatory democracy" that was expressed most clearly by the Workers' Self-Defense Committee (KOR).[20] It is important to emphasize that Solidarity was not simply a movement for higher wages or lower prices. It had economic, social, and national components, but fundamentally, despite the rhetoric of "antipolitics," it was a political movement, challenging the existing system of the communist monopoly on power by demanding free trade unions and the right to strike. It therefore both challenged the state and attacked the existing trade unions and workers' councils for being inadequate to represent workers' interests. Within four months, it had grown to include some ten million members in all branches of the economy. For sixteen months, the government with much unease recognized Solidarity as legitimate, and even though it was repressed by martial law in December 1981, it would shape Polish politics throughout the 1980s.

After Solidarity was forced underground, the party-state in Poland did try to reform the unions and the councils to appease the workers, but it could not regain even a semblance of legitimacy. Its economic reform plan was rejected by voters in November 1987, and by 1988 a new wave of strikes, led by younger workers loyal to the Solidarity ideal but not controlled by Solidarity, rocked the country. Seeing the desperateness of the situation, the government agreed to talk to Solidarity, and Lech Walesa, Solidarity's leader, agreed to enter the dialogue, claiming he'd talk to the devil himself if it would save Poland. Ultimately, Solidarity and the party-state, with the Church as a mediator, forged a "neocorporatist" settlement,[21] which ultimately led to new elections, the total delegitimation of the Party, and the first emergence of a noncommunist government in the region in September 1989.

Solidarity's victory demonstrated the power of civil society in general and organized labor in particular, but labor could not translate the defeat of communism into its own empowerment. In fact, many Solidarity leaders, including Walesa, even eschewed the goal of creating a strong union, for fear that this would disrupt the reform project. For some, this is the tragedy of Solidarity. It became after 1989 both a political party and a labor union, and the latter, which had millions of supporters and was built on an ethos of participatory democracy, delegated its power and authority to the former, which led a government committed to bringing capitalism to Poland without trouble from the working class. Although the goals of market reform were initially supported by a majority of workers,[22] as the results of reform caused dislocations, splits emerged within Solidarity. This led to a wave of strikes in 1992–1993 led in part by Solidarity directed against its own erstwhile allies. This ultimately brought down the ostensible Solidarity government and paved the way for the return to power in 1993 of the former communists, who were backed by the All-Polish Trade Union Alliance (OPZZ), the old communist-successor unions, which in fact outnumbered Solidarity in official membership figures. The main point here is that Solidarity created a window of opportunity to craft a new order in which unions would be real and active participants in policy making, but it failed to seize this chance. Labor was marginalized prior to 1980; it would be so again after 1989.

Poland, while certainly the most dramatic case of labor militancy, was not the only one in postcommunist Europe. Labor became an important political player in the USSR, when Mikhail Gorbachev's reforms failed to turn the Soviet economy around.[23] Initially, evidence suggests that Gorbachev's ideas of glasnost and perestroika had substantial workers' support, and there was even an increase in production in 1986. Gorbachev intended, arguably, to empower workers, but he did not foresee the consequences of perestroika. His attempts to decentralize the Soviet economy gave authority to managers, and his cost-accounting schemes gave managers an incentive to cut costs, often at the expense of workers' welfare. The Law on State Enterprises provided for the election of management and bolstered the position of work-collective councils (first created in 1983), which in principle were to contribute to self-management. This, however, failed to happen, as these councils remained subservient to management, elections were easily manipulated, and perestroika remained limited so that ultimate authority remained with the ministries. By 1990, new laws ended the election of management, and worker-collective councils were stripped of much of their authority. As the system began to move toward its ultimate denouement, managers profited much more from the chaos than the workers, and the pilfering of state enterprises (the *nomenklatura,* or spontaneous, privatization) began.

Workers, however, were not entirely passive. In July 1989, a wave of strikes among coal miners in Russia and Ukraine offered a stiff challenge to Gorbachev and the Soviet trade unions. This strike was, according to one set of analysts, a direct result of the failures of both rational and enterprise-level reforms to live up to the aspirations of the workers.[24] It also was a repudiation of the unions, which were rejected by the workers as tools of management.[25] These strikes, however, were not just a local phenomenon: the strikers demanded (in addition to lower prices and more consumer goods) more political and economic reform. Some concessions were given to the miners, but the lasting legacy of this wave of strikes was the formation in the fall of 1990 of the Independent Miners' Union (NPG). This union would remain small, with its president conceding a membership figure of only thirty-five hundred in the spring of 1991, which Simon Clarke et al. contend may have been an *overestimate!*[26] However, the workers remained restless as the economy continued to deteriorate, striking again in 1991, this time demanding Gorbachev's resignation and privatization of the mines, in the belief (based on faulty reasoning) that mine workers would be better off under a capitalist system.[27] The NPG formed an alliance with Boris Yeltsin, which would last into 1993, and despite low membership figures, became the most vocal, if not visible, union in the USSR.

The NPG was not the only new union to be formed as the USSR began to collapse. Independent unions were formed in a number of localities, including Sverdlovsk and Leningrad. Intellectuals, professionals, and those in cooperatives came together to form the Association of Socialist Trade Unions (*Sotsprof*). Air traffic controllers and railroad drivers also formed their own trade unions, breaking with the old communist-controlled unions. However, all of these unions remained very small. Sotsprof claimed as many as 250,000 members, but Clarke et al., based upon survey evidence, suggest that the total may have been closer to 1,000.[28] Sotsprof did, however, secure positions for itself in Yeltsin's government, although this did little to bolster its credibility once Russian-style shock therapy was introduced. These and other small, independent unions continue to exist, but they remain essentially marginal players in all but a handful of sectors.

While the strikes in the USSR, particularly those of the miners, were significant events, their primary importance may have been symbolic, showing in a clear fashion that the Party was not fulfilling its promises to the workers. Most workers, it bears mentioning, did not strike, and most did not join new unions. The old all-Soviet unions renamed themselves, eventually becoming the Federation of Independent Russian Trade Unions (FNPR). While the FNPR's links to the Party were formally broken when the August 1991 coup failed and the Communist Party was outlawed, its ties to management and functions at the enterprise level were not substantially changed in the immediate post-Soviet period. As a report by Alexandr Tarasov notes, FNPR leaders were unchanged, still part of the "flesh and blood of the upper stratum of the Soviet bureaucracy."[29] The FNPR has been forced to make some adjustments in more recent years and has emerged as a critic of the government, but it has not spearheaded an empowered labor movement in Russia.

Events in Ukraine mirrored those in Russia. Small independent unions were formed in the same sectors as in Russia, and these were by far the most active labor groups in the 1990–1992 period. The republican-level union organization declared itself independent from the center, becoming the Federation of Ukrainian Trade Unions (FPU), a largely conservative organization that did little more than issue hollow proclamations while millions of workers were pushed into poverty.[30]

Other countries also witnessed labor mobilization and a splintering of the old, monolithic communist unions. In the late 1980s in Hungary, for example, the government began to allow new unions to form. In December 1988, workers from scientific enterprises and other organizations formed the Democratic League of Independent Trade Unions (LIGA), which became part of the opposition roundtable, negotiating with the government in 1989. Several other unions were formed from fractures within the old communist-dominated unions. These included the Trade Union Cooperative Forum (SZEF) of public sector employees, the Federation of Autonomous Unions (ASZSZ), drawing mainly from the Union of Chemical Workers, and the Academic Employees Union (ESZT). The main union reconstituted itself as the National Confederation of Hungarian Trade Unions (MSZOSZ), was composed mainly of workers in manufacturing industries, and forged links with the Socialist Party, the former communists. [31] There was also a new Hungarian Work Councils Association (MOSZ). However, in the transition phase, unions remained bit players, with a taxi driver strike in Budapest constituting the most publicized case of labor militancy. Thus, unlike in Poland, there was no neocorporatist approach in which unions were central to helping extricate the country from communism.

In Bulgaria, an independent union, *Podkrepa* (Support), formed in February 1989 and was an integral part of the anticommunist Union of Democratic Forces (UDF). It was, and arguably remains, more a political entity, with a clearer program on liberalization and human rights than on economic questions. During the upheavals in Bulgaria from November 1989 to March 1990, there were over five hundred cases of labor conflict, a flood of labor unrest, but most were spontaneous and led by no union federation. As in other countries, the old unions renamed themselves, now operating under the moniker Confederation of Independent Bulgarian Trade Unions (KNSB), but at the grassroots level this new body was not very successful in purging itself of communist-era connections and methods of operation.[32] While the Socialist Party (the former communists) won elections in 1990, the UDF prevailed in 1991, and Podkrepa formed a block of about seventy members of parliament. This could have been a decisive moment, but instead of focusing on economic questions Podkrepa was more interested in purging the country of communist influence by confiscating property, and when the government, with the backing of the IMF, began to pursue antiunion policies, the Podkrepa lobby disappeared.[33]

Czechoslovakia may have witnessed the least amount of labor activism in the region, arguably due in part to the relative health of the economy. However, in the decisive moments of the November 1989 "Velvet Revolution," there was a general strike and workers gave their support to students and intellectuals who spearheaded change. The union federation, however, did not experience a serious splintering. It formally disbanded itself and reformed with a new democratic charter as the Czech and Slovak Trade Union Confederation, now the Czech and Moravian Confederation of Trade Unions (CMKOS) after the breakup of the country. Its Slovak equivalent formed the Slovak Confederation of Trade Unions (KOZ), and like other unions in the region, it has not been empowered in the postcommunist period.[34] CMKOS, however, unlike most unions in the region, has maintained a politically non-aligned character, with only an informal and loose allegiance to the Social Democratic Party.

This review has been admittedly cursory, and those interested in the immediate postcommunist period can consult the numerous more detailed studies cited throughout this work. For my purposes here, however, the point is clear. While the collapse of communism gave rise to new unions and labor activism, there was no solid breakthrough for labor in any country. Most workers continued to belong to the old, more inert unions that were far from the cutting edge of democratic change. They remained (and arguably still remain) more interested in protecting their privileges under the old system than promoting anything new. While labor activism was not universal, many workers did break out of their lethargy, engaging in protests, supporting other elements in civil society, and looking for new forums to organize themselves. Had this been sustained, the whole postcommunist period would be very different from what it is today. However, labor's presence on the stage of history turned out to be brief, even in Poland, where labor retreated in 1990–1991 when shock therapy was introduced. While some workers formed new unions, they generally were unable to offer a powerful or even articulate program that could make them important players. Organized labor, as a collective entity, did not profit from the collapse of the old system. While voters and consumers are now more empowered, workers—*as workers*—are not. While labor's relative power during and after communism cannot be debated, the general picture is that a system that repressed and contained labor has been replaced with a system, although less obviously brutal and authoritarian, which also works to marginalize labor, this time in the name of building capitalism.

Trade Unions' Collapse after Communism

Despite unions' role in helping bring down communist governments and, in several states, their alliance with the new postcommunist political elites, unions have not fared well in the postcommunist period. A full list of their failures would be too long to mention, but would include the following: policies enacted by government have ended job security for millions, ripped apart the social safety net, contradicted their pledges to workers and voters in general, and ended a host of privileges for unions and workers' councils. Yet, unions' protest has been muted, and only on exceptional occasions have they been able to get their members on the streets to protest these measures. While there is some variance across the region (labor activism has been most notable in Poland, Russia, and Romania), organized labor stands out not for what it has done, but for what it has failed to do despite deteriorating economic conditions and government assaults on its position. As Stephen Crowley and David Ost note, "Contrary to what many expected, unions seem to be among the weakest institutions of the new civil society—weak in terms of gaining influence over policy-making or securing material rewards for workers."[35] One Ukrainian observer goes even further in her assessment, noting "if labor were really powerful, then [because of its sheer size] there would be no need to talk about any other political force at all."[36]

Readers may want to see evidence of union weakness, including how to measure it. This latter issue has dogged studies of unions in advanced industrialized states as well, but there have been efforts to measure union strength and overall effectiveness.[37] Essentially, union strength has two components: resources and impact on policy. Resources are those assets that allow unions to organize and articulate interests to policy makers. The impact on policy is a reflection of unions' ability to marshal resources and to achieve their positions. Impact on policy can also be measured by union's access to decision making itself, often through corporatist or tripartite institutions that seek to bring the state, employers, and labor together. There are four ways in which unions in postcommunist countries are weak: on the resource front, declining membership and the inability of unions to mobilize their members; on the policy front, the array of policies that have been adopted despite union objections and the lack of institutionalized access to decision making because of the weakness or ineffectiveness of corporatist institutions.

Membership

Membership is the sine qua non of a powerful union. Without members, unions will lack both financial resources and the ability to claim that they speak for a substantial part of the population. Without members, unions die. Thus, union density—the percentage of workers in a given sector or country who are union members—is often taken to be a primary variable in assessing union strength. It also happens to be the most quantifiable, which no doubt adds to its appeal as an indicator of organized labor's power.

Data for union membership in postcommunist states during 1990–2001 are presented in table 2.1. These data, I should add, are largely self-reported and cannot be independently verified—the International Labour Organization (ILO) and governments are forced to take unions at their word. Most observers, moreover, maintain that the figures are highly inflated. With that caveat in mind, a few items in the table stand out. One is that membership, compared with many Western countries and with other nongovernmental organizations in postcommunist countries, is still rather high. Unions claim as their own millions of workers, who in theory provide unions with a potent base through which they could exercise an important political role. Nonetheless, there has been a steep membership decline in many countries, particularly in Eastern Central Europe, where reforms have progressed further than in Russia or Ukraine. Finally, the communist-successor unions have many more members than the newer or independent unions. This is even the case in that former bastion of free unionism, Poland. The dominance of successor unions among workers helps perpetuate some of the communist legacy, although it is debatable how much these legacies still hamper unions a decade after communism's fall.

Beyond these observations, however, it is not self-evident what these membership data mean. Unions dwarf all other groups in civil and political society in all states. Their members in many states are in the millions; other groups, particularly political parties, have membership figures with only four or five digits. Union density figures of even 30 percent compare favorably with union density in the United States, France, and Japan. Thus, it is possible to suggest that unions are not really weak.

Few, however, make this claim. When looking at these figures, more attention is given to the *decline* in union membership since the collapse of communism, not today's membership. Indeed, it is notable that union decline in postcommunist Europe has been more marked than in any other region of the world.[38] This is particularly evident in the non-Soviet cases; Russian and Ukrainian unions have managed to, on paper at least, hang on to their members, in part due to the limited reforms in their economies but also due to workers' inertia. Numerous hypotheses might explain why this is the case, and union attrition is probably natural as membership is now voluntary, rather than mandatory or automatic. This study will focus on the effects of privatization and market liberalization. Thus, rather than conclude that large membership figures mean powerful unions, those worried about the fate of organized labor should be alarmed by this precipitous decline in member-

Table 2.1 Membership in Postcommunist Unions

Country	Union	Membership (in thousands)				Approximate Union Density, 2001 (%)
		1990–1991	1993	1995–1996	1999–2001	
Bulgaria	KNSB*	3,600	1,664	1,070	680	35
	Podkrepa	250	500	510	154	
Czech Republic	CMKOS*	4,500	3,500	2,300	1,500	35
Hungary	MSZOSZ*	2,700	1,300	892	235	20
	SZEF*	557	550	500	300	
	ASZSZ*	374	410	280	120	
	LIGA	70	250	100	50	
	MOSZ	106	160	80	30	
Poland	Solidarity	2,200	1,500	1,300	1,200	25
	OPZZ*	6,000	4,782	2,500	1,700	
Russia	FNPR*	66,000	64,300	45,000	38,000	70
Slovakia	KOZ*	—	1,500	1,200	830	35
Ukraine	FPU*	26,000	21,295	18,000	14,500	80

Sources: Numerous sources, mostly from author's contacts with unions, or unions' self-reported data given to state ministries or the ILO. Some figures may include pensioners, who are occasionally counted by unions as members. Some data come from chapter studies in Crowley and Ost, 2001.

Note: *Communist Successor Unions

ship. If this trend continues and unions find no way to add to their ranks, it is hard to imagine how they can reemerge as powerful factors in these states.

If, however, it is still tempting to conclude from these figures that unions really are not that weak, then how can it be explained why unions have been such marginal political, economic, and social players in the postcommunist period? The answer in part is that membership figures exist only on paper; it is something far different to turn those members into activists willing to lobby, strike, and protest to get their way.

Worker Mobilization

Union members are not likely to do unions much good if they are members in name only. They should feel part of an organization they can trust and be willing to participate in union activities. If unions cannot turn their members out to protest, vote, or engage in other collective action, then unions are not truly powerful. It is on this score that postcommunist unions reveal many of their weaknesses.

A large part of the problem is that workers (and the population in general) do not have much regard for unions. This phenomenon has been reported in virtually every country in numerous public opinion surveys.[39] While most institutions in postcommunist countries elicit little public enthusiasm, unions —both the communist successors and the new ones—rank near the very bottom of all groups in society in terms of public trust. In Ukraine, Russia, and the Czech Republic, the surveys show unions trusted by roughly 10 percent of the population, and even the old unions rank higher than the new, ostensibly more "democratic" ones in Russia and Ukraine. In Poland, unions are viewed somewhat more favorably, but it nonetheless must have troubled Solidarity to see its level of public trust, as Pankow reports, plummet from 69 percent in 1989 to 26 percent in 1993, a mere two points ahead of the OPZZ. Enterprise-level studies also confirm that workers are apt to see management as more effective in defending workers' interests and unions as largely ineffective.[40] An omnibus survey of the region in 1994 found that 91 percent of respondents expressed little or no trust in unions.[41] What cannot be said with certainty, however, is whether these findings are based upon perceptions of unions' performance in the postcommunist period (which is likely in the case with Solidarity, given its credibility in 1989) or a cultural carryover from low confidence in unions during communism. One effort to test competing explanations is made by Carola Frege and Andras Tóth, who argue that the low level of trust in Hungarian textile unions is based far more upon assessments of the union today than past experience under communism.[42]

What is just as troubling is that union leaders envision no way of getting out of this predicament and make little effort to try to recruit more members to energize the base. Ost reports that union leaders are almost embarrassed to be affiliated with the union and they make no special effort to reach out to workers.[43] Anna Pollert reports that only 7 percent of all Czech union members have been recruited since 1989.[44] In many countries, the private sector remains almost completely nonunion. Unions are thus "holding on" in the decrepit and ever shrinking state sector. In my own work in the four countries covered in this book, again and again I was struck by a sense of hopelessness among union leaders, a recognition that all was not right, that the unions needed "good cadres," but they had no notion how to acquire them. In a sense, the unions have fallen into a catch-22, recognizing that they need committed members to be strong, but in order to have committed members they must be capable and have something to offer them.[45]

This is not to say that unions have been completely incapable of mobilizing their members. The clearest example of grassroots labor activism has been the periodic strikes that have rocked the region. These have been far more prevalent in Poland, Russia, Ukraine, and Romania than in Hungary, Slovakia, or the Czech Republic. Table 2.2 provides strike data for selected years. The high number of strikes in Poland, Russia, and Ukraine is a reflection of the counting procedures. Most of these strikes were by doctors and teachers (both in the state sector), and the strike at each school or hospital was counted as one strike—hence the high total. Moreover, strike waves are evident, most clearly in Poland in 1992–1993 and Russia in 1995–1998. These waves are a reflection of both the political and economic environment, but in Poland, at any rate, the situation has been more peaceful since 1994. Finally, the short duration of strikes in Hungary and the Czech Republic can be interpreted as a sign of low labor mobilization.[46] Some strikes in the region, however, have been notable, including those in Romania and Russia that turned violent, those that shut down the Trans-Siberian Railway in 1998, and the strikes that helped bring down the Polish and Bulgarian governments in 1993.

Again, there is the question of what to make of these data. Ost rightly notes that strikes can indicate union weakness as well as union strength, a reflection that they are not getting what they want at the bargaining table and are forced to strike because of desperation.[47] He also observes that in many cases workers, not unions, have been the leaders of the strikes, and the unions go along with the strike call only to avoid undermining their credibility completely. Others who have examined the Polish case contend that these strikes show union strength, insofar as most result in concessions from the state or management, or both.[48] However, the strikes have not led to general empowerment of workers in Poland, and plans to close coal mines (which caused the most politically significant strikes) have gone ahead. In Russia and Ukraine, much of the strike activity is "repeat," meaning workers who were not paid struck, were then paid (at times from funds designed to help restructure their industries), suffered another round of wage arrears, and then struck again. Efforts to eradicate the root causes of workers' suffering have not been undertaken. In Romania, one report acknowledges that there is "an inverse relationship between the number of strikes and improvement of workers' conditions."[49] As for the possible argument that these numbers show a lot of

Table 2.2 **Strikes in Selected Postcommunist Countries**

Country	1993			1996			1999		
	# Strikes	# Strikers	Days/p.p.	# Strikes	# Strikers	Days/p.p.	# Strikes	# Strikers	Days/p.p.
Poland	7,443	383,200	1.51	21	44,300	1.69	920	27,149	3.94
Russia	264	120,000	1.97	8,278	663,900	6.04	7,285	238,400	7.66
Hungary	5	2,574	1.92	8	4,521	.53	5	16,685	14.5
Czech Republic	2	2,500	.12	2	11,500	1.43			
Ukraine	462	260,400	10.28	1,269	171,400	12.45	290	42,029	10.54

Source: ILO, *Yearbook of Labour Statistics, 2000* (Geneva: International Labour Organization, 2000).
Note: p.p. = per person.

strikes, the point is that strike activity has involved only 1–2 percent of the workforce in Russia and Ukraine (and admittedly more than this in Poland). This low percentage is, I would venture, less than could be expected given the privations suffered by the workers. Labor activism has been meager, not marked, and it certainly has not produced lasting, significant results for most workers. To the extent that many strikes have been difficult, if not impossible, to organize (due to a number of factors, including classic collective action dilemmas, the poor state of the economy, and strike fatigue for some workers) and are more spontaneous outbursts of workers' desperation than a consciously planned event by the unions themselves, *organized* labor is a paper tiger, and this no doubt undermines its ability to reach agreements with the state and management and exert broader political influence.

State Policies and Economic Outcomes

The most obvious way of gauging organized labor's power is to look at the economic environment of the region as well as government policy. In other words, strong labor unions should be delivering benefits for their members. However, even a cursory glance at the region shows that unions have been unable to do this. The postcommunist period has been disastrous for many workers: double-digit unemployment is the norm, real wages have fallen, the social safety net has immense holes in it, minimum wages are below subsistence level, and privatization has led to corruption and the rise of oligarchs, not an equitable distribution of wealth. These problems, admittedly less serious in Central Europe, are well known and need no elaboration. Of course, unions are not wholly to blame for this, just as unions cannot take complete credit for good economic conditions. What is noteworthy is the combination of economic catastrophe and general union quiescence, bordering on hopelessness. This cannot speak to union strength.

More disturbing have been the numerous antiunion policies taken by governments throughout the region. These policies are discretionary, and unions could have exercised more influence to prevent them. The list of government antiunion actions is very long, and almost every union leader has something to say on this score. In Hungary, for example, the 1992 Labor Code "severely curtailed the rights of unions at the workplace level," ending their role in overseeing managerial practices and in grievance procedures.[50] Similar measures have passed in other countries. Moreover, legislation in Hungary has promoted work councils, typically more docile institutions, so they have a share of power at the enterprise. This move is seen by some as a gambit by management to weaken or circumvent unions.[51] In the Czech Republic, legislation has chipped away at the issues and the number of workers covered by collective bargaining.[52] In Ukraine, the government officials, particularly at the local level, have worked with the FPU to hamper the development of independent trade unions.[53] A restrictive strike law has also been passed there, as well as in Romania, where several labor leaders have been arrested. In Russia, one report suggested that the unions were "one hundred percent ineffective" under Yeltsin's shock therapy, unable to advance much of their agenda or even see to it that existing laws are enforced.[54] Under Putin, a new labor code has been proposed that could weaken workers' protections at the workplace, such as giving management the right to change the terms of work and shuffle personnel in the enterprise.[55] Notably, governments have attacked unions even when union leaders have assumed prominent posts in government, as has been the case in Poland, Romania, and Hungary. This point is worth noting because *unionists* in power do not automatically lead to *empowered unions*. Ost notes that in the Polish case organized labor has "won little except the regular co-optation of its leaders,"[56] and a Russian author, V. G. Rupets, suggests that some unions in Russia "paid for their proximity to power with the downfall of the mass of workers."[57]

The action that may be the most debilitating to unions is privatization. Privatization, a major concern of this work, poses many challenges to labor, and the results have to this point rarely been to labor's liking. On the macrolevel, it has led to the concentration of wealth by a few individuals, banks, or investment houses, and the average person has profited little, despite, in several countries, provisions to facilitate workers' purchase of shares in their enterprises. On the microlevel, privatization has led to hierarchical management practices, the disempowerment of workers at the enterprise, as well as in some cases the outright disappearance of trade unions.[58] It has also fostered a decentralized system of collective bargaining, one that theoretically could respond both to workers' concerns and market conditions. Reports on the bargaining processes in the region are mixed, but some caution that a decentralized approach will play into the hands of management and make workers' solidarity impossible.[59] These issues at both the macro- and microlevels are crucial to the future of unions.

Some might note, however, that unions have not been disenfranchised. Rather, through neocorporatist or tripartite (labor-state-employers) bodies they have been empowered in all countries in postcommunist Europe. These forums provide unions with an institutionalized voice and often a very visible role.

Corporatist Institutions

Corporatist institutions,[60] which provide unions with an institutionalized role in policy making and a set of legal rights and responsibilities, are commonly taken to be an indicator of union effectiveness or strength.[61] Typically in corporatist regimes, workers are represented by a single, national union association, and this union is empowered by the state to negotiate on behalf of the workers and to bargain with state agencies and employers on various tripartite bodies that establish economic and social policies. Corporatist institutions are also assumed to be key components of a social democratic model of capitalism, which is assumed to be more egalitarian and inclusive of different interests than the Anglo-American variants.

There are problems with this line of argument, however. First, institutionalized access to policy making does not guarantee an *effective role* in policy making. Corporatist institutions may exist, but negotiations within them may have a negligible impact, or rules governing them may not be followed to the letter. Additionally, corporatist institutions have arisen in the past *because* of strong unions forcing concessions from the state, but in postcommunist Europe, they have been created largely "from above," not as a result of union pressure or empowerment. In fact, in some countries such as Bulgaria and Poland, unions have lobbied *against* the creation of corporatist bodies. Given this background, these institutions will therefore likely work differently from their counterparts in Western Europe.

It should not be surprising that corporatist institutions, although they exist almost universally in the region, are not very effective. The two most comprehensive, comparative investigations of corporatism both note that they play a marginal role in policy making, either because the preconditions of mature capitalism have not been established or state elites manage to control, manipulate, or simply ignore the unions and tripartite institutions.[62] According to one investigation, corporatism is but a facade, and tripartite bodies are used to give legitimacy to neoliberal, often antiunion policies, or to keep unions under control. In contrast to institutions in Western Europe, those in Eastern Europe are in "no position to bring about the politically stabilizing and economically inclusionary class compromise that was West European neocorporatism's great achievement."[63]

Numerous examples of corporatist failure have been documented. For example, in Russia the Russian Tripartite Commission, formed in 1992 as the main tripartite body, has not been integrally involved in policy making. Decisions are made elsewhere, and even in the rare event that debate does occur within the Committee, the norm is that "government leaders hope to press partners for approval of policies already formulated."[64] In a detailed study, Walter Connor contends that although the institutions are in place to lend a "surface plausibility" to a corporatist system, in reality corporatist structures are a "disorganized sideshow," essentially unworkable in the absence of a consensus on the proper reform path.[65] Given the role of the oligarchs in Russia, the centralization of power under Russia's constitution, and Putin's recent promotion of military and KGB officials into leading policy-setting roles, it is doubtful whether these bodies have been invested with any more importance.

The Czech Republic has also established corporatist-style committees, but under the reign of Thatcherite Vaclav Klaus they assumed very little importance. The CMKOS is viewed with suspicion by the government as an element of the *stárá struktura* (old structure).[66] Klaus has flatly declared that he prefers other means to determine economic policy, and the result is that Czech unions have been politically marginalized. In 1994, the economics minister brushed aside the possibility of union protests over low wages by asking, "Trade unions? What's that?"[67] A representative from the Czech National Bank concludes that the experience of the CMKOS on the Council on Economic and Social Agreement has been "embarrassing, its influence near zero."[68] Even a report that tried to find something positive to say about trade unions concluded, "trade unions have no choice but to accept government decisions."[69]

Hungary represented one of the best opportunities for corporatism, given its more gradual move to the market, its extensive set of institutions for workers' participation under communism, the early (1988) creation of a National Council for the Reconciliation of Interests (NCRI), and the election of a socialist government in 1994 with solid union support. However, corporatist institutions, despite an impressive array, have not worked very well. In part, they are constrained by union pluralism, the lack of strong, centralized employers, and ambiguity as to the institutions' jurisdiction. More to the point, however, the unions have been run roughshod by the government. Prior to 1994, the government demonstrated little willingness to take unions seriously, preferring a statist or technocratic approach to policy making.[70] The elections of 1994 brought new hope that labor could institutionalize a political role for itself by virtue of its connections with the Socialist Party. However, in 1995 the government imposed an austerity program without consulting the unions, and tripartite negotiations were suspended. Efforts to revive them yielded few results for labor, and the new government elected in 1998 has essentially abandoned the corporatist path.[71]

Last, the Polish case is instructive because it was here, by virtue of the Solidarity movement, that corporatism may have stood its best chance. Solidarity could have forced a corporatist path upon the postcommunist governments, but it elected not to do so. Thus, Poland remained, until 1994, one of the few postcommunist countries without even the trappings of corporatism. The return of the former communists to office did lead to the creation of tripartite bodies, but these have not been central to policy making. In the polarized Polish environment, corporatism has been hampered by the rivalry between Solidarity and the OPZZ, with each boycotting tripartite bodies when its opponent's partner was in power. While there was some agreement and cooperation during 1995–1997, this broke down when the Solidarity-backed electoral coalition won elections. By 1999, "tripartite activity had almost completely broken down,"[72] and this coincided with growth in strike activity.

The situations in Ukraine, Bulgaria, and Slovakia are hardly better. Suffice to say that unions cannot make these corporatist institutions function properly without the ability to mobilize their members and make governments suffer the consequences of unpopular or antiunion policies. The corporatist institutions exist not so much to serve workers, but to give elites an ability to say that they are conforming to European standards and to offer a virtually cost-free gesture to workers, while still doing largely whatever they want.

Why Are Unions So Weak?

While virtually all observers can agree on the general weaknesses of postcommunist trade unions, there is debate on the root causes of the unions' predicament. The varying conclusions reached by scholars can be accounted for by the countries or cases they choose to study or the level of analysis of their research, or both. That is, scholars focusing on enterprises tend to focus on enterprise-level factors, whereas those investigating unions on the national level tend to stress more general political or economic factors. Nonetheless, several theories that have been put forward can help account for labor weakness. They are not all mutually exclusive, and often accounts of trade unions will weave together a mixture of explanations.

These approaches can be roughly placed into two categories. The first category, more of a "path dependent" approach, identifies the root causes of postcommunist labor weakness in labor's inheritance from the communist system. In other words, labor is handicapped today because certain legacies and choices made in the past make it far more difficult for it to overcome its communist history and become an effective political, economic, and social actor. The second category focuses more on the peculiarities of the postcommunist period, arguing that the uncertainties, unfamiliarity, and dislocations of the new political and economic system have hampered labor's ability to organize and defend its position. Multiple theories can be identified in both categories and deserve closer inspection.

With respect to the path-dependent approach, two main arguments have been advanced. One highlights the persistence of "residual corporatist" institutions that have been inherited from communist times and are sometimes little altered by postcommunist governments.[73] This argument is different from what was mentioned above about corporatism, where the point was that the corporatist institutions built on Western European models and designed to give workers a real, institutionalized voice are not working. Here the main argument is that the persistence of communist-era unions and ways of doing business that are akin to state (authoritarian) corporatism work against the emergence of a vigorous, independent labor movement. The troika of union leader/manager/state (formerly party) official (in which the unions were in the subordinate position) has not been entirely broken, as it operates both informally and through corporatist institutions of "social partnership," nationally and at the enterprise level. Many unions are also rather "unreformed," and corruption—both real and perceived—works against them in dealings with the state and in retaining and mobilizing members. One report from Russia noted that the FNPR reflects the "flesh and blood of the upper stratum of the Soviet bureaucracy" and that the union leadership is more loyal to management or state ministries than to its membership.[74] In the Czech Republic, the CMKOS survived the end of communism largely intact, but as a consequence it was treated with suspicion by the promarket government of Vaclav Klaus and thus, according to one report, "emasculated" and "marginalized."[75] In some cases, unions have not been entirely freed from a dependent relationship with the state, especially as the state can take away union property or pass laws that would seriously undermine the ability of these holdover unions to retain their dominance over the labor force. Thus, the unions are not in a position to resist vociferously state efforts to enact policies that are sometimes hostile to workers. At the same time, however, these holdover unions can forge alliances with more conservative governments to prevent the emergence of independent unions that would be more interested and perhaps capable of mobilizing workers. Thus, unions are trapped in a peculiar bargain with the state akin to state corporatism, one that reflects more elements of the old system than a pluralist, democratic one.

Another type of structural explanation has been proffered by Crowley, whose research on the branch- or mesolevel asks why coal workers strike and steel workers do not.[76] His answer, based upon resource mobilization theory, identifies a crucial difference between the two sectors: coal miners receive high salaries but fewer fringe benefits (the mines are now far less able to provide housing, schools, consumer goods) whereas steel workers, albeit lower paid, do get these benefits in kind. Benefits, however, are distributed at the discretion of management and through largely obedient trade unions. This union-as-social service organization is, of course, a direct holdover from the Soviet system, as discussed previously. Miners have only their salaries to lose, and thus they are more likely to strike when they are not paid. Steel workers, however, stay on the job for fear of losing their more valuable benefits. Unions' "Soviet" role as a social service department, a task that many unions have fought to preserve, thus ironically works against their ability to mobilize workers. Crowley's theory could also be invoked (although he does not do so) to explain why the majority of strikers in postcommunist states have been teachers and doctors, employees in the state sector who receive few side benefits and cannot be paid in kind from their place of employment. Crowley's approach, however, is not without its critics. Ashwin notes that if Crowley is correct then the workers with the least pay and benefits—female textile workers —should compose the vanguard of workers' mobilization.[77] They do not. Thus, it cannot be said that Crowley's theory has universal validity.

Not all explanations rely so strongly on path dependency. Others focus more on the particular and peculiar features of the postcommunist transition. This comes across most clearly in the work of Debra Javeline.[78] Her research asks why Russians do not protest more, given the appalling economic conditions and massive wage arrears. Unlike Crowley, she puts no stock in explanations relating to the level of fringe benefits that workers receive. Armed with survey evidence, she claims that workers (and Russians in general) do not protest because they are unable to assign blame for their predicament and thus do not know to whom they should direct their protests. She presents an array of data from 1996 to 1998 showing that the ability to blame an actor (together with education, urban residence, and confidence in the Communist Party) accounts for propensity to protest, more than delayed wages, nonwage benefits, a second income, political efficacy, and political interest. She argues that there has been little protest precisely because Russians do not know who to blame for the economic disaster that has befallen them: the president, the Duma, local authorities, the mafia, management, their unions, or the IMF? Each possible culprit, of course, can plausibly blame someone else—the result is confusion and, eventually, passivity.

The same argument could be made in different terms, maintaining that the underdevelopment of capitalist institutions creates ambiguity with respect to ownership and responsibility. The corollary to this would be that Javeline is highlighting only a temporary phenomenon and that as time passes, workers will be better able to determine their own interests and who is to blame for their problems. The survey data, of course, tell us only part of the story, and left largely unanswered is how Russians are able to learn to assign blame. Arguably, for instance, trust in the Communist Party could be a proxy for ability to blame. Or, protests themselves could "teach" people who is to blame, so the causal arrow is actually the other way. However, enterprise-level studies, such as those by Ashwin,[79] also capture this sense of confusion among workers, so Javeline's points cannot be so easily dismissed. There is not, however, appreciably more protest in countries such as Hungary or the Czech Republic where, admittedly, economic conditions are not as dire as in Russia, but where ambiguity and confusion should be less pronounced due to greater progress on reforms. Whether Javeline's arguments can therefore be applied to a more "normalized" situation as in Poland or Hungary remains to be seen.

Crowley and Ost have put forth another argument that gets at this notion of confusion, albeit a case in which the confusion is in part shaped by history as well as the present.[80] Their contention is that labor lacks a voice today because it lacks a discourse or ideology that would enable it to articulate a specific *labor* agenda. Thus, it is hamstrung in any effort to appeal to workers as workers. This argument is developed most clearly by Ost in the case of Solidarity. He contends that workers in Poland today essentially lack "class consciousness" since the structure and discourse of communism delegitimated the emergence of *class* identity because class-based rhetoric had been appropriated by the regime. Therefore, the anticommunist struggle and the Solidarity movement itself were based, he claims, on universal, not class, claims. Solidarity was therefore less a trade union than a social movement, and this can be seen by the formation of agrarian and student Solidarities, groups that have interests distinct from workers. Moreover, by looking at Solidarity's demands both in 1989 and after, there is little that is distinctly *worker* about it. Indeed, in the middle of the 1990s Solidarity spent far more energy on questions of abortion, Church–state relations, and lustration of former communists, not to mention efforts to get its candidates elected to office, than battling for *worker* issues. Thus, Ost claims, because workers did not think of themselves as a class yesterday, they are less able to think and act as a class today with a coherent ideology. This legacy is compounded by the particularities of the postcommunist period and the hegemony of capitalist or neoliberal discourse. There is no alternative to this new ideology, save the discredited old one, and thus Solidarity has been compelled to go along with shock therapy reforms because it had no vision of an alternative and it cannot back social-democratically oriented initiatives from the party of the Democratic Left because it is still obsessed with fighting the communists.

This argument can also be supported with evidence from other countries. In Russia, its essence is captured by comments from Aleksandr Sergeev, a leader of the NPG in Russia, who noted that the NPG supported the new bourgeoisie and Yeltsin because there was no alternative.[81] This union also supported mine privatization, in the now apparent naive belief that privatization and market liberalization would allow mines to sell coal on the open world market at higher prices and thus ensure profitability. They clearly underestimated the problems of mines in the former USSR, and now that some privatization has occurred and problems continue to mount for many mines, they have found themselves in an awkward position because they have no "Plan B" to fall back on.[82] One Russian writer documenting the problems of all the independent unions contended that they have been hampered in appealing to workers because they have been unable to free themselves from a "hypnotic official ideology" that presents any opposition to reforms as communism in new garb.[83] In the Hungarian case, one expert on labor relations notes that the several independent trade unions formed when communism began to collapse were designed to serve more a political than an economic purpose.[84] Thus, they have been unable to articulate a solid vision of their role once the Communist Party was removed from power. In the Czech Republic, the CMKOS has, as one union leader admits, a "schizophrenic" character as it is compelled to support reform but objects to certain key elements of it.[85] It cannot, however, find a way out of this conundrum by articulating a credible program that would allow it to present a labor-based or labor-friendly reform.

Crowley and Ost argue that in the postcommunist period, the rhetoric of the working class is passé and cannot be put into a framework that differentiates it from communism. They conclude, based upon the several country studies in their volume, that union leaders have little notion of where their interests lie and have essentially jumped aboard the capitalist bandwagon without much thought. They note, "East European labor seems to believe that weak unions are precisely what capitalism is all about. They tend to see unions as rearguard institutions for the weak, relevant chiefly for obsolescent state-sectors, rather than as vital representatives of labor against capital, let alone agents of expanded citizenship."[86] Taking the argument further, they would contend that all the counterproductive legacies of the communist period create a path dependency that weakens unions and that even when the effects of the legacies are no longer discernible, labor will find it difficult to "right" itself because of the path it put itself on (or, in some cases, was put on). If true, this type of explanation would go a long way in explaining the lack of labor mobilization and the relative ease politicians have in disregarding trade unions.

While these specific arguments may apply better to the new, independent, democratic trade unions that have tended to side with market reformers, the old, "official" unions are not immune to myopic visions. They, however, tend to be caught in the past or at least *perceived* in this manner. This helps explain both why they cannot mobilize their members and why free marketers such as Balcerowicz and Klaus can so easily dismiss them as relics of a past age that have little or no business in shaping the capitalist future. Moreover, their ideological blinders have prohibited them from engaging on the main issues of the day. For example, in Russia, the FNPR continued to defend wages, job security, and fringe benefits for the workers, when, according to one Russian labor activist, the real question was property redistribution.[87] In general, these unions—and not just in Russia—are in a very defensive position, trying to hang on to remnants of the old system without much conception of how to shape a new, market-oriented system that will be more respectful of workers' interests.

Another approach contends that the problem of organized labor is not so much that it is unable to find its own voice or discourse but that it has been led astray and betrayed by intellectuals and politicians who have used workers for their own ends but then turned their backs on them once they came into power.[88] This argument has been pushed most forcefully in the case of Poland, where for years there was a tension between workers and anticommunist intellectuals. Solidarity's success in 1980–1981 was, arguably, due in part to a coalition made between the two groups, but after 1989 this alliance began to break down. Finance Minister Balceworicz became a lightning rod for criticism by workers, who accused him of betraying them by implementing shock therapy and not telling them the real consequences of the reforms. According to this view, once in power these former Solidarity leaders, many without workers' roots, became advocates for a still nonexistent capitalist class and did whatever was necessary to weaken or coopt workers' organizations.[89] Solidarity leaders, to the extent that they gave their blessing to the first postcommunist governments, were deemed culpable in this betrayal. Thus self-described "pure-worker" elements in Solidarity formed their own union, Solidarity 80, breaking with what they perceived to be a union leadership in cahoots with the neoliberal new elite. Wildcat strikes—not approved by the Solidarity leadership—ensued, Walesa began to attack the leadership and initiated his "war from above" to assert presidential power, and trust in Solidarity plummeted. Other analysts, in a slight twist, blamed the IMF and international advisers for forcing the government's hand in adopting the reforms.[90] The results, however, were deemed to be the same: betrayal.

Similar arguments have been made in the case of Russian independent trade unions, which backed Yelstin in his struggles with Gorbachev and later the Supreme Soviet and also gave him carte blanche to adopt his own version of shock therapy. Clarke et al. contend that the independent labor movement, particularly the NPG and Sotsprof, had to rely on political patronage because they lacked resources at the grassroots level, particularly access to the fringe benefits controlled by the official unions. They remained loyal to Yeltsin, hoping that he would both adopt worker-friendly policies and change the rules of the game so that they could compete more favorably with the old unions. Neither happened. Shock therapy led to impoverishment of millions, and Yeltsin later tried to court the official unions in corporatist institutions, leaving the independent unions politically marginalized.[91] Sergeev of the NPG conceded that politicians had tossed workers "bones, slogans with no economic basis" and that intellectuals had purposefully tried to restrict the number of workers elected to the Supreme Soviet. He added that the elite could get away with this because of workers' ignorance about how a market economy operates. He stated, "Someone who has spent six hours at physical labor and has to worry about where to get food naturally doesn't think about these things [economic reform models]. They [the politicians] tell him, 'Here's your chance to become [an] owner. Until now you've worked without being the owner.' And he says to himself, 'Hey, maybe that's the truth! Who the hell knows?'" Sergeev also asserted that he was under no illusions about Yeltsin. Nonetheless, in an interview in 1992 he continued to offer him support, even though it was apparent that Yeltsin had little time for trade unions or any voices from below.[92]

Last is the James Carville argument: It's the economy, stupid. Economies throughout postcommunist Europe have shrunk an average of 25 percent since 1989, although the fall has been twice as high in the two largest countries, Russia and Ukraine. Workers have been devastated by this catastrophe: savings have been wiped out by inflation; real wages have plummeted; economic security has disappeared with the loss of social safety nets; and many firms have gone bankrupt, dismissed workers, or are unable to pay their workers on time. Worker quiescence in the face of this disaster is a puzzle, but perhaps one with a simple answer: this environment is ill suited for any sort of workers' organization or activism. Labor markets in all countries are slack. In many countries, production is only a small fraction of capacity. Workers who strike or otherwise protest against management can be dismissed without real costs to management given the fact that many workers are available to replace them and the company itself may want to downsize anyway to get rid of unproductive workers. Workers thus have no clout or meaningful resources that they can withhold from their employers, and they strike or protest only when they are most desperate. Moreover, because individuals are under such duress, many are choosing the option of "exit" (into the burgeoning informal economy) rather than the more costly and risky action of exercising a collective "voice" via trade unions or other organizations. Informal work, however, often is quite derogating and takes place in arenas where workers have little or no rights. It also exacerbates problems of collective action by isolating workers in more individualistic economic pursuits.

While these arguments no doubt hold a certain degree of intuitive appeal, it is worth echoing Ost and Crowley who contend that this hypothesis does not stand up to even the most basic test.[93] For example, by the reasoning of this argument, more labor activism would be expected in countries with healthier economies, such as Hungary and the Czech Republic. This is not the case—in both states, labor has been more quiescent than in countries with worse economic problems such as Romania, Bulgaria, and Russia.

What is striking about all these arguments in both categories is that they imply most of labor's problems are transitory, either the result of vestiges of the past still present today or because of problems unique to the transition period itself. Both elements will eventually erode and lose explanatory power, which is clearest in the case of arguments about residual corporatism. While these observations may have had some resonance with the immediate post-communist period in countries such as Russia and Ukraine, it arguably was and is less applicable in more reform-oriented states, where communist residue has been mopped up to a much greater extent. Moreover, even in Russia and Ukraine, the communist-era "way of doing business" should begin to change as private ownership becomes more widespread and the state retreats a bit from the economy. Crowley's arguments may hold up better, but his points will become less applicable as fringe benefits are taken out of the hands of enterprises and unions and given over to providers on the open market or taken over by the state. Already there is ample evidence that private employers in Russia do not want to be burdened with being a social service agency.[94]

Arguments about confusion, ideological blinders, or betrayal may also become less relevant over time as workers and unions adjust to the new conditions, become able to articulate their interests, target protest, and become less reliant on communist-era discourse. The neoliberal moment in several states, notably Russia, has ended, and thus alternative discourses should be able to emerge. True, path dependency may still hamper union development, but to the extent that the "ideological legacy" of communism identified by Crowley and Ost is being overcome, more labor activism might be expected if, to put it simply, labor's problems were more psychological or ideological than structural. Put another way, human agency should be able to overcome many aspects of this form of path dependency. Moreover, this point can be extended further into a hypothesis that given time workers and unions will rebound from their current problems and find ways to assert themselves in a marketized, more adversarial (worker-owner) economy. True, we may be left with a hangover from the communist era for many years to come, some of these points may remain only possibilities, and all obstacles to union development may not come down entirely swiftly in all countries, but the prevailing explanations of labor weakness do offer some grounds for hope. Indeed, Crowley and Ost's "path dependency" argument is far from optimistic, but they should be able to recognize that path dependency need not imply determinism and that new ideas and approaches can emerge, especially given changes in the political economy. They fail to give due consideration to discourse of a Third Way and to the hope among labor activists of replicating the Austrian or German experience, two developments which demonstrate that labor is *not* wholly captive either to neoliberal discourse or its own past. Looked at from this perspective, then, there might be hope for postcommunist labor.

Be that as it may, the central hypotheses of this work reflect a less sanguine view of the future, albeit one that is not rooted in explanations of discourse or ideology. The rosy forecasts ignore some important facts about the effects of structural economic change. First, capitalism in the West evolved gradually; in the East it is being imposed by the state where some of the prerequisites of the market may not have been met.[95] Capitalism in the West led to the gradual empowerment and enfranchisement of workers; in the East, a bourgeoisie is being created largely from scratch and the existing workers are being asked (or told) to surrender some of the perks that they had under the previous system. Additionally, social democracy and democratic corporatism (the German model for labor leaders in postcommunist Europe) arose in Western Europe due to strong unions and social movements. Lacking these conditions, it is hard to see how institutions that give labor a prominent voice and political role will emerge. It is not exactly a chicken-and-egg argument; rather, it is an observation that postcommunist Europe has neither the chicken nor the egg and thus to expect either to spontaneously appear may be wishful thinking. Also, and perhaps most important, the Germany or Austria dreamed of by some in Eastern Europe is not what it once was. Organized labor in advanced industrialized states is far weaker than it once was, and thus as postcommunist countries begin to look more like Western Europe, labor may not be saved at all. Rather, the twin forces of marketization and globalization, accused by many of weakening labor's standing in the West, may also work against labor's emergence or reemergence in the East. Thirkell et al. suggest, "It is perhaps particularly ironic that, just as trade unions in the East glimpse the possibility of obtaining some of the advantages of Western European systems, scholars in the West are increasingly identifying the fracture and decomposition of Western European models of labour relations in the context of economic globalization."[96] Prima facie, this seems plausible given the fact that union membership (perhaps the most crucial component of union strength) has dropped more precipitously in those postcommunist states that have gone furthest with reform. Thus, labor's ultimate problem is less the communist past or the confusing and turbulent present, but the future that will be defined by market relations. In this view, labor will not find it easy to adapt to the market, even when it frees itself from the fetters of the past.

This is, of course, not what union leaders or supporters of strong unions want to contemplate. It is always preferable to dream of a better tomorrow.

3

East Meets West

IT IS IRONIC THAT POSTCOMMUNIST labor leaders are looking more and more to the experience of their colleagues in the West, just as organized labor in most advanced industrialized countries is experiencing a marked decline. However, there is little doubt that some of the very same processes that are helping to erode trade union power in the West, and their concomitant neocorporatist, social-democratic policies, are also present in Eastern Europe. Viewed from this perspective, unions' problems in the region—at least over the long term—may stem less from the past legacies of communism than from movement to a marketized, globalized economic system. Looking at the new political economy in the region thus frees the analysis from exclusive reliance on the past or path dependency and helps integrate the postcommunist experience more into the broader sphere of comparative politics.

The literature is extensive on labor's decline in the advanced capitalist states. The central argument is that postcommunist Europe is being molded, both by design and by default, into an image of the West. True, it is not a mirror image, and no doubt some countries still have a long way to go to even approach the standards of a developed capitalist economy.[1] Critics might even suggest that most of these states will be condemned to live on the semi-periphery of the global economy. Moreover, with variants of capitalism and systems of industrial and labor relations, there is no single Western sociopolitical system. Nonetheless, in important respects, the capitalist system of the West—broadly defined—will be the future of the East, particularly in that efforts to establish a humanistic Third Way, prevalent in much of the dissident writing in the communist period, have been essentially abandoned.[2] Although there may be room for each state to develop some unique institutions or features, free markets and open economies will be the norm, and all the more so with several postcommunist states joining the European Union. This fact is recognized—often with little enthusiasm—by trade union leaders in the region.

Thus, if the premise is accepted that many of the overarching structures of political economy will be similar between East and West, it could be posited that the results will be similar for labor. This hypothetical condition is convergence and is clearly a more pessimistic prognostication than assuming that postcommunist labor will one day be able to find its voice and overcome the legacies of path dependency once the situation becomes "normal." However, matters are not all that simple or predetermined. A crucial point to keep in mind is that even though the destinations in both cases are the same, the starting points are different. Unions in the West moved from a position of relative strength to weakness. Unions in the East are starting with a heritage of weakness (Poland being the main exception). It might be argued that in the former case unions had nowhere to go but "down," whereas in the latter they have nowhere to go but "up." The emergence of capitalism and democracy could thus provide unions with an opportunity to reach out and mobilize workers as they were unable to do in the communist past. Hence, it is possible to look forward to resurgence for organized labor in postcommunist states.

Accounting for Unions' Decline in the West

The deterioration of organized labor in the West is beyond much dispute and can be seen most clearly in union membership in various countries. Table 3.1 illustrates the extent of union decline in several countries based upon union membership. Although there have been fluctuations across time, and some countries continue to have high union membership (notably Sweden), membership decline has been an ongoing process in most Western countries for several years, gaining more momentum with the establishment of neoliberal norms in the 1980s. Membership, of course, should not be construed to be the only indicator of union strength. However, as David Peetz notes, "declining union density may raise major problems of legitimacy for the union movement as a whole. It can be used as a weapon by employer groups and others to argue that the 'privileges' afforded unions, and denied the majority of the workforce, should be withdrawn. Declining union membership may lead to cutbacks in staff and resources in unions and thereby to reductions in the union organizing effort and services provided to members."[3]

Another problem for unions in Western states is the low level of public

Table 3.1 **Loss of Union Membership in Advanced Industrial States**

Country	Union Density (% of workers belonging to a union)					
	1950	1960	1970	1980	1990	1997
Austria	66.3	65.8	63.6	59.6	56.2	46.6
France	30.2	19.2	21	17.1	9.2	8.6 (1995)
Germany	40.8	38.7	37.7	40.6	38.5	33.4
Italy	43.8	28.5	38.5	49	39.2	38 (1995)
Japan	36.5 (1953)	31.3	34.1	30	24.5	—
Netherlands	44.2	44.2	39.8	39.4	29.5	28.9
Sweden	67.3	70.7	66.6	78.2	82.4	86.4
United Kingdom	44.3 (1955)	44.5	48.6	54.5	38.1	30.2
United States	31.1 (1952)	29.4	25.9	20.2	14.8	13.5 (2000)

Source: Jeremy Waddington and Reiner Hoffmann, "Trade Unions in Europe: Reform, Organization, and Restructuring," in Waddington and Hoffman, eds., *Trade Unions in Europe* (Brussels: European Trade Union Institute, 2000), 54; and Miriam Golden, Peter Lange, and Michael Wallerstein, "Union Centralization among Advanced Industrial Societies: An Empirical Study," 1997, at www.shelley.polisci.ucla.edu/data.

trust in unions. Data from the 1999–2000 European Values Survey (table 3.2) show that solid majorities (West and East) do not have much confidence in unions, with confidence in several EU states lower than that in postcommunist states—a phenomenon that rarely happens in such confidence indices. Moreover, confidence in unions ranks lower than confidence in the press and civil service—popular targets for public skepticism. While time-series data are lacking, it nonetheless is clear that unions do suffer from a low public standing in many Western countries, which is no doubt both a symptom and a cause of their general malaise.

Furthermore, in other measures typically associated with strong unions— in particular neocorporatist structures and policies that provided unions with an institutionalized role in policy making and sought full employment with social redistribution—there is also little dispute that unions have declined.[4] The post–World War II Golden Age for organized labor is now over, evi-

Table 3.2 **Public Confidence in Trade Unions and Other Entities, 1999–2000**

	Respondents expressing "not much" or "none at all" confidence in select institutions (%)		
Country	Trade Unions	The Press	Civil Service
Great Britain	72.0	84.2	54.1
France	65.2	64.3	54.1
Germany	62.2	64.0	61.2
Italy	71.3	64.8	66.8
Spain	72.6	58.7	59.5
Netherlands	41.4	44.6	62.5
Sweden	57.5	54.2	51.2
Austria	68.6	68.1	57.6
Poland	66.0	53.2	67.5
Hungary	76.3	69.2	50.4
Russia	69.5	70.0	62.2
Ukraine	62.4	53.5	61.0
Survey Average	64.8	61.2	60.3

Source: Loek Halman, *The European Vaues Study: A Third Wave* (Tilburg, Netherlands: Tilburg University Press, 2001). The European Values Survey was conducted in thirty-one countries continentwide in 1999–2000.

denced by a shift in policy making to arenas far less amenable to corporatist-style bargaining.[5] Unions have also declined politically, as witnessed by the arms-length distance that unions are now held by several of their erstwhile political allies (e.g., the British Labour Party, the German Social Democratic Party). While some particular unions do remain powerful forces, there is nonetheless little doubt that as a whole organized labor has been in decline in the West.

While it is relatively easy to note labor's decline, it is far more difficult to account for it. Union membership and overall strength depends upon a variety of individual, workplace, organizational, national, and even international factors. Numerous arguments have been put forward to account for the rise and fall of trade unions, including historical institutionalist approaches,[6] cultural theories,[7] and success of social-democratic parties.[8] Others might be tempted to adopt a country-by-country approach and stress the role of political leadership or particular ideological programs in combating organized labor (these points crop up with regularity in discussions of the United States under Ronald Reagan and the United Kingdom under Margaret Thatcher). For example, governments' pursuit of price stability and the abandonment of full employment policies could be considered a phenomenon that was especially damaging to unions.[9] These policies—part of the so-called Washington Consensus—have been exported to postcommunist states. All this being said, few would doubt that we are witnessing at present a process with deeply rooted structural causes that go beyond mere policy shifts or preferences. Some of these causes, it is true, are not objective in the sense that they have been promoted by advocates of neoliberalism and thus can be construed as a policy choice,[10] but fundamentally the assault on trade unions in most Western countries can be attributed to shifts in the mode of production, a reflection of changing global markets, and introduction of new technologies.

What precisely are some of these factors? One, which has been noted in numerous works, is the deindustrialization of the West and the rise of the service sector. Some have labeled this a shift from "Fordism" to "post-Fordism," signifying that the nature of work has fundamentally changed.[11] It has long been a maxim that certain types of enterprises (large-scale manufacturing, mining, energy, construction) are more amenable to unionization. Due in part to the physical nature of work, a rather homogeneous set of workers' interests, more adversarial worker-management relations, and the sheer size of these enterprises, unions are more likely to emerge in these settings. Indeed, workers in large industrial enterprises have formed the backbone of trade unions throughout the world. As traditional manufacturing jobs have gradually disappeared in many advanced industrial states, jobs have been lost and union membership has fallen because displaced workers take up jobs in sectors less conducive to unionization. Moreover, given the weaknesses of this sector, it is arguable that the remaining industrial unions are often on the defensive, recognizing that they have a weaker hand to play against management.

The flipside of the decline of manufacturing has been the rise of the service sector and its appendage, the much ballyhooed New Economy. Workers in the service sector are, on average, less likely to join unions. The reasons are many: there is more work based on individual workers or small teams; more temporary employment; flexible hours; and a less clear distinction between worker and manager, both of whom may wear white collars. To put it in Marxist terms, it is doubtful that an insurance salesman, an accountant, or a retail clerk has the same sense of class consciousness as a coal miner, who, at least traditionally, knew that he could aspire to little else than being a miner. Of course, certain service sector employees are unionized—airline pilots, teachers, public utility workers—but many of these (again, not all) work in the public sector. In general, studies find that the changing composition of the workforce, as evidenced by movement into the service sector, accounts for a large chunk of the decline in union membership.

This leads to an additional factor: private ownership. Indeed, at least one author, Jonas Pontusson, points to how the dynamics of the service sector and private ownership work together against unionization.[12] Private owners, far more than the managers of state or publicly owned enterprises, can afford to be antiunion: they do not answer to a political constituency, and in some cases they may possess the wherewithal to buy off workers and prevent unionization. Moreover, because private firms are beholden to profit and loss under hard budget constraints, owners lack the means or incentive to cut a deal with the workers and "bill" the state, which may only weakly or nominally supervise activities at a publicly owned enterprise operating under softer constraints. In addition, unions can use their position in the public sector— for example, teachers, government civil service—to impose closed shop requirements, thereby maintaining their membership. Private schools, for the most part, and subcontracted workers (such as airport security workers prior to 9/11) are typically nonunion. Moreover, privatization disperses economic resources into several hands, and with the decentralization of ownership it may be harder to organize corporatist-style tripartite bodies of government, labor, and owners, which often serve to provide labor with an institutionalized voice in management of the economy. For all of these reasons, it should not be surprising that unions typically have resisted privatization efforts in the West (e.g., in the United Kingdom under Thatcher), and there remains a prevalent assumption that measures to promote or empower private owners will be detrimental to organized labor.

In addition, even if privatization does not lead to deunionization, it is to be expected that it changes union-management relations and that relations in private firms will differ significantly from state firms.[13] Again, part of the issue is the constituency of the owner and political accountability, but the form of privatization may also matter, with better worker-union relations expected at firms that are privatized with manager-worker buyouts (a common practice in Russia and Ukraine). However, once privatized, the singular drive for profits in private companies may compel owners to take an active role in work reorganization, particularly in cases (as in most postcommunist countries) where workers de jure had a lot of power on the shop floor. This could, of course, lead to conflictual relations, ones that might empower labor. However, disputes are likely to be localized and tied to the practice of the firm, not the practice of the state. Thus, privatization, while preserving unions, may prevent the emergence of a unified union movement.

Finally, the shrinking size of enterprises is a variable that has had demonstrable effects on organized labor's position. Large enterprises based on mass production figured prominently in the story of trade union development. In this case, size is an advantage, because larger enterprises are better able to foster class consciousness, shrink the costs of collective action, and create greater homogeneity of interests. Large firms are also more capital intensive, and hence the wage bill is a smaller share of costs, making unions less costly to management. In the 1960s, however, the average size of industrial plants in the West began to shrink, due both to the infusion of labor-saving technologies and desire for smaller, more nimble firms. Studies confirm a link between plant size and unionization.[14] Smaller firms not only present coordination problems for unions in a particular branch of the economy, but they also encourage a more heterogeneous workforce. Competition among firms also may lead to competition among workers (e.g., which company will survive in the marketplace), and this would undermine labor solidarity.

Thus, labor is weakened by deindustrialization, growth of the service sector, expansion of private ownership, and decrease in enterprise size. All of these elements have been witnessed in the West in recent years and in some corners are taken to be part and parcel of a postmodern, competitive, dynamic economy, as opposed to the behemoth state-owned smokestack industries of a bygone era. To the extent postcommunist countries are transforming their economies in this direction (which is largely the case, albeit in some cases a slow process), labor, weak today, may find itself in an even weaker position tomorrow.

While there is general consensus on the above claims, we should also take up a far more controversial, albeit relevant and interesting, argument: the effect of globalization on organized labor. In the past, some maintained that open, trade-dependent economies were more likely to produce corporatist systems that helped empower unions.[15] Now, however, some maintain that globalization is eroding the power of organized labor. Juliusz Gardawski, for example, is most emphatic on this point. He claims that "In the first place, among the reasons causing the crisis of trade unions belongs the deepening of international division of labor and the globalization of world markets."[16]

This often made argument is based on an extensive literature and has several strands.[17] One is that labor's status and its rights are based upon its capacity to exert pressure in the domestic political arena. To the extent that state power is eroded by globalization, the state must answer to foreign constituencies (e.g., other states, investors, the IMF), and when decision making occurs in forums where labor has no voice or leverage, labor loses an important means of protecting itself.[18] Another argument is based on convergence: globalization forces states to adopt similar policies, and competitive pressures will result in a "race to the bottom," which will erode labor's rights and power.[19] Finally, it can argued that global markets—which largely lack the regulations of domestic ones—will, ceteris paribus, favor capital over labor because the former enjoys mobility and thus is in better position to respond to, and dictate to, markets.

Different actors in, or levels of, globalization that supposedly threaten labor can be identified, and these elements provide a means for measuring the extent of globalization in a given country. First, there are organizations such as the IMF, other international financial institutions (IFIs), and faceless international markets that apply conditionality and put pressure on states to adopt austerity programs and business-friendly legislation, often undermining the position of trade unions and the ability of governments to negotiate with them on social and economic policies. Many have argued that countries subjected to IMF structural adjustment programs typically experience increases in unemployment and inequality, and declines in real wages, social expenditures, and legal protection for workers.[20] Moreover, to the extent that institutions such as the IMF wield decisive influence and decision-making power, they erode not only labor's position but also that of domestic voters, hence compromising democracy.

Moreover, international trade is a factor. Several decades ago, import substitution policies were the norm in many states, and these policies were designed to protect workers from foreign competition and often went hand-in-hand with state policies to incorporate unions in policy making. This changed with the turn toward export-oriented industrialization, in which the watchwords were specialization, competitiveness, and engagement with the world economy. Subsidies to labor were scaled back, and the openness to world markets was designed to challenge local production, potentially forcing cuts in wages and benefits or prompting decentralization of labor relations in order for local industries to be competitive or flexible enough to survive in a more dynamic marketplace. Lowell Turner, based upon a study of the United States, Germany, and Japan, argues that globalization has led to a reorganization of production and work in advanced capitalist states, often directed toward goals of production and efficiency and a subsequent weakening of the traditional role of trade unions.[21] David Peetz, examining the Australian case, also notes how domestic and international forces are helping promote a shift toward decentralized, more flexible employment relations.[22] George Ross and Andrew Martin identify this decentralization as an important "shift" to the company level where "unions' influence could be diluted."[23] Philip Cerny identifies this broader trend as the rise of the "competition state," in which states, under international pressure, are compelled to abandon policies and practices (e.g., wage stability, centralized wage bargaining, full employment) that attempted to protect citizens from market fluctuations. Deregulation and decentralization have become the new watchwords, neither of which is particularly conducive to organized labor.[24] Moreover, globalization may help divide labor within a given country, as workers in export-oriented firms, or those in a sector with a "competitive advantage," will have very different interests from those demanding greater tariffs and protection.[25]

Last is the role of direct foreign investment of multinational companies

(MNCs). Driven for profits, MNCs are accused of employing (or, perhaps, exploiting) cheap labor outside their home countries, and using their immense financial power and threat to pack up shop to prevent governments from adopting measures that would strengthen workers' and unions' rights. As countries outbid each other to attract this investment, labor becomes a loser in the process. Pointing to the problems of labor in the more vulnerable states in the developing world, Henk Thomas contends that labor now faces "total elimination as a significant social institution" as national-level unions cannot exercise sufficient influence on international capital.[26]

True, these arguments are derided by critics defending globalization, who deny there is any race to the bottom and praise global markets and free trade as bringing enhanced opportunities for growth.[27] Some scholars, bringing empirical evidence to bear on these questions, have noted that union and neo-corporatist decline has not been universal, meaning that in principle unions and their allies on the social-democratic left can resist any push to global convergence along a more marketized system less advantageous to labor.[28] The ILO, discussing nascent globalization in postcommunist Europe, duly notes that globalization could bring significant benefits to the people in the region: higher wages, better training of workers, technology, gains in efficiency, access to markets, and adoption of Western-style labor standards.[29] Randall Stone, in a study of the IMF in Eastern Europe, praises the IMF's efforts in the 1990s to combat inflation, which he sees as the single biggest threat to economic stability and growth in the region.[30] However, it is necessary to distinguish among direct benefits *to individuals* (e.g., higher wages), diffuse benefits *to society* as a whole (e.g., lower inflation), and benefits *to labor* as an organized, coherent actor in civil society. It is easy to imagine, for example, that MNCs offer higher wages, but the quid pro quo is that workers will surrender their right to unionize and thus, potentially, lose ability to influence political, economic, and social questions on a national level. Thus, for our purposes, we must identify what globalization is doing to *workers' organizations*. Evidence to date on this front is rather inconclusive. Eddy Lee, reviewing much of the literature, notes the plethora of anecdotes but concludes that systematic evidence of globalization being a cause for the erosion of labor standards or trade unions is lacking.[31]

One other factor should be mentioned. While, potentially at least, the pernicious effects of global market forces can be identified, there are countervailing forces as well that might offer labor some protection. Some of these, of course, are ILO Conventions, which have been adopted by most postcommunist countries and are used by trade unions to assert their rights. More important, however, may be the role of the EU as a supranational organization with legal authority above that of member states. True, some do blame the EU for taking decision-making power away from member states (and, consequently, away from voters and organizations such as trade unions) and for making demands for privatization and fiscal responsibility that echo much of what the IMF and international markets would prefer. Recently, however, unionists have looked with some hope toward the EU, especially after the conclusion of the Social Charter in 1989 that has become part of the *acquis communitaire*. The concept of social dialogue has also been supported at the EU level, including a provision mandating a European Works' Council for large multinationals operating in the EU, which would give workers the opportunity to be informed and be consulted on the operation of the company. Moreover, the European Trade Union Confederation (ETUC), a transnational alliance of unions from EU countries supported by the European Commission, could be an important resource for postcommunist trade unions. To the extent that some postcommunist states will join the EU in 2004, they may have to adopt more labor-friendly legislation to meet EU standards embodied in the Social Charter and other statutes than if they were responding only to their own preferences, market forces, or the neoliberal dictates of the IMF. Moreover, some analysis has suggested that EU membership —because it obligates states to certain rules—may actually strengthen member states (and, consequently, unions) because MNCs cannot extract concessions (e.g., on matters such as labor law) that would run afoul of EU standards.[32] All these considerations involving the EU will be especially relevant to Poland and Hungary, which will join the EU in May 2004. It would thus be interesting to see how labor views the EU and whether the efforts of Brussels may compensate for labor weakness in the domestic arena.[33]

That being said, we can still posit some standard antiglobalization hypotheses: pressures of international markets will encourage the adoption of antilabor legislation in postcommunist Europe; global forces will limit the ability of governments and enterprises to offer significant concessions to the demands of labor; globalization will undermine workers' solidarity; and global forces will facilitate deunionization.

Finally, does unions' decline really matter? What, if any, effects have organized labor's problems had on the economic, social, and political fabric of

Western societies? This, of course, is another immense topic, and opponents and defenders of unions have joined in debate over what the erosion of labor's position really means.[34] I will suggest only that even if the causes of labor's decline in Western Europe are similar to those in Eastern Europe, this need not mean the results will be the same. Western states enjoy stable democratic institutions, organizations to provide checks on state power, and well-developed (if shrinking) social welfare protections. Postcommunist states are in an entirely different situation, both politically and economically. Labor weakness in rich states may thus produce entirely different—and perhaps less serious—results than labor weakness in poorer states trying to establish a new political, economic, and social system. Bela Greskovits and Dorothee Bohle note that the postwar corporatist development paradigm of Western and Northern Europe appears to be closed to postcommunist states due to a variety of domestic and international factors and thus the latter constitute an "unexplored development paradigm."[35] Whether this is for good or ill, and how labor weakness affects various issues of democratic consolidation, remain to be explored.

Convergence with the West?

Is there any reason to think what happened to organized labor in advanced industrialized states could be repeated in those states just now making the transition to capitalism? There may be compelling ground to think so. It is clear that the economies of postcommunist Europe, in several important (but certainly not all) aspects, are looking more and more like those in the West. Table 3.3 provides data to document the progress many states have made in dismantling a system of state ownership and opening up to the world economy, and more recent data would likely point to a continuation of these trends. These processes have also been accompanied by deindustrialization (by choice and by market-compelled bankruptcies), movement to new jobs in the service sector (e.g., travel and tourism, banking, insurance, security, retail), and a reduction in the size of enterprises to provide more flexibility. Data have not been systematically gathered, but existing data from several countries do point to a trend toward smaller enterprises,[36] many of which were formed after the fall of communism, and thus do not enjoy (or suffer from) residual trade union membership found at the older, larger enterprises. Moreover, there are millions now working in microbusinesses such as kiosks and small-scale trade, and few (if any) of them are union members for obvious reasons. Although it can by no means be precisely quantified, the shadow economy, especially in Russia and Ukraine, is overwhelmingly small-scale business in the service sector.

Several forces and choices have put these states on the market path. First, although many postcommunist states are still in transition, it is clear that capitalist, market relations are the destination. For both political and economic reasons, this is the goal of most major political actors in the region, and the trade unions themselves either support such moves or concede that they are inevitable. A full-fledged communist revanche is not in the cards. True, this need not mean that states will adopt the more liberal Anglo-American variant of capitalism that has been particularly harmful to trade unions. Many in the region are attracted to the Continental system of the "social market economy" (itself of course under assault by many of the same forces discussed in the previous section), and there are occasional discussions of the Japanese system as well. However, while the institutionalized form that capitalism will eventually take is debatable, there is no doubt that free markets, private ownership, and openness to the global economy will be the norms.

More important, there are vast differences across these countries. These differences concern the timing, form, and results of marketization, as well as the scope of foreign involvement in these states' economies. These differences are the manifestations of path dependency and objective economic conditions, as well as the constellation of interests and their proximity to power.

As for the timing of market reforms, Poland, the Czech Republic, and Hungary took the lead in creating a capitalist system. They moved immediately after the collapse of communism to construct a new socioeconomic system, building upon (in the case of Poland and Hungary) some years of experience with reforms. Russia, together with Slovakia and Bulgaria, can be said to have followed behind a bit (often in an erratic fashion), with Ukraine even more of a laggard. The data in table 3.3 reflect this in part, although it is apparent that Russia has made progress in areas such as transferring property from state ownership, and during 1999–2000 Ukraine embarked on a more decisive reform path under Prime Minister Viktor Yushchenko. The larger point about the timing, however, is that the main elements of the transition have been completed in Central Europe, whereas there is less institutionalization and stability among states in the former USSR (the Baltic states

Table 3.3 Extent of Economic Reforms in Postcommunist Europe

Country	Change in Manufacturing Employment, 1990–2000 (%)	Change in Employment in Trade and Services (%)*	Average Annual Growth in Trade, 1990–1998 (%)	Net FDI, 1993–2001 ($ billions)	FDI Per Capita, 1989–1999 ($)	Industry Share of GDP, 1998 (%)	Services Share of GDP, 1998 (%)	Private Sector Share of GDP, 2000 (%)
Bulgaria	-53 (1990–1999)	—	+2.3	3.7	284	26	50	70
Czech Republic	-28	0 (1993–2000)	+7.0	25.7	1,447	37	—	80
Hungary	-32	+9 (1995–2000)	+4.9	16	1,764	26	60	80
Poland	-13 (1990–1999)	+12 (1992–1999)	+12.3	35.6	518	28	70	70
Romania	-41 (1990–1997)	0 (1994–2000)	+7.5	7.5	252	28	48	60
Slovakia	-18 (1993–1999)	+28 (1993–1999)	+12.1	6	391	26	62	80
Russia	-34 (1993–1998)	—	+2	12	71	29	49	70
Ukraine	-58	—	-3.2	4.1	55	25	48	60

Sources: EBRD Transition Report, 2000 and EBRD Transition Report, 2001 (London: European Bank for Reconstruction and Development, 2000, 2001); World Bank Development Report, 99/00 (Washington: World Bank, 2000); and ILO Yearbook of Labour Statistics, 2000 and ILO Yearbook of Labour Statistics, 2001 (Geneva: International Labour Organization, 2000, 2001).

*Note: Trade and services is defined as retail/trade, transport, finance/investment, and communal and social services, from the ILO.

excepted). For our purposes, what this means is that in Poland and Hungary, where matters have more or less normalized, it is already possible to speak of a posttransition environment (*post*-postcommunism) and thus assess more clearly what the future holds for organized labor since, in a sense, the "future" has already been realized.

The varying forms of marketization are also something that we must keep in mind. There was no single postcommunist process of transition to the market. At a general level are differences among Poland's shock therapy, Hungary's gradualism, Russia's on-again, off-again course of reform, and the tortoise-like pace of movement in Ukraine. More specific are important differences in the processes of privatization and ownership change among these countries. It should be recognized that there were many available paths for divesting the state of enterprise ownership: competitive, open auctions (as in Hungary); mass privatization through voucher programs (as in the Czech Republic); special rights and privileges given to insiders at the enterprise, namely the workers and the management (Russia, Poland, Ukraine); and leasing or cooperative arrangements (done in several countries). Of course, these processes could also be combined, at the same time, or used individually at different stages of reform or with different types of enterprises. Moreover, the forms of privatization may not have been well specified or centrally controlled, leading to "spontaneous," "vulture," "bottom-up," or "*nomen-klatura*" privatization in several cases, particularly early in the process.[37] In addition, ownership change has been more contested in some countries (Poland, Russia) than in others (Hungary, Czech Republic). These differences warrant our attention, in particular on issues such as workers' involvement in the privatization process and the degree to which legal rules were actually enforced.

There are also obvious differences in the results of privatization and economic reform more generally. These are noteworthy at the macro- and micro-level. At the macrolevel, a number of indicators (GDP per capita, GDP growth, the Gini index of inequality, poverty levels) show that the countries of East Central Europe have been far more successful than Russia or Ukraine. The data presented in table 3.4 point to real differences across the countries in the region. True, it could be argued that the laggards are catching up and making real progress (GDP growth in both Russia and Ukraine from 2000 to 2003 has been sizable, but even a casual observer would note that something has gone very wrong in these countries and that they have years to go to ap-

Table 3.4 Economic Indicators in Postcommunist States							
Country	GDP in 1999 (1989 = 100)	First Year of + GDP Growth	GDP per Capita, 1999 ($)	Poverty %, 1999	Avg. Inflation, 1991–2000 (%)	Avg. Unemploy. 1991–1999 (%)	Gini Index, 1996
Poland	122	1992	3,987	13	27.2	13.18	30.2
Hungary	99	1994	4,853	2	20.3	9.21	34.8[a]
Czech Rep	95	1993	5,189	1	14.2	4.65	25.4
Slovakia	100	1994	3,650	1	15.9	14.11	—
Bulgaria	67	1994	1,513	33	188.2	13.45	29.1
Russia	57	1997	1,249	35	319.9	8.24	48.3
Ukraine	36	2000	619	41	746.1	1.43	41.3

Sources: EBRD, Transition Report, 1999 and Transition Report, 2000 (London: European Bank for Reconstruction and Development, 1999, 2000). Data from 2000 are EBRD projections.
[a]1997

proach the levels of development in East Central Europe. However, even the more successful cases, Poland and Hungary, have significant economic problems, particularly unemployment, although it could be added that the figures in those countries are well within the current standard for continental Europe. Thus, it should not be anticipated—at least for the foreseeable future—that such countries will enjoy a Western standard of living.

The point, though, is that structurally, in terms of ownership patterns, employment profiles, and integration into world markets, postcommunist states are moving in the direction of a capitalist-market system. On the microlevel, the discussion revolves around new systems of labor relations, which depend both on the macropolitical and macroeconomic environment, but perhaps just as important, on choices made by owners, management, and workers. On this level, relative successes or failures (from labor's perspective) within various countries are a result of microlevel processes and decisions. Thus, privatization is a highly differentiated process in form and results, and it is therefore easy to agree with J. E. M. Thirkell et al. that "it cannot be assumed that privatization will have uniform effects on labour relations either from country to country or from organization to organization within a country."[38]

Finally, the differences in these states concerning the role of global economic forces should be recognized. As noted, the IMF and other international financial institutions have been active in the region, often provoking the indignation of some who believe that government directives and laws are essentially cut and pasted from IMF policy briefs.[39] However, IMF advice was not followed in all cases, due more often to the influence of nascent business interests than that of organized labor.[40] International trade has grown in most countries (Ukraine being the exception), but trade's share of GNP varies markedly: 123.8 percent of GNP in the Czech Republic, 115.5 percent in Hungary, 96.5 percent in Ukraine, 61 percent in Russia and Romania, and 44 percent in Poland.[41] Some states have successfully attracted foreign investment (Hungary is the clearest case) and are moving toward integrating into European and world markets. Others, notably Russia and Ukraine, have taken only modest steps in this direction, less because of their own choice and more because capital has been reluctant to locate in countries with greater political and economic instability.[42] Moreover, as was the case with ownership change, there are many possible forms of foreign involvement, ranging from joint ventures with a local partner, to buy-outs of local companies, to the creation of wholly new enterprises (usually subsidiaries of the parent MNC and often called a "greenfield" investment). The role of foreign capital will therefore largely depend on the form it takes. Overall, scores on the EBRD's foreign exchange and trade liberalization scale (on a four-point scale) are another measure of globalization: 4+ for Hungary (since 1994) and Poland (since 1996), compared to scores of 3.0 for Ukraine (since 1995) and only 2.3 for Russia (since 1998).[43]

It is far from obvious that movement to a market-based or globalized system need lead to the same results for organized labor in the East as has occurred in the West.[44] The key here would be the nature of the *ex ante* system: the West was moving to a marketized system with preexisting, strong unions, whereas postcommunist states are moving to the market from a system that lacked an autonomous labor movement. The potential relevance is clear if we consider the effects of privatization, perhaps the central component in the new political economy of former communist states. Now, there is a clear owner-worker relationship that did not previously exist. Unions should therefore not have the divided loyalty they had in the past. Unions are not bound to ideologies emanating from structures of collective ownership, as they were before. Adversarial, market conditions may help yield a "class consciousness" (to use a rather hoary term) that could stimulate the development of trade unions and a union movement in a manner that was heretofore simply impossible. In other words, unions may be handicapped now, but this may be largely a heritage of past weakness, and as interests become normal and workers and union leaders begin to understand the market system, they will be able to articulate their own interests and form stronger organizations. Simon Clarke et al. predict, "when the much heralded 'transition to a market economy' does get under way [in Russia], there will be no doubt that conflict within the enterprise will increase dramatically, and that workers and worker activists will have an important role to play in such conflict."[45] David Mandel, despite documenting labor's multiple failures in the postcommunist period, anticipates change to a market-oriented system and asserts in his conclusion "that the working class of the former Soviet Union has not yet spoken its last word, not by a long shot."[46] Certainly the same can be hoped for in other countries as well, and union leaders naturally look forward to a better tomorrow when the uncertainty of the transition is over and they will play an important role in both a new system of industrial relations and in the political life of the country.

This hypothesis, that privatization will actually *promote* trade union strength and development and help mobilize workers, stands in direct contrast to the one of convergence that privatization will undermine unions in the East as it has in the West. Over a decade after the fall of communism, we can assess whether there are signs of this occurring.

Similarly, a counterargument can be made for globalization, which is a controversial topic in its own right. Previously, these states were cut off from the world economy. Global economic forces could promote labor's decline, but they also may help workers and their unions by bringing these countries closer to "world standards" that, in important ways, would be an improvement for workers compared to what existed before. This is not to say that globalization will somehow significantly empower labor. Rather, the contention (similar to what MNCs claim in less-developed countries) would be that the importation of foreign capital and business practices might help labor take a few steps up from its previously lowly position. Additionally, the EU and its Social Charter will, potentially, ameliorate the unbridled forces of capitalism by providing for a number of protections for workers. Thus, movement to Europe may compensate for movement to the market and allow some aspects of European social-democratic systems to take hold in the East.

Various forms of path dependency may also help postcommunist labor. An American capitalist, for example, unencumbered by a communist past, might be more willing to treat unions as representatives of workers than, say, a Russian entrepreneur, who may be used to thinking of unions as only playthings of management. To the extent that new businesses allow labor to reinvent itself or create organizations from scratch, labor may be able to shed some aspects of its debilitating communist heritage. Thus, I will posit as a counterhypothesis: globalization will bring new opportunities for workers; globalization will bring with it new norms that help raise standards in postcommunist Europe; and foreign capitalists will treat unions better than their local counterparts.

The point of emphasis is not so much how unions are encumbered by their past (which does remain a relevant concern) but how the structural economic changes adopted under the rubric of reform are affecting workers' organizations. While consideration of all factors may prevent drawing clear-cut conclusions with respect to the points to be examined, it may allow positing, upon investigation, more refined arguments and hypotheses. Moreover, if organized labor is highly differentiated, subjected to various forces, and pushed and pulled in numerous directions by markets, governments, and foreign capital, that in itself is an important conclusion with respect to *labor movements* and workers' ability to exercise influence collectively at the national level.

4

Organized Labor in Poland

ANY STUDY OF POSTCOMMUNIST LABOR must give concerted attention to developments in Poland. The reasons are not hard to find. Poland was, of course, the birthplace of Solidarity, the largest independent trade union-cum-social movement in Eastern Europe and an actor often credited with precipitating the fall of communism. In 1989, Solidarity, by then part trade union and part political party, assumed leadership of the country. Many who championed notions such as "workers' self governance," a "Third Way," or even generic "social democracy" or "democratic corporatism" took heart from the victory of Solidarity and what it portended for the position of workers in the postcommunist period.

Of course, these hopes were quickly shattered, which also makes Poland such an interesting country. Rather than seizing the opportunity to defend and enhance workers' rights, the Solidarity government launched a program of economic shock therapy, which was designed to eradicate many of the vestiges of communism favorable to labor and to lay the groundwork for the emergence of a capitalist class that would preside over what was touted to be a more efficient economic system. Many, however, questioned this decision, and the Solidarity movement that had united Poles against communism split into a variety of factions. From 1990 to 1993, under a government that claimed the moniker of Solidarity, the union struggled between the goal of building capitalism and serving the needs of its core labor constituency, with the former priority generally winning out. David Ost writes, "Just when it seemed that they [workers] could pursue their class interests with unencumbered commitment, workers watched passively, even approvingly, as their former rights were whittled away."[1]

In 1993, a government of Solidarity-successor parties was defeated at the polls by the former communists who received significant backing from the All-Poland Alliance of Trade Unions (OPZZ), the former communist-dominated union federation. Since then, there have been alternations in government (no incumbent party or coalition has retained control of the Sejm, the lower house of parliament), but the procapitalist course of the country has been altered only at the margins. Despite the initial promise of organized labor in Poland, no labor leader looks back on the past decade with much fondness, as economic changes have resulted in high unemployment (18 percent in 2002),[2] declining union membership, and a palpable loss of workers' rights at the enterprise level.

The final irony, however, is that despite all the well-documented problems in the postcommunist period, labor remains visible, unlike in the Czech Republic, Hungary, or Ukraine where trade unions are at best occasional and bit players on the political stage. Of course, many would take umbrage with my claim that labor has been weak and marginalized in Poland. After all, Solidarity's leader, Lech Wałesa, served as president 1990–1995, and Marian Krzaklewski, the post–Wałesa Solidarity leader, was the driving force behind the bloc Solidarity Electoral Action (AWS), which governed Poland during 1997–2001. Some speak of a "unionocracy" in Poland.[3] Moreover, outside the political arena, unions of all stripes have organized protests and strikes, making Poland (particularly in 1992–1993) the site of the greatest amount of labor militancy in Eastern Europe. In other words, unions have not been entirely passive.[4]

However, labor won limited gains from these actions, many actions were led by Solidarity and other unions in order to demobilize discontent,[5] and the unions' ability to place people in high positions in government has not translated into strengthening its organizations at the grassroots level. Unions are still derided as dinosaurs. In the words of one analyst, Tomasz Inglot, unions are "hopelessly suspended between the ambition to become significant players in national politics and their routine role of social partners in the postcommunist system of labor relations."[6] Most relevant, perhaps, Poles, when queried whether unions have too much, too little, or about the right amount of authority in the country, have overwhelmingly stated that unions have too little influence.[7]

There are a variety of reasons for labor's relative failure (relative at least compared to the hopes of some) in the postcommunist period. Solidarity's past as a universalist social movement and its virulent anticommunism set the table for the initial shock therapy reforms that lowered living standards and created disillusionment about unions.[8] However, my concern is how Solidarity, the OPZZ, and other unions have been affected by those reforms themselves. In particular, I want to examine if and how privatization and incipient globalization are handicapping labor in the postcommunist period. Some seem to imply that unions in Poland are caught in a funk and will gradually learn to reassert themselves. Others believe that the political economy has so changed that labor is left to wax nostalgic on its victory in 1989 and struggle in a system designed to benefit capital and integrate Poland into the world economy. Does the answer lie somewhere between these extremes? And what are the broader political consequences of organized labor's predicament?

Issues in Poland

Although there are over one hundred different union confederations in Poland, the trade union movement, such as it is, is dominated by two: Solidarity and the OPZZ. Despite sharing the label "trade union," the two organizations are markedly different and have frequently been heated rivals.

Solidarity's history is well known: it was formed "from below" by workers themselves, maintained its independence from the communist authorities, mobilized thousands in anticommunist protests in 1980–1981, was repressed under martial law in 1981, reemerged in 1988, and since 1989 has continued the fight against vestiges of the communist system. It has played a prominent role in several of Poland's postcommunist governments. As a trade union, Solidarity, in its pre-1989 form, joined together intellectuals and more qualified workers, although by the end of the 1990s a majority of its members, according to surveys, classified themselves as "workers" (*robotnicy*).[9] Over time, it has played more and more to a pro-Catholic agenda and has consistently tried to thrust itself onto the national political stage.

The OPZZ, in contrast, was formed in 1984 by the communist authorities, as a decentralized federation and a party-backed alternative to Solidarity. It attracted a large number of managers and supervisors, as well as more passive, less qualified, older elements of the "lumpenproletariat," who were unwilling to risk joining Solidarity. Juliusz Gardawski calls these workers "socially disadvantaged," more interested in social funds (which OPZZ initially had, thanks to government support), and notes that the leadership of the union was clearly that of the party elite.[10] Previously cited surveys from 2001 confirm that the membership profile of the OPZZ relies more heavily on managers and specialists (13 percent) and service employees (27 percent) than on physical workers, particularly skilled workers (21 percent of the OPZZ compared to 41 percent of Solidarity).[11] It has also tried to appeal to those more in favor of a leftist, social-democratic agenda.

Despite their rivalry and historically acrimonious relations, these confederations share several things in common. By several measures both are weaker today than they were in the last years of the communist system. The clearest sign of union decline is the drop in membership. If Solidarity could claim a membership of ten million in 1980–1981 when it was initially formed—a figure that reflected its status as an all-Polish social movement and not just a union for workers—it claimed a quarter of that in 1989, and by 2001 its membership had shrunk to just over one million members in fourteen thousand local organizations, which in turn are organized into thirty-eight regional unions and sixteen national branch secretariats (miners, chemical workers, transport workers, etc.). The OPZZ claims a higher figure (approximately 1.2 million in 2002), but some consider this an exaggeration, as surveys from July 2001 reveal more Polish workers claiming membership in Solidarity (5.4 percent in Solidarity vs. 4.9 percent in OPZZ unions). Total membership in the OPZZ is therefore estimated by some outside sources to be only 700,000–800,000 members, and its eleven thousand local unions are grouped together under a regional structure as well as under a branch structure of over one hundred different unions, ranging from miners to dairy workers to a separate union for trade union employees.[12] However, even the self-reported OPZZ membership figure is far lower than the 4.5 million claimed in 1990. Hence, regardless of the precise figure used, no one disputes a precipitous membership drop.

Overall, the estimate from survey research is that union density in Poland in 2001 was just under 14 percent, down from over 60 percent ten years before and one of the lowest rates of unionization in all of Europe.[13]

There are, of course, other unions. A radical off-shoot of Solidarity, Solidarity 80, gained supporters in the initial postcommunist years by mobilizing actions against Leszek Balcerowicz's shock therapy plan, but by the end of the 1990s it had lost relevance on the national scene.[14] Andrzej Lepper's anti-European, rural trade union-cum political party, Self-Defense (*Samooborona*), emerged in 2001 as a potent political force, but this is best viewed as a farmers' organization. In some sectors, especially mining, railroads, and health care, there are dozens of different unions, usually uniting one particular profession. In 2002, there was an effort among eighteen different trade unions to establish a new confederation, Forum, composed of disaffected groups in the OPZZ and Solidarity (most notably railway workers and nurses) and unions of white-collar workers (managers, engineers, coal service employees), which would join together over 300,000 workers. One inspiration for this movement was to avoid the eternal bickering between Solidarity and the OPZZ, as well as to gain representation on the national Tripartite Commission, which requires a high (300,000) threshold of national union membership.

Of course, loss of membership and creation of a more pluralistic trade union system may be perfectly natural and even democratic. In the past, workers had no choice: there was one union, and they had to join. Now, they can form unions as they want, or not join one at all. Moreover, economic restructuring has meant displacement for millions, and the general trend has been out of the old smokestack sectors of the economy and into the service sector and privately owned microbusinesses, which proliferated after 1989. Indeed, given the fact that a majority of Poles work in the nonstate sector and that surveys from 2001 reveal that only 6 percent of workers in private companies claimed union membership (only 11 percent of workers in private enterprises indicated the enterprise had a union), as opposed to 33 percent of their counterparts at state-owned enterprises (where 81 percent of workers claimed there was a trade union at the enterprise), privatization as a cause of union decline is generally acknowledged by all observers.[15] Moreover, survey research indicates that size is a factor, meaning that unionization rates at small- and medium-size firms with fewer than 150 employees (one of the fastest growing sectors of the economy) are significantly lower than membership rates at larger firms. For example, in surveys across various sectors, the mean size of unionized firms in forestry is 530, in chemicals is 296, in autos is 1,404, and in health is 190, whereas the respective mean sizes of non-union firms in these same sectors are 89, 43, 75, and 44.[16]

Equally problematic, however, has been the unions' general lack of interest in organizing to retain or attract members. Ost documents that Solidarity divested itself of many assets, such as housing, vacation homes, and spas, which were important and often very visible reminders of the side benefits of union membership. He also suggests that the union had a very passive approach to recruiting members, typified in a union leader's comment that "They'll [workers] join us if they like what we're doing." However, what they did was play politics, a strategy union leaders themselves acknowledge was a mistake and may have turned off workers.[17] As for the OPZZ, it too has been politicized, and critics within the OPZZ itself note that it lacks an impulse to form new unions, or to strengthen existing structures by expanding into new companies or linking together workers across traditionally defined branches. As a result, it remains rather passive and defensive.[18]

The financial constraints of the unions are a hindrance in recruiting new members and forming new company unions. In Poland, the majority of the money collected as union dues (80 percent in OPZZ, 60 percent in Solidarity) stay with the primary (enterprise-level) organization; the rest is distributed nationally and regionally, but only 2 percent goes to the branch-level organization, meaning the branch union has little wherewithal to engage in basic tasks such as training, lobbying, organizing, and even paying for international memberships. The contrast with Germany—where there are strong branch unions that gather the dues of members—is marked and leads to a situation in which it is very difficult to form branch unions at enterprises that lack a company union because there is no organizational base. Solidarity officials concede that this structural problem—that privileges the regions over the branch structures—is a handicap to strengthening the union.[19]

Along with union decline came the disappearance, particularly in private firms, of workers' councils, structures that received much rhetorical attention under communism and held, perhaps, some promise to become a vehicle for workers' self-management or stakeholder governance in the postcommunist period. These organizations did offer another means for workers' voices to be heard within the enterprise. While these organizations could be viewed as a rival to unions in the late communist period and in the early postcommunist period, Solidarity, in particular, worked with workers' councils on organizational and management issues. However, in the name of creating a market economy with clear lines of management, Solidarity pushed for these councils to be eliminated from privatized companies.[20] Now they have been eliminated from most Polish enterprises, and workers have one less institutional mechanism for exercising their voices. Interestingly, there are proposals to allow them—or something akin to them, such as an advisory council—to exist at nonunionized firms, but Solidarity is opposed to this because it could lead to the manipulation of labor relations by management.[21]

More serious than the drop in membership, however, has been the decline of trust in trade unions in the postcommunist period. This development has been occurring for some time—Wlodzimierz Panków reports a decline in trust for Solidarity from 69 percent in 1989 to 26 percent in 1993, with the drop for the OPZZ in the same period from 35 percent to 24 percent.[22] Gardawski, reporting CBOS (the Public Opinion Research Center, in Warsaw) surveys among workers in 1991–1994, also notes that a consistent majority of workers —nonunion workers, Solidarity members, and OPZZ members—stated that no one in the country represented the interests of workers, and at their enterprises solid pluralities (33–56 percent) stated that no one (neither management, nor unions, nor employee councils) represented their interests.[23] By 2001, CBOS surveys revealed an even more bleak perspective from the unions' point of view: only 8 percent of respondents thought the OPZZ represented people like themselves, 6 percent picked Solidarity (down from 21 percent in 1993), and 51 percent said no trade union did. More tellingly, perhaps, trade union members were more likely than nonunion members (82 percent vs. 73 percent) to state that unions were not competent to defend the interests of workers.[24] Pankow and Barbara Gaciarz label this phenomenon the "abandoned employee syndrome," evidence of an asymmetrical industrial relations system in which workers are forced to play a much weaker hand.[25] More to the point is how long unions can survive given their standing with their own members.

Pankow's research among workers in 1998 (from the survey Trade Unions 1998) points to more causes of concern. His main research questions are what effects trade unions have on firms and on work conditions. Several items are notable. One is that the gap between what workers believe unions should be doing at the enterprise (e.g., defending workers against dismissal, providing financial assistance, increasing social benefits, promoting modernization, enhancing work safety) and what they perceive unions as actually doing is quite large. For example, solid majorities thought unions should be influential on all issues just mentioned, but typically less than a quarter of workers thought unions did have substantial influence on these matters. More interestingly, perhaps, are the findings that workers in unionized companies were more likely to report the financial condition of their enterprise and their own compensation as worse than workers in nonunionized enterprises, and workers in nonunion enterprises were more likely to be satisfied on issues such as respect for workers (91 percent vs. 86 percent), ability to critique work conditions (72 percent vs. 64 percent), technical aspects of work (81 percent vs. 68 percent), and salaries (48 percent vs. 25 percent). Pankow and Gaciarz use this and other evidence to argue that Poland suffers from "enlightened paternalism," meaning that workers hold relatively positive views about management: more (55 percent), for example, would turn to their supervisors at work than to unions (6 percent) if they had a problem at work.[26] The implications for unions are obvious. On a related note, Bernadeta Waszkielewicz, citing CBOS surveys, reports that union members earn about 25 percent less than nonunionized workers and union members are also more likely to fear layoffs.[27] True, Pankow's research does show that unionized enterprises rate higher on social questions such as enterprise-supplied housing, health care centers, and resorts (all vestiges of the communist system), but in general unionization does not rate highly in providing great benefits to the workers.[28]

Of course, unions may not be at fault for these problems—unions may simply be more likely to exist at "loser" companies, or perhaps unionization increases workers' expectations and thus exacerbates a sense of disappointment. However, given the fact that unions appear to be best at preserving or managing the social properties inherited from the old system and (perhaps) that they are more prevalent in less successful companies or sectors, this speaks volumes about the staying power of unions and their ability to expand to currently nonunionized enterprises, where workers may (rightly) ask what the union can do for them.

Whereas Polish labor unions in general are experiencing a general malaise or "identity crisis," the problems within Solidarity are more acute. Surveys from CBOS in 2001, for example, find that more workers (as well as the population at large) believed that the OPZZ better represents their rights and interests than Solidarity (22 percent of workers favored OPZZ, 17 percent named Solidarity). OPZZ members were more likely to value their organization (49 percent) than Solidarity members valued theirs (39 percent), and twice as many Solidarity members (57 percent) claimed that no union represented their interests compared to members of the OPZZ (28 percent). Almost twice as many Solidarity members (45 percent) than OPZZ members (24 percent) believed that at their enterprise there was no effective way to defend the interests of workers. Moreover, the survey reveals that the OPZZ unions have been far more successful in attracting newer, younger members, whereas 25 percent of Solidarity members are over fifty (only 8 percent of OPZZ members were this old), which is a significant break with the past. Finally, and perhaps most surprisingly, Solidarity members were found to be more distrustful of Solidarity leader Marian Krzaklewski (63 percent) than Leszek Miller (44 percent distrust), who led the Democratic Left Alliance (SLD) to electoral victory in 2001. In a remarkable shift, the surveys found Solidarity members equally disposed among the left, center, and right, which would have been unthinkable during much of the 1990s.[29] These data do much to explain the AWS's electoral woes, as well as the widely perceived notion that Solidarity no longer connects with Polish workers on bread-and-butter economic issues.

Leaving aside the unions' internal problems, what can be said of interunion relations? Until recently, the answer was not much, at least at the national level. Solidarity treated the OPZZ as a pariah, deeming it a haven for communists, a retrograde, backward looking organization, and not a true voice of the workers. The OPZZ, for its part, was willing to acknowledge the historical role played by Solidarity but claimed that Solidarity lost touch with workers and pointed to its (self-proclaimed) higher membership numbers as proof of its own legitimacy. The two now compete for members at the enterprise level, as the law on trade unions allows a group as small as ten workers to form a union. However, the membership profile and ideological slant of the two have differed, meaning that cooperation at the enterprise level is reported by both sides to be rather commonplace. However, some reckon that negotiations are easier if there is only one union in an enterprise, and certainly the presence of numerous unions in some sectors and enterprises has complicated conclusion of collective agreements.[30]

Relations were virtually nonexistent at the national level in 1989–1993, with Solidarity boldly declaring, "NSZZ Solidarnosc does not cooperate with any national trade union center."[31] In 1994, when a Tripartite Commission was established under the first SLD government, Solidarity rejected cooperation with the OPZZ on this body, preferring instead direct talks with the government. From 1995 to 1997 there were periodic and ephemeral agreements made through the Commission, but they unraveled as elections approached. Under the AWS government, the OPZZ took a harder line, treating the government and its Solidarity ally with suspicion. Clearly, the two sides viewed themselves in a zero-sum game, in which anything offered or supported by the other side had to be bad.

There are some signs that this is changing, perhaps as a result of Solidarity's electoral defeats, disillusionment with the government, and shifts in viewpoints among Solidarity members. In 2001–2002, there was talk of cooperation between the two confederations in debates on a revised labor code, with the unions agreeing that basic rights of workers must be defended against government assaults. Maciej Manicki, leader of the OPZZ, openly welcomed Solidarity-OPZZ cooperation on this question, and there have been joint activities to pressure the government to amend its proposals, although Solidarity officials remain a bit skeptical of OPZZ activities.[32] Arguably, however, the battles of the past are slowly being forgotten (although the dispute over management of the communist-era workers' holiday fund remains a sticking point, one that has held up OPZZ's accession to the ETUC), and Solidarity may be beginning to depoliticize itself, contributing to a sense that unions must defend themselves against encroachments by the state. It is not known, of course, how long this can last, and whether any cross-union alliance can make significant changes in the Polish political economy. No doubt, these developments are positive from the perspective of organized labor, but compared with what a unified movement could have accomplished years ago, it is disappointing that these unions are trying to join hands only after years of bitter animosity that coincided with marked erosion in organized labor's position.

Trade Unions and Politics

Union-government relations have been a prominent leitmotif in postcommunist Polish politics, not only under Solidarity-led governments (1989–1993 and 1997–2001) but also under the SLD. Both Solidarity and the OPZZ have close ties with political parties, and unions have often figured prominently in policy discussions. According to Article 19 of the Act on Trade Unions, unions even enjoy the right to review legislative proposals. However, despite fears of unions' ability to undermine reforms, union-government cooperation (at times at the expense of union members) has been just as prevalent a theme (if not more so) as union-government confrontation. These issues have been ably covered by several observers, and I will reprise many of their points.[33]

The gist of the story is relatively simple: when Solidarity assumed power in 1989, its leaders were intent on pursuing rapid marketization, which was the culmination of a change of approach from the initial (1980) aims of self-management, labor rights, democratic socialism, and egalitarianism. Agreeing with the elite that the communist system needed to be dismantled, Solidarity the trade union gave the new government a blank check, or a "protective umbrella," to allow it to carry out market reforms. There was little secret that these reforms, which would cut social subsidies, raise prices, create unemployment, and limit wage increases, among other things, would be particularly harmful to industrial workers. However, Solidarity, which had always envisioned itself serving a dual role of both protecting workers and doing what was best for Poland, decided it would not stand in the way of what were widely regarded as necessary and progressive measures and would refrain from advocating any "Third Way experiments." Moreover, shock therapy was seen as the best means to garner international financial support, and indeed Western institutions and advisers (most famously Jeffrey Sachs) touted radical reform as the best solution to Poland's economic troubles. Social networks and personal ties facilitated elite-union cooperation for a couple of years, giving the government a window of opportunity to dismantle much of the old system.[34] The costs were high for many, and the question of reform strategy caused splits within Solidarity. As one Solidarity member asked, "How is it that Solidarity can at the same time be the government, a trade union, the nation, [and] me?"[35] Obviously, Solidarity's many hats forced it astray from a purely worked-based agenda, but most Solidarity leaders, however, stuck with the government and worked to defuse workers' protests and strikes. Ost and Marc Weinstein, drawing upon survey research of union activists in 1994, find that activists in both Solidarity and (rather surprisingly) the OPZZ were much more likely to cite "support of market reform" and "speed privatization" as reasons for union activism, as opposed to "fight the Balcerowicz program."[36]

This decision would prove to be of great consequence. In contrast to the previous ethos of self-organization, Solidarity would now encourage demobilization and popular withdrawal from the political arena in favor of a technocratic government (albeit one with a democratic mandate). Yet, this was a crucial period, as new institutions were being built, and the lack of societal voice would have consequences, particularly for the workers, who were dismissed (in a twist on Marxist thought) as a backward, retrograde class of yesterday, whose strength would have to be diminished to make way for capitalism. However, the problem that Solidarity faced (and to a great extent continues to face) is that while it was clear what it was against (communism) it was not clear what the union was for, at least for its worker members. This lack of purpose is, of course, a problem for trade unions throughout the region, arguably even globally. In Poland, if 1989–1991 can be celebrated by Balcerowicz and company as a "window of opportunity" that they seized to create capitalism,[37] the irony is that Solidarity, which also had an opportunity to assert itself, failed to take advantage of the period and press an agenda for its members.

With time, the consensus within the Solidarity leadership began to break down. Lech Wałesa won the Polish presidency in 1990, acknowledged discontent in the ranks, and promised to adopt more proworker policies. However, Wałesa's "war at the top" was more about augmenting his own power than slowing down the course of reforms, as he remained committed to the destruction of the communist system. By 1991, Solidarity, now under Krzaklewski, declared the "umbrella" was closed and supported strike action against the government, especially on the issues of unemployment and the added wage tax (*popiwek*). Solidarity, of course, was also under pressure from the OPZZ, which was profiting from its lack of support for shock therapy and its accusations that Solidarity was betraying the workers. Calls for moderation or patience had ceased to placate workers, and by 1992–1993 strikes increased twentyfold compared to those in 1991.[38] However, Carol Timko convincingly argues that these strikes were disorganized, often wildcat activities directed against unions as much as management, and Solidarity assumed "leadership" of them to ensure its own survival and thus prevented the emergence of a unified, coherent labor movement with a clearly defined program. Hence, Solidarity was, in Timko's terms, "*dis*-organizing" the workers that it had so efficiently organized years before.[39] However, fearing the worst, the government did make some overtures to the workers, resulting in the State Enterprise Pact, which eliminated the *popiwek* and provided more influence for workers on questions of privatization. However, Solidarity remained unconvinced that the government had really changed course, and the union's representatives in the Sejm helped bring down the Suchocka government in May 1993.

In parliamentary elections later that year, the various Solidarity factions failed to unite, opening the door for a coalition government led by the SLD, the former communists. Solidarity's defeat would be complete when Alexander Kwasniewski of the SLD defeated Wałesa for the presidency in 1995. The SLD was strongly backed by the OPZZ, and it made an explicit effort to appeal to workers by promising to assuage problems of unemployment and living standards and to give unions more say in policy making. Thus, in 1994 Poland became the last Eastern European country to adopt a corporatist-style Tripartite Commission, an institution long deemed by Solidarity governments to be unnecessary and risky for the reform process itself.

While this institution did succeed in decreasing strikes (although Solidarity's own weaknesses may have prevented workers' mobilization), its ability to work effectively was limited by a politicized environment, particularly from the side of Solidarity, which kept the SLD government at a distance. For its part, the OPZZ did not benefit much from the SLD ascendancy. Gardawski argues that the OPZZ lacked its own program, was too dependent upon its political allies, and did not enjoy a deep reservoir of workers' confidence. Once in power, the SLD embraced the transformation to capitalism, and unions, "representing the 'anachronistic' milieu of employees shaped by People's Poland, had about as little say as Solidarity had when representatives held seats in the previous Sejm."[40] Julian Bartosz concurs that the OPZZ, backing away from its pledges during the campaign, began to acknowledge "economic necessities," including the dismantling of social services and reductions in pensions. Ultimately, he argues, the "marriage of convenience between the OPZZ and the SLD has condemned the trade union to impotence," and the OPZZ unions have "compromised themselves more in the past few years (1993–1996) than they ever did in the 1980s."[41]

The issue was similar to what happened with Solidarity: the union leadership failed to present an alternative to government proposals, and the base of the union suffered and grew disillusioned and resentful. The remainder of the story is, in some sense, an echo of the past. The SLD was unable or unwilling to deliver on many of its campaign promises. Solidarity, now in opposition, organized large-scale strikes and protests among education and health workers in 1994–1995, miners in 1997, and Gdansk shipyard workers (the vanguard of Solidarity, whose enterprise had great symbolic importance) in 1997, the last of which ended with violence and a temporary workers' takeover of government buildings in Warsaw. In elections in 1997, the AWS, a vehicle designed by Solidarity President Krzaklewski, unified various anti-leftist forces and won a plurality of seats in the Sejm.

The AWS, however, did not offer a sharp change in the economic course from the previous Solidarity governments, with Solidarity now increasingly concerned with protecting the "holy grail of national and Christian values."[42] While in government, the AWS coalition partner was the Freedom Union, whose leader, Leszek Balcerowicz, the architect of shock therapy, reclaimed his previous post of finance minister. Tripartism worked no better—the OPZZ was now the one boycotting sessions of the Tripartite Commission, accusing the government of violating the law by refusing to consult unions on its proposals and freezing discussions in the Tripartite Commission on an OPZZ-backed Pact for the Polish Family. The OPZZ declared that the AWS coalition was a "government of social monologue," complained to the ILO, and in April 1999 suspended its participation in the Commission, noting it did not "intend to legitimize government's activities which try to create an appearance of participation in social dialogue, when this dialogue has been in fact liquidated by the government."[43] Even Solidarity representatives sympathized with the OPZZ's course of action, complaining about the arrogance of "our ministers" who present unions with "take-it-or-leave-it-policies" and claim they do not want to "waste time" talking with the unions.[44] Thus, market-based reforms continued, with minimal concessions to the workers, and restructuring in one major sector, steel, led to a 50 percent drop in union membership (due to redundancies) in both Solidarity and OPZZ unions.[45] Not surprisingly, then, many workers turned to the SLD in 2001 and abandoned the AWS, leaving the Civic Platform, a grouping of "pro-business liberals," as the last vestige of the once powerful Solidarity movement.[46] However, even the OPZZ is not happy with the current SLD-led government, and Balcerowicz, always the lightning rod for protests, sits as head of the National Bank, where he continues to pursue, in the unions' view, antiworker policies.

Although it may be premature to announce the death of Solidarity as a political movement, it is clear that over time organized labor has lost its central role in Polish politics. Recognizing their weakness, recently Solidarity and the OPZZ have backed away from politics and have been more willing to discuss a common agenda. As one OPZZ official suggested, "At least we can now sit in the same room together."[47] Even Lech Wałesa, no fan of the OPZZ or the SLD government, sounded a corporatist note and conceded that the moment required elements of Polish society to come together and that the various unions, business interests, and government would have to manage economic policy together.[48] Whether this can come to pass remains to be seen. There was some hope that disputes over the new Labor Code would at a minimum bring the OPZZ and Solidarity together to fight against what critics of the government proposal viewed as a curtailment of workers' rights, particularly on the issue of dismissal from work, the offering of short-term contractual work (which can inhibit unionization), and overtime pay. Envisioning such cooperation, one newspaper headline was "Miracles Are Possible."[49] In the end, however, the OPZZ allied with the Polish Confederation of Private Employers, supporting efforts to create a more flexible labor market, with Solidarity backing an alternative proposal that it claimed would more adequately defend the workers and not give employers a free hand to fire workers and otherwise treat them poorly.[50] By 2002, union leaders on both sides noted many common interests, but real steps toward cooperation (at least on the national level) were rather meager.

Trade Unions and Privatization

Since 1989, there have been sweeping changes in the Polish economy. State control has largely given way to market forces. Shock therapy did worsen the economic crisis inherited from the communist regime, but by 1992–1993 there were signs that shock was giving way to therapy: inflation was declining, and the economy was growing. For several years in the mid-1990s, Poland's economy was the fastest growing in all of Europe, led by a nascent private sector and spurred on by foreign investment. Still, many Poles have not seen the promised benefits of capitalism: unemployment is high, and the social safety net has collapsed for many. As a consequence, surveys reveal that Poles themselves do not concur with the conventional wisdom of outsiders that Poland has been an economic success story.[51] Trade unions, of course, have had to adjust to this new environment, which has been, according to many union leaders, full of both opportunities and challenges.

The one change that has probably had the most impact on trade unions and their members has been privatization. Instead of dealing with a single owner-state, most Polish workers now confront private owners, and the pursuit of profits by the latter has led to conflicts with the former. While all post-communist Polish governments have encouraged the creation of small, private businesses and attempted to sell state-owned industries to individual or collective buyers, this fundamental shift in the political economy has not been a boon to trade unions. As noted previously, surveys find union membership much higher among workers at state enterprises and institutions than at private ones. Moreover, surveys taken in July 2001 among manual workers reveal vast differences in union membership across sectors of the economy, with the highest unionization in transport and communication (35 percent), agroindustry and forestry (34 percent), and education, science, and culture (29 percent), all sectors that have substantial state ownership, compared with a paltry 6 percent in trade and services and 8 percent in construction, both sectors overwhelmingly made up of small, private businesses.[52] Moreover, the most mobilized unions are those comprised of workers in the state sector—teachers, miners, steelworkers, nurses, and railway workers. However, given that some of these sectors are in the process of a long, painful death or severe downsizing (particularly mining and heavy industry), an observer might wonder how much weaker unions might become in the near future.

Why is there such a correlation between private sector employment and low levels of unionization? Part of the answer is historical: most private businesses in Poland are new (formed after 1989) and did not inherit trade unions, as did the state sector, where unionization under communism was nearly 100 percent. Moreover, private owners have shed workers in an effort to make their enterprises more profitable, and this move has undermined continuity in the workforce. Also, many union leaders note that pay in the private sector is typically higher than in the state sector, so workers feel less need to form unions. This is supported by surveys, in which 46 percent of workers in nonunionized enterprises said they have no unions because there is no need. Unions thus die of atrophy in many settings. Thus, even without evoking arguments about antiunion managers or owners, it is understandable why unionization is not high in this sector.

However, anecdotal evidence from many union leaders points to more subjective problems of forming unions at both new and privatized companies. Supporting such claims, the same July 2001 survey found that 16 percent of respondents noted that there had been an attempt to form a union at their enterprise but that the directors or the owners, or both, would not permit it.[53] Such actions, of course, are a clear violation of the law but reflect the fact that management is often in a strong position to assert itself, workers do not feel confident pressing claims for union representation against their bosses, and court cases require time and money.

Aside from malevolent managers, another problem has been the transitory nature of employment in the private sector. Studies confirm that workers in the private sector change employment more than workers in the state sector (for understandable reasons), and thus the nature of employment itself (not to mention the small size of many microbusinesses) inhibits unionization.[54] Union leaders are not ready to give up on unionization in the private sector—in 2001–2002 there was a major effort to unionize workers in Polish supermarkets—but clearly they recognize that recruitment and retention of workers in this sector is a major problem if they want to boost union density in the country.

The story of privatization in Poland, however, is worth recounting from a workers' perspective. The Solidarity leadership, of course, saw it as a necessity, as did the IMF and numerous Western advisers in the country. Start-up and privatization of retail, trade, and service enterprises were foreseen under the initial reform program in 1990, and few questioned the rationality of taking the state out of these mostly small enterprises for the sake of efficiency and potential workers' gain (particularly if they obtained a share of ownership). However, the bigger political question was the privatization and restructuring of the large industrial enterprises owned by the state. Surveys among Poles in 1990–1994 indicated declining confidence that privatization would be advantageous for their place of work, and surveys from both 1990 and 1993 revealed that to the extent they favored ownership change at all, they favored schemes for employee ownership and self-management. There were differences among Solidarity and OPZZ members, the latter preferring state ownership to private (as opposed to employee ownership) by 40 percent to 10 percent, the former more in favor of privatization (21 percent) than continued state ownership (10 percent).[55] However, at least initially, the government "rather than leaving reform to interest group politics . . . declared the privatization of the economy as the only available option."[56]

However, all did not proceed as planned from either the government's or the workers' perspective. The plans for privatization through commercialization and public sales faced a number of technical obstacles (e.g., valuing the firm, lack of domestic capital), and thus it proceeded slowly. Government targets for privatization were not met. Bela Greskovits and Dorothee Bohle note that privatization in Poland was largely "by default," and that all rhetoric of shock therapy aside, the private sector's percentage of GDP lagged behind its Central European neighbors in the 1990–1993 period.[57] Writing in 1995, Ryszard Rapacki noted that grassroots, small-scale privatization (often spontaneous, as entrepreneurs were allowed to start up companies), rather than top-down privatization of large enterprises, has been the "driving force for Polish transformation."[58]

Moreover, the government was forced, due to the heritage of workers' self-management procedures inherited from the communist era, to make concessions to workers. Specifically, the workers' councils were empowered to initiate and approve privatization plans, as well as given powers to appoint directors and make resolutions on planning and investment in the firm. In addition, while outright transfer of enterprises to the workers was adamantly rejected, in the 1990 Law on Privatization the government granted workers the legal right to buy a fixed share, 20 percent, at 50 percent of the nominal cost. Workers (and managers) could also participate in "direct privatization" (*prywatyzacja bezposrednia*, sometimes referred to as "liquidation"), which envisioned a number of procedures, including a leasing arrangement that would transfer assets to the employee-managers. However, the government also passed a measure mandating that employee councils would be abolished upon privatization, a measure that was supported by the Solidarity leadership. But, in general, these concessions gave Polish workers (on paper at least) more say over privatization decisions than in most other countries in the region.

These moves did not get rid of all the snags in the privatization process. Public support for privatization continued to decline. While workers did have certain privileges to purchase shares, most lacked sufficient funds to take advantage of their rights, a fact that surely was well known to policy makers.[59] A Mass Privatization Program that was to distribute certificates for share purchases, adopted in 1994 as a way to bolster public involvement in the process, floundered due to lack of public knowledge about the program and poor performance of share values.[60] Government plans for privatization through commercialization (turning enterprises into joint stock companies and selling the shares with proceeds going to the state treasury) were continually underfulfilled due to lack of capital and the unattractiveness of tendered companies.

However, workers and managers did utilize the procedures of direct privatization, which envisioned liquidation of the firm and transfer to a new owner (often workers) through purchase, contribution in kind to the company, or (most commonly) leasing. Over fifteen hundred enterprises (mostly small- and medium-sized ones, particularly those that were less capital-intensive and thus had lower lease payments) were privatized in this manner from 1990 to 1997. In theory at least, these procedures could have led to employee-owned and -managed companies. However, research indicated that, over time, workers sold their shares and the raising of capital (issuing of new shares) diluted the power of the shares workers initially obtained. This produced a trend toward "formation of a very narrow ownership elite and pauperization of the remaining part of employees."[61] This phenomenon can be found throughout the region, and its presence in Poland underscores that rights on paper have not always produced positive results for workers. More disturbingly, from the trade union perspective, there has been a marked de-unionization of these firms (from about 50 percent to less than 30 percent), which now operate as "typical capitalist enterprises." According to one observer, "employees [in employee-owned firms] think that unions do not meet their needs, that they engage themselves in nation-wide actions, and that they do not protect their members as well as this form of privatization." Casting aside traditional trade unions, many such firms have joined a Union of Workers' Ownership, which primarily dispenses legal and investment advice.[62]

What have been the overall results of privatization? One trend, due to workers' opposition and investor reticence, has been a marked difference between sectors viewed as potentially profitable, where there has been near complete privatization, and the "sunset sectors," such as mining and metallurgy, which have few prospects and have generated no interest for privatization. Rapacki notes that this "contributes to social and political tensions, and exacerbates such macroeconomic problems as budget and imbalances and inflation," as the state must still care for these loss-producing behemoths.[63] At the end of 1999, Solidarity reports, 2,599 enterprises, roughly one-third of the 1990 total slated for privatization and over half of the figure left to be privatized in 1995, were still in state hands.[64] These major enterprises include the steel works in Katowice and Krakow (Nowa Huta, or the Sendzimir Mill), the Ursus tractor factory in Warsaw, the Cegielski railroad car and ship engine factory in Poznan (all of which have been hotbeds of labor militancy in the recent past), and large chemical works throughout the country, which have been transformed into state-controlled joint stock companies, but for which the state has yet to find outside buyers so it can divest itself of these holdings. Probably the most dire sector is coal mining: the number of miners has shrunk by one-third, and there are no prospects for privatization, as the industry survives on state subsidies of some $200 million a year. Restructuring has been on the table for years, but more mine closures are inevitable.[65]

Should these delays be viewed as a victory of the workers, who because of their rights on paper have been able to delay, prevent, and at times direct the privatization process? Certainly many workers, particularly miners, have successfully used the strike weapon to protest privatization or restructuring proposals, and in the case of the Ursus factory, Solidarity has had a dominant position in the company, using its power to dismiss directors and reject several restructuring schemes. However, their "victories" are more often negative, meaning *against* something, than positive by bringing about substantial improvement. The problems with privatization, though, are several and are readily enumerated by union leaders: corruption, inequality, breakdown in solidarity, lack of productive investment, and unemployment due to cutbacks in the workforce at privatized firms. Job losses, especially in heavy industry, have resulted in a severe drop in union membership. Moreover, privatization has produced divisions between workers in companies with a future (many of which have abandoned trade unions) and those unemployed or stuck in dead-end enterprises. Broadly speaking, then, workers can be classified as winners and losers, the former less likely to be unionized or, even if still in a union, finding little in common with those unionized workers in the state sector. Obviously, this situation hampers prospects for a union movement in Poland and may belie any claim about workers' solidarity.

Of course, some observers praise the Polish economic "miracle" of the 1990s and note that the growth of private businesses has opened up numerous opportunities for would-be entrepreneurs and workers.[66] Solidarity itself notes that experience shows the "rightness" of Polish privatization and that "it is difficult to state that privatization itself (as transformation of owner's subject) is a reason for worsening living, employment, and working conditions, as it depends directly on the capabilities of the private owner."[67] However, surveys from workers themselves paint a less rosy picture. Lena Kolarska-Bobinska reports from a 1993 CBOS survey of workers in privatized firms that many workers remained unimpressed with the results. Over 40 percent of workers reported layoffs and limits on employee decision making, and only 13 percent reported that social welfare provisions at the firm level have improved.[68] Lest we think that this research is dated and that workers have "learned to love" privatization, the August 2001 survey of workers by CBOS asked about their preferred form of ownership for their enterprise. Close to a majority, 42 percent, favored state ownership, 19 percent favored worker ownership, and only 30 percent cited private employers (26 percent favoring Polish owners, 4 percent foreign). Interestingly, union members favored state ownership even more, 67 percent, whereas only 2 percent of unionists claimed they would want to work for a private employer! Significantly, these findings stand in stark contrast to earlier surveys that showed general workers' approval for moves to a marketized economy.[69]

Individual workers aside, the main question of the study is the effect of privatization on unions and workers' organizations. Al Rainnie and Jane Hardy, focusing on the collective rights of workers, offer a rather skeptical assessment, noting that the promises and "influence of self management legislation has certainly not been that envisaged by the legislators, insofar as it has [produced] . . . a pattern of change in the direction that mostly involves relatively unfettered management."[70] Ost and Weinstein, utilizing survey research of union leaders in privatized firms, note that at the firm level privatization has stripped away workers' rights, leading to a system of "hierarchical and non-participative industrial-relations institutions." Interestingly, they note that this has emerged due to "acquiescence from below," meaning trade unionists themselves have backed these changes. Among the consequences, they note that managerial control over basic issues such as wages have harmed workers by "promoting internal competition [among them] and reducing employee solidarity."[71] Monitoring violations of the labor law, Solidarity noted in 2001 that "employers constantly violate the provisions of the act on trade unions," including harassment of union leaders and failure to provide unions with space, technical means of support, and information about the company.[72] Notably, branch collective agreements—there have been a mere sixteen in Poland from 1994 to 2002—are all in sectors where the state remains dominant.[73] Private employers, *if* they have to deal with unions at all, have thus far managed to avoid any agreement "from above" that would affect their enterprises. And, union membership has eroded even in firms subjected to direct privatization by the workers.

What do union officials themselves say of their experiences at privately owned firms, and how do private firms differ from state- or employee-owned firms? Given the results of some of the above surveys, it might appear that union leaders report only problems with private employers and wish that privatization could somehow be rolled back. However, union leaders from both Solidarity and the OPZZ in general view privatization as a mixed bag, something that was necessary and has brought benefits to some but in general needed and still needs better oversight by the government with the goal of boosting enterprise productivity and job security for workers. In other words, a desire to return to the past or somehow undo privatization is not encountered, at least in the OPZZ and Solidarity leadership. Typical is the view of Zdzislaw Tuszynski, head of the OPZZ-affiliated union Metalowcy: he maintained that there was nothing wrong with privatization per se, only that in many cases privatization was pushed too fast in Poland or without sufficient guarantees of investment.[74] His counterpart at the rival Solidarity metallurgical branch union agreed, noted that privatization could be conducted successfully, and pointed to the purchase of the Warsaw Steel Works by the Italian conglomerate Lucchini (although this plant has seen its workforce shrink by over half since privatization and its workers protest just after the takeover in 1992). However, he too was concerned that privatization has often been accompanied by layoffs, pronounced violations of labor law (such as at the Bison-Bial plant in Bielsk Podlawski, owned by the Warsaw-based Metalexport, which had not paid workers for several months, leading to strike action), and dismantling of firms.[75]

Despite well-placed concerns, however, union leaders have learned to accept privatization as the norm. When asked to comment about the demands that the Szczecin shipyards be renationalized, a Solidarity representative noted that "we know from the past that we cannot create utopias (through these means)," and a vice chairman of the OPZZ conceded that even if renationalization might make some sense in this particular case, that it could not become a widespread policy, given the problems at numerous Polish companies and Polish commitments to adhere to European standards.[76] However, it bears mentioning again that the rank and file have more positive views toward state ownership, and based upon anecdotal evidence, they remain very fearful of plans to privatize or restructure their enterprises—hence part of the reason why major steelworks and coal mines in particular remain in the hands of the state.[77] Moreover, the next wave of reforms in Poland will likely tackle labor market issues such as granting more flexibility in wage determination and greater ability of employers to use fixed-term contracts in an effort to "improve the entrepreneurial climate" for small- and medium-size enterprises that have the most interest in flexibility.[78] This will likely have negative repercussions for unions.

Thus, Polish unions must live with privatization, whether they like it or not. The question is what can be done now? Is there any reason for hope? Small enterprises will likely remain nonunion, if for no other reason than that Polish law requires ten workers to form a union, thus preventing union membership at microenterprises (where unionization is likely not logistically possible anyway). On the broader front, however, Ost notes in his most recent work that unions are changing, emphasizing servicing their constituencies instead of engaging in political work and trying to play the role of a social movement. He also points to efforts by Solidarity in 2000 to 2001 (made with assistance from the AFL-CIO) to organize workers in foreign-owned "hypermarkets" (large retail outlets) in Poland, a sector that was notoriously antiunion.[79] This new round of activism produced a response from the OPZZ, which is now sponsoring the Labor Confederation OPZZ (*Konfederacja Pracy OPZZ*), a new structure that allows for quick membership (through this confederation a worker can join a union without jumping through a number of legal hoops) and bypasses the existing OPZZ bureaucracy. It is an interesting development, one that might give some hope to unionization from below, but in the two years since its inception it has attracted only a few thousand members.[80] However, despite these small examples, unionization continues to plummet, and few wax truly optimistic about the predicament of organized labor. Pankow suggests that talk of union reform or union comeback is unduly optimistic, since economic conditions have changed so as to prevent unions from being able to exercise their traditional role. Years of "passive acceptance" of various reform programs and management strategies have undermined unions' ability to press forward a prolabor agenda.[81]

What of workers' mobilization and activism? Given their disappointment with many of the changes they have witnessed in recent years, it is easy to think workers would be willing to adopt a more militant position to press their claims against employers and the government. This, however, seems unlikely. Not only is unionization down, not only are workers divided across and within enterprises, but even union members reject this option. Surveys of Solidarity and OPZZ members from 2001 reveal that 0 percent of each suggested that organizing strikes and protests would be the most effective form of defending workers' interests. This could, of course, be taken as a positive sign (workers do not need to strike and can defend their rights through negotiations), but the fact that 45 percent of Solidarity members in the same survey (24 percent of OPZZ members) contended there was no effective means to defend workers' interests must be viewed as disheartening.[82] Hence, it should not be surprising to learn that a major strike at the Szczecin shipyard in 2002 was initiated by workers themselves, leaving unions (as was often the case in the strike-heavy years of 1992–1993) to catch up.[83]

Mere survival may be the best unions can do, and radical changes do not seem very likely. Speaking in 2001, Wałesa himself could say only that the workers would have to learn to be "well-behaved parasites," garnering what they could from the capitalist organism, but at the same time ensuring they would not destroy it.[84] This may be prudent and pragmatic, but not something likely to inspire a workers' movement in Poland today.

Trade Unions and Globalization

If the battles over privatization are essentially over and workers must play on the new field of industrial relations (even if it is not to their liking), the effects of globalization are only beginning to be felt and receive attention from the trade unions. True, foreign investment has been a growing component of the economy for some time now, and Polish workers are employed by a host of multinational corporations. However, it has only been in the past couple of years, with Polish accession to the EU seen as a near certainty, that the consequences of opening the Polish economy to global markets have been a major subject of political debate within the country and among trade unions.

There are really three components of globalization that have the most effects on trade unions and their members. The first is the role of international financial institutions (IFIs) such as the IMF. Conventional wisdom is that the fingerprints of IFIs and their advisers, most famously Jeffrey Sachs, are all over the early Polish reforms.[85] In turn, these programs have been blamed by some as resulting in decreased living standards for most Poles, as they required wage freezes and cuts in social programs.[86] As noted, however, Solidarity backed the shock therapy program, and observers have noted that the genesis of the program may lie less with the IMF than with individuals within the Solidarity camp ideologically committed to the rapid dismantling of communism. In other words, the IMF may not deserve blame for all of Poland's ills. At worst, perhaps, IMF support for reforms may have given the government some leeway to avoid political accountability for the reforms (e.g., the IMF made us do it). Moreover, in the Polish case (notably *not* in others), international creditors also forgave much of Poland's international debt, and this approach helped the government carry the reform program through to an eventual economic upturn in 1993.[87] Thus, it is arguable that IFIs had, despite the pain of shock therapy, a long-term positive impact upon the Polish economy and that Polish success, compared to the experience of other postcommunist states, vindicates the shock therapy approach. However, even if we grant the positive long-term impact upon Poland as a whole, that does not erase the fact that IMF support for shock therapy helped undercut any potential policy-making role for the trade unions and workers in the early stages of postcommunist Poland (e.g., powerful corporatist institutions), thereby in turn creating conditions that have been less than amenable for trade union development.

Debates over the IMF, however, have largely receded as the Polish economy became one of the most vibrant in Europe. By 2000, the role of competitive international market forces and foreign trade is coming to the fore. An obvious example is Polish agriculture and accession negotiations for the EU, but it is also important in the industrial sector, where Polish enterprises, due to lower levels of technology, outdated production, poor quality, and problems of distribution and marketing, often cannot compete with Western firms. This is most clear in industries such as chemicals, coal, and steel production, which have fallen on very hard times. Unionists therefore blame international markets for many of their problems. This is a very thorny issue, and "restructuring"—often a euphemism for radical cuts in the workforce—is a major preoccupation of several unions. Of course, the role of competitive market forces does hinder unions in less successful sectors (while opening up possibilities for workers in other sectors), but many of the fundamental problems of Polish industry cannot be laid at the door of the world economy. Such arguments overlook the fact that current problems of competitiveness are directly related to the failures of the communist regime. Moreover, the policy of the government and National Bank, which is to maintain a high value for the zloty, has also harmed would-be Polish exporters, and in 2002 unions from the OPZZ in particular have rallied against this policy, blamed on Balcerowicz, now head of the National Bank. True, certain factors, such as European restrictions on steel imports and U.S. tariffs, do not help, but competitive pressures may put the Polish economy on a more sustainable course than was the case in the late communist years, when the government borrowed heavily to boost consumption and prop up unprofitable sectors of the economy. A Solidarity representative, speaking about the Polish accession into the EU and into the broader world economy, conceded that there would be short-term costs to some, but that the union could not lose its focus and overlook the long-term benefits to the Polish economy.[88]

The role of multinational corporations in Poland is also of great interest to this study. Foreign companies and foreign investment are an increasingly important part of the Polish economy. Figures on foreign investment do vary, but the Polish Agency for Foreign Investment announced that by the end of 2000 foreign investment in Poland topped $49 billion, with $13 billion coming in 2000 alone.[89] This dwarfs investment in Poland's larger neighbors to the east, Ukraine and Russia, and unlike in those countries the investment is widely distributed throughout the economy, with the largest investments in food manufacture, transportation equipment, banking and finance, trade, and communication. The list of the largest investors reads like a Who's Who of the world economy: Citibank, General Motors, Nestle, Heineken, France Telecom, General Electric, Phillips, Shell, and Volkswagen. This investment has made a big difference in many cases, saving many companies on the brink of collapse. One report suggests that privatizations involving foreign investors, because of capital and know-how, are in general "more successful than those privatized companies that remained under local management and control," whereas others calculate that foreign investment has accounted for one-third of Polish economic growth and even by 1997 was responsible for 21 percent of employment and 34 percent of output in the nonagricultural sector.[90] Gardawski, stating the opinion of several economists, claims that in ten years there may not be any large enterprise in Poland that is "purely Polish."[91]

The fact that MNCs are active in Poland is hardly news, but it is far less clear what effect they have on trade unions. Indeed, trade union officials refused to paint a black-and-white picture, noting that it was virtually impossible to make generalizations. Ryszard Lepik, vice chairman of the OPZZ, stated that in the majority of cases his unions have "normal" relations with foreign owners and that he could not say there was a big difference in behavior between Polish and foreign firms (although the latter are in possession of more capital and technology).[92] Examples of companies held up as positive models by union officials include Philip Morris, Bombardier Aircraft, Siemens, Phillips, Danone, Lucchini in the Warsaw steelworks, and Volkswagen, whose unions at plants in Poznan and in Polkowice are among several dozen in Poland that participate in the European Works Councils of various multinational firms. Frank Hantke at the Warsaw Friedrich Ebert Foundation, who has worked with Polish unions for several years, maintains that companies' attitudes toward unionization depend in large part upon home company practice and on the sector of the economy. Large plants are far more likely to be unionized, as well as older plants, as many foreign buyers inherited trade unions.[93] Indeed, one Solidarity official who has tracked MNC presence in Poland noted that the closest thing to a rule is that unions are absent in greenfield plants, such as Pepsi in Szczecin and Levi-Strauss in Plock.[94] Coca-Cola, Frito-Lay, Marriott, and, most especially, various European "hypermarkets" (e.g., Giant, Hit, Metro A. G., Carrefour) are also held up by union leaders as negative examples, where management has done all in its power to prevent unionization or existing unions have been subjected to extensive harassment. However, in the case of the hypermarkets, a problem that was mentioned by virtually every trade union leader I met, some suggest that it was the local Polish management, perhaps in an effort to prove its capitalist credentials, that was more antiunion than the foreign ownership.[95]

Of course, not all has gone well for the unions inherited by MNCs. Some MNCs—most notoriously the Daewoo plant in Warsaw and Daewoo-owned subsidiaries throughout the country—have harassed unions, failed to engage in social dialogue, and even failed to pay salaries on time. In other sectors, foreign involvement has meant breaking up the existing conglomerates into smaller firms and subcontracting work, meaning that workers are no longer treated as employees but as self-employed contractors. This has been especially prevalent in shipbuilding, metallurgy, and aircraft construction. Some, such as GM/Opel in Gliwice and Danone, have shown enthusiasm for reanimating structures such as an "advisory forum" or a "Danone Committee" for workers in order to, potentially, bypass trade unions. One pattern that has been repeated in many sectors is that the investor signs an agreement on social guarantees and job protection for three to four years, but when that contract expires, significant downsizing occurs.[96]

On the positive side, however, trade unions may have more recourse at an

MNC than at a Polish-owned enterprise if the MNC has signed on to an international code of conduct and has unions in other countries. Polish unions have used bilateral contacts with their counterparts and lobbied through international bodies such as the ETUC to help support activities of trade unions at Nestle and IKEA subsidiaries.[97]

Moving away from union headquarters and talking with unionists closer to the enterprise level, I heard fewer and fewer negative stories about foreign capital. Indeed, many of these union leaders, particularly in sectors where job loss has been significant, would welcome foreign ownership. They would note that as Polish patriots they would prefer to see Polish ownership but concede that Poles lacked the capital to invest in the largest enterprises. The purchase of the Warsaw Steelworks by Lucchini was again held as a very positive example—despite the significant downsizing there—and unionists in the steel industry also looked with envy on the purchase of the largest Slovak steelworks by U.S. Steel.[98] The head of the Solidarity coal miners union noted that he would most definitely welcome purchase of mines by foreigners, but he lamented that no foreigner would be "stupid" enough to buy them.[99] A placard held by one worker at the Polish-owned Ozarow cable plant, which was experiencing union-management conflict leading to strikes and protests, was telling: "We want an investor, not a liquidator."[100] Of course, for many sectors of the Polish economy there is no other solution but foreign investment, so even if not ideal foreign investment is accepted. Rather than stopping the takeover of Polish firms, unionists see their role as protestors for the workforce, trying to get the best compensation packages and (inevitably) severance pay for the workers that must be laid off in order for these firms to become more profitable. The problem, of course, is that finding the balance between would-be investors' interests and workers' interests has been very difficult, and thus many large firms remain on the trading block.

To illustrate the point that it is hard to generalize about the experience of foreign-owned firms, let us consider the automobile manufacturing industry, one that has seen substantial foreign investment, has been privatized, and is one of the most competitive in the country. In this sector have been very different union experiences with MNCs. The best, as noted, would be Volkswagen, which created a joint venture with an existing Polish plant (Tarpan) in Poznan and has built a brand-new, state-of-the-art engine plant in Polkowice. Both plants have strong unions (Solidarity), with the unionization rate in

Poznan above 60 percent. In Poznan, due to union lobbying, Volkswagen agreed to hire most of the Tarpan workers. There have been no mass layoffs, and in fact the plant is expanding. Wages have gone up 300 percent since the takeover in 1993, and union representatives from both plants sit on Volkswagen's European Work Council. Union leaders in Poznan report successful negotiations with management on pay raises, inflation adjustments, and bonus pay, all basic economic issues. Solidarity representatives in Poznan noted that their primary issues revolve around the plant and its workforce, and they do not get involved in more political issues outside the plant. In all, it would be difficult to imagine many better union-employee relationships in Poland.[101]

At the other end of the spectrum is the experience of Daewoo, which took over a Polish automobile plant in 1996 and created "daughter companies" for equipment and service throughout the country. While the privatization pact did include a social pact with a three-year moratorium on layoffs and a no-strike pledge for five years, union-management relations have been anything but harmonious. Unions and workers in all of these plants have been plagued with problems: mass layoffs of about half the workforce, harassment of union leaders, refusal to engage in social dialogue, and problems over payments of back pay. Workers at several enterprises have gone on strike and protested to Polish government officials, as well as Daewoo officials in Korea. Of course, part of the problem is that Daewoo itself is in serious trouble, and in Poland its operations have been unprofitable because its products (designed primarily for the internal Polish market, as opposed to Volkswagen's, which are mostly for export) cannot compete with the influx of European used cars into Poland. As of this writing, there was a search for new investors for the Warsaw and Lublin plants (Rover is rumored to taking over the former), but it is clear that this company has been one of the most antiunion in the country and is held up as the archetypical bad foreign investor. In the words of the chairman of Solidarity's Inter-Enterprise Commission at Daewoo, the company promised "to Polonize the production of Korean automobiles" but instead they have "Koreanized" Poland.[102]

In between these two extremes is Fiat, which has been producing cars in Poland since 1934 and had important investments even during the communist era. In 1992, Fiat took over two Polish factories in Tychy and Bielsko-Biala, despite union opposition. Strikes, led by a politicized branch of Solidarity 80, followed the takeover. This strike not only soured worker-management relations but also led to splits among unionists, so that (in stark contrast to Volkswagen, where there is only a Solidarity union) there are over ten unions in Polish Fiat factories, with mainstream Solidarity totally absent in Tychy and many of the unions very politicized, with ties to far-right political movements. Hostility and mutual suspicion between workers and management was the norm, and one study suggested that resentment of foreign ownership and Polish nationalism played a role in workers' militancy.[103] Matters did improve in 1998, when a collective agreement for the company was signed and the company agreed to a more formal system of communication with unions. While some of the radical unions do remain suspicious of management, the OPZZ-affiliated union at the Tychy plant (Metalowcy) has come around to a promarket and even pro-Fiat position, expressing sympathy for Fiat's need to be competitive while downplaying any element of class conflict. However, there are still real problems. The economics of the plant are still poor (and Fiat itself has had some problems), and downsizing of the workforce and outsourcing to nonunionized plants continues.[104]

What accounts for the differences across this sector? While unionists may in some cases point to the success of "their strategy," it seems plain that a company's relative success and corporate culture are very important factors, with a stark contrast in attitudes toward unions between Volkswagen and Daewoo, with Fiat somewhere in the middle but nonetheless often suspicious of unions. Not to take anything away from the unionists in Poznan, but their success is directly tied to the success of the firm, a fact that they readily acknowledge. Interestingly, despite high levels of unionization, there have been no collective agreements for this sector, reflecting the competitive pressures faced by companies and unions, both of which have been reluctant to cooperate with each other, focusing instead on plant-level concerns.[105] Thus, despite labels to the contrary, "solidarity" is difficult to find.

In Poland, there is one other major international factor that creeps into almost any conversation about political and economic life: the European Union. Polish accession to the EU occured in May 2004. Accession talks tackled a number of controversial issues, among them agricultural subsidies from the Common Agricultural Policy (which has been the cause célèbre of Lepper's *Samoobrona*) and mobility for Polish labor within existing EU countries. The latter has been a major issue and source of disappointment for trade unions, since there will now be a seven-year transition period for the free movement of peoples. Despite this defeat, however, both the OPZZ and

Solidarity embrace the idea of joining the EU. Union leaders list several reasons for this position, some with obvious relevance to unions (access to markets, job opportunities in other countries, even direct EU aid for depressed areas) and others more general in nature (the desire to "return to Europe" and "Christian civilization").

As far as the impact on unions themselves is concerned, union leadership sees long-term benefits for their members, and they participate in drafting position papers and in a Liaison Committee that is consulted by the Polish government and EU representatives.[106] However, faith is also placed in the social *acquis* of the EU, including construction of social dialogue at the European level and adoption of the Social Charter (with all its various protections) by the Polish government.[107] Interestingly, branch or enterprise union leaders did not mention as important the legal changes necessary to bring Polish law up to EU standards, perhaps because in some areas (e.g., grievance procedures on dismissals), Polish law remains rather prounion, a heritage of the communist past that still exists, at least on paper. The EU itself, however, in a recent report on Poland, did note that Poland is lagging behind on the adoption of legislation for social policy, employment, and occupational safety, all of which directly affect the unions.[108] This is rather strange and perhaps represents the fact that the EU has more faith in a legal regime than Polish unionists, who often lack the wherewithal to fight for their existing rights against antiunion employers or stubborn government bureaucrats.

On balance, one report concludes that the possible consequences of EU membership for Polish unions appear to be "ambiguous."[109] Certainly, there will be advantages: Polish participation in European Works Councils (EWCs) of MNCs, access to information and training, and EU support for social dialogue within Poland, which has already borne fruit (on paper at least) with the creation of regional commissions for social dialogue. However, there are reasons to be skeptical. One risk is that of a division between workers represented on EWCs and those working for smaller, domestic producers who depend upon national-level agreements and whose interests will diverge from those working for MNCs.[110] Above and beyond short-term costs of dislocation due to competitive pressures, there is the issue of national sovereignty and adding another layer of decision makers further away from voters and social actors. If the Polish government's hands become tied by EU legislation (e.g., it can no longer offer tariffs or subsidies to certain industries), unions will be less able to lobby Warsaw and will have to either lobby at the European level or focus on enterprise-level concerns. The European focus on cross-border issues and negotiations that "ignore traditional territorial divisions" signifies a "commitment to disseminate corporatist type labor relations within member countries."[111] By itself, this may not be a terrible thing for Polish unions, given the ineffectiveness of corporatist structures in Poland, but it does suggest that unions will have to reconsider their traditional approaches (and find some avenues closed) after Polish accession to the EU.

5

Organized Labor in Russia

RUSSIAN TRADE UNIONS HAVE NOT BEEN nearly as prominent in the postcommunist period as their Polish counterparts; not one of them has lent its name to a party that has ascended to the heights of political power. Their political identity is ambiguous, and their electoral campaigns in alliance with other groups have won them little. They, unlike the oligarchs, do not curry favor in the Kremlin. They stood paralyzed in the wake of the massive theft that accompanied privatization, and they have been unable to consistently mobilize workers even as millions went unpaid and slid into poverty as the result of what David Mandel describes as "an open, massive offensive against workers' living standards."[1] Laws and regulations often do little to mitigate the *bardak* (chaos) in the realms of industrial relations and corporate governance. For many Russians, unions are not even on the radar screen. Throughout my stay in Russia, when I told people I was investigating trade unions, a typical reaction was "Why?" or even "Trade unions? I thought they had been disbanded years ago."

The saddest part, perhaps, is that relative to unions in several Eastern European states and throughout the former Soviet Union, Russian unions and other workers' organizations have been relatively active. Certainly, the strike waves of 1989–1991 were an important link in the chain that caused the collapse of communism and the Soviet Union, and spontaneous workers' strikes and protests in 1998 shut down railroads and contributed to the collapse of the short-lived Kiriyenko government. True, the level of activism has been low given the deprivations suffered by most Russians, but there has been activity.[2] Such protests, to be sure, are often rather perfunctory, performed on May 1 or other holidays out of a sense of nostalgia, but at times, as in 1998, workers have demanded attention from the authorities. Aside from action on the streets, several institutional arrangements also exist for the unions to consult with the government, practice collective bargaining, and forge general agreements. True, these tripartite structures do not work as well as unions might like, but unions have not given up in this sphere or in their work with the Duma, and they can point to some small successes from their efforts in these arenas. In this very limited sense, Russian unions are relatively active.

While Russian unions still, for the most part, remain rather weak, it is not entirely their fault. They have been hampered by the bardak that was the first ten years of the post-Soviet period. In contrast to Poland, where the capitalist path was immediately and clearly blazed, the situation in Russia is not so well defined. Basic principles of shock therapy were halted within months of their initiation, privatization was then rushed through, laws were contradictory or simply never existed, bargains were made between political authorities and oligarchs, and economic progress remained elusive. Forceful resolution of political crises gave way to political incapacitation, and a series of halfway reform measures yielded government bankruptcy. Unions, as their leaders themselves admit, were handicapped both by the crisis itself and the unfamiliar, ill-defined terrain of a pseudomarketized system. Defining what course to take was a difficult task. In short, unions (like the government, and like most observers of Russia) knew things were not as they should be but had little notion how to go about fixing them. As a result, unions at best reacted to events rather than playing an important role in shaping policy, both at the national and at the enterprise level.

The new millennium has brought with it, arguably, some improvement in Russia's economic and political situation. Economic growth has averaged 6 percent since 2000, real wages have increased, confidence in President Putin remained high and he was easily reelected in 2004,[3] and the wage arrears crisis has considerably abated from its epic proportions in 1998.[4] Putin has put a team of reformers in place and has centralized power. There is, more than before, a sense of optimism, a notion that Russia may have turned a corner.[5] Chechnya aside (a terrible mark on Russia's record, to be sure), there is greater political stability. True, Russia may not be heading in a democratic direction, but this may not bother the majority of Russians.[6]

What does all this mean for trade unions? To understand unions today requires determining whether they have overcome their past troubles, what the transition has left them, what role they played in the construction of the new socioeconomic system, and whether they now have any capacity to play an important political and economic role in the country.

Union Issues in Russia

While Russia did witness labor activism in the waning days of communism, this did not lead to a massive split in the union movement, as in Poland. True, there are literally hundreds of unions and over a dozen national confederations of unions in Russia today, but the main player in the workers' movement is the Federation of Independent Trade Unions of Russia (FNPR) and its constituent unions. The FNPR, formed in 1990, is the successor to the old All-Union Central Committee of Trade Unions (VTsSPS), and like its predecessor it is organized along both branch (sector) and territorial principles. It unites forty-three branch unions, and even though its membership has fallen steeply, from approximately sixty-six million in 1991 to thirty-eight million ten years later, it still claims to represent well over 95 percent of the unionized workers of Russia.[7]

Life has not been easy for the FNPR in the post-Soviet period, however. It has found itself confronted by two major challenges. The first concerns its own preservation, meaning its membership, organizational unity, and property. On this front, it has been largely successful. When union leaders are asked their achievements in the past ten years, invariably the first answer they give is "We survived" (*my sokhranilis'*). Membership is down, but by most accounts this is because of job losses or people voluntarily changing jobs, usually taking jobs in the shadow economy or in new, nonunionized enterprises; in most major sectors of the economy (transport, energy, heavy and light industry) unionization rates, according to the FNPR, continue to be 80–90 percent.[8] In addition, the federation has preserved its unity (or least the appearance thereof). Although there have been some defections of individual unions (the unions at the Kirov factory in St. Petersburg and at Norilsk Nickel being the largest ones in industrial sectors), the largest union to leave the FNPR, the Union of Miners and Metallurgical Workers, returned to the fold in 2000, and in 2001 the Union of Railway Workers (which existed outside the VTsSPS in Soviet times) entered the FNPR. Moreover, the FNPR has maintained control over a vast network of property, including offices, print houses, banks, cultural institutions, and, most important, resorts and hotels. One estimate put the value of FNPR property at $6 billion, with an annual income of $300 million a year, although the FNPR itself claims a far lower figure.[9] Critics charge that this property, state assets unjustly seized by the FNPR, has turned the union into a commercial enterprise, allowing it to live independently of workers and their union dues.[10] The FNPR would dispute this claim, but its leaders do note that this property, and its availability to offer benefits such as vacation discounts to union members, is crucial to attracting and keeping members in the union.[11]

Of course, the FNPR has not been able to preserve everything. One item that has been lost is control over social insurance funds, including pension, unemployment, and health funds. In Soviet times, these funds were managed directly by the unions. In 1993, they were formally taken away from the unions, but they continued to be administered through the enterprise, and de facto the FNPR continued to exercise significant control over them. Effective January 1, 2001, there is now a "unified social tax" in Russia, and these funds are put under government budgetary control through the Tax Service. The FNPR lobbied unsuccessfully against this move, claming it would result in benefit cuts for workers,[12] and some rivals hope that this change will make it impossible for the FNPR to use control over these funds to coerce or persuade workers to join or remain in the union.

Moreover, there are schisms within the FNPR itself. Many of these are rooted in regional or branch differences, and some have emerged quite clearly during parliamentary elections, when local or branch FNPR unions have ignored the central FNPR and made their own political bargains, typically allying with the party of the regional governor.[13] These schisms are also reflected in a battle against the FNPR leadership waged by some constituent unions, particularly those with leaders allied to neocommunist groups. Vladimir Makavchik, head of the Shipbuilders Union, has been one of the most vocal critics, calling the FNPR "oversized," "unguided," and "ridiculous," demanding the ouster of its leadership, and stating "the faster it is dismantled, the better."[14] Less dramatically, there are also schisms between unions, particularly those in the public sector and those in the competitive sphere, with the public sector unions (education, medical, and cultural workers) forming their own working group within the FNPR. This split could become a significant obstacle to all-union solidarity.

If the first challenge to the FNPR was preservation, the second, and more difficult one, is breaking with the past in order to gain independence from management, adopting democratic practices, and winning the confidence of the members. In other words, the FNPR must reform itself. As mentioned, in the past Russian (Soviet) unions were largely transmission belts of the Party and management and did little except to administer social programs. Now, it seems, they need to reconstruct themselves so that they can play a genuinely representative function. On this score, there is less evidence that they have had much success, at least in terms of convincing people that they really have broken with the past and are prepared to play a new role. One report in 2001 dubbed the FNPR "old school," still beholden to old methods and ideals. It noted that "the spirit of a Soviet institution is hard to remove, and it is very difficult to imagine that these people [leaders of the FNPR] represent the interests of the workers."[15] This misgiving is reflected in many ways, but most clearly, perhaps, in the fact that throughout the post-Soviet period, trust in trade unions has been abysmally low and few believe that they are capable of defending workers' interests.[16] This lack of confidence is perhaps unions' most serious problem, as it hampers their ability to mobilize workers and press claims against owners and the state.

Critics charge, however, that the real problem is that the FNPR unions—or at least many of them—have no real interest in defending workers against management, preferring instead to continue with the old system while stifling initiatives for change from below. One worker from the Perm Motorworks, a delegate to the FNPR's Third Congress, walked away with a quite unfavorable impression. "I did not expect anything different from the Congress. Look at who sits in the hall. The majority are people from the past. They don't need any reform of the union movement. To them, it is only important to preserve their leadership positions."[17] Many actions of the FNPR, including strikes, lobbying, and even political campaigns, have been done in concert with management or employer organizations.[18] Some would thus question whether these unions deserve the label *nezavisimyi*. Notably, unions—those of the

FNPR and the newer, alternatives—were not, at least initially, on the side of workers during the "railway war" of 1998, and when the unions tried to jump on the bandwagon, the striking workers chased them away, accusing them of repeatedly selling out the workers.[19]

Other observers are more generous to the FNPR and note that it is difficult to change such an ossified structure in a short period of time and that the unions and their members are in a tough position given the financial standing of many enterprises. Militancy in most cases will only get workers thrown onto the streets, and thus unions cannot do much but hold onto the little they have. Simon Clarke notes:

> The primary organisations of the trade unions expressed the dependence of the employees on their employers and so were in no position to articulate the conflict that could be expected to arise as employers chose or were forced by market pressures to cut costs by intensifying labour, cutting wages and reducing employment. . . . It is still almost universally the case that the trade union organization only ever opposes the administration when it is able to ally with an opposition management faction or an external force.[20]

It is worth noting as well that management retains the right to join the trade union itself, as directors technically qualify as hired workers of the owners. This could easily constrain union independence.

The FNPR does attempt to mobilize workers on the obligatory holidays and on other occasions to protest socioeconomic conditions (particularly wage arrears), but the numbers drawn to these protests are fewer and fewer each year.[21] The peak of such activity was 1997–1998, during the height of the wage arrears crisis, but even then the FNPR's actions expressed rather limited demands (typically payment for the wages owed to workers), pointedly eschewed radicalism (no effort was made to involve the Communist Party, for example) and proposals for far-reaching reform, and were construed by some as attempts by the FNPR leadership to fend off complaints from local affiliates and grassroots unions that it was not doing enough for the workers.[22] Even during this period, however, the FNPR could only get less than 1 percent of its members on to the streets for its national days of mobilization, and the radical actions in May–June 1998 that did get the attention of authorities were spontaneous, desperate acts of protest, not union planned or union led. Studies suggest that disgruntled, impoverished workers are exercising the option of "exit" through wage substitution and supplementation in the shadow economy rather than exercising "voice" through the unions to press for broader environmental change.[23] The FNPR's failures to win over the rank and file are underscored by its abysmal electoral performance in political formations in national parliamentary elections and in surveys of workers. To put the matter simply, if unions really commanded the respect of their members, unions would represent an immense, if not invincible, force. The FNPR is still a behemoth, to be sure, but largely toothless and often ignored.

The FNPR is the dominant union structure in Russia, but it is not the only one. Independent or (in FNPR lexicon) "alternative" unions do exist. Many were formed toward the end of the Soviet Union and have their genesis in the strikes of 1989. Most of these unions are now affiliated with one or another confederation, including Sotsprof,[24] the All-Russian Confederation of Labor[25] (VKT), and the Confederation of Labor of Russia (KTR).[26] They are Lilliputian compared to the Brobdingnagian FNPR.[27] Efforts to forge a united group of independent unions have floundered due to leadership squabbles, although there are some individual unions with crossover ties, and the VKT and KTR have formed a Coordinating Committee. For the most part, the independent unions unite workers with a high degree of qualification (pilots, railroad drivers, underground miners, aviation mechanics, air traffic controllers), are based upon profession (as opposed to industrial sector), and are centered in strategic branches (transport, energy) in which strikes can cripple the economy.[28] For this reason, these unions have been less reticent in using strikes as a weapon and have taken a more adversarial position than the FNPR vis-à-vis management. However, unlike the FNPR, these associations have had to build themselves from scratch, lacking the property to give members substantial fringe benefits or "selective incentives." Start-up costs are also high for workers willing to leave the preexisting union or attempting to launch a union at a nonunionized enterprise. Such efforts are smiled upon neither by employers nor the FNPR, and local authorities have also helped stifle the development of new unions.[29] Unlike the FNPR, these unions do not allow management to join and typically do not, unlike the FNPR, operate from a principle of congruent interests between the enterprise and the workers. However, in public opinion surveys they do not rank much higher—if at all higher—than the FNPR.[30]

Relations between the FNPR and the other unions have been tense, if not hostile. Disagreements are rooted in both ideology and more mundane concerns such as control over union property. The basic ideological division has been on questions of economic reform and relations with the political authorities, and this has been particularly pronounced in the immediate post-Soviet period. The FNPR was far more critical of economic reforms, while most of the independents offered support to government efforts to marketize the economy. Igor Klotchkov, former head of the FNPR, accused the new unions of being a tool of the government, "puppet unions" allowing the authorities to "divide and conquer" the trade unions.[31] At this time, the FNPR was also worried that the independents would use their allies in the Kremlin (particularly Yeltsin adviser Gennadi Burburlis and Labor Minister Aleksandr Shokhin) to gain a sizeable portion of FNPR property.[32] However, now that the FNPR feels its dominance of the trade union movement in Russia is assured, some of the fiery rhetoric has cooled down. FNPR officials informed me repeatedly that they recognize the rights of the alternative unions to exist, they try to cooperate with them, but frankly, as one official contended, "Their influence is meager. They are really just chump-change (*meloch'*)."[33]

In turn, the independents tend to have a rather unfavorable view of the FNPR. However, as Boris Kravchenko of the VKT and Nikolai Shtirnov of the NPG noted, there has been some cooperation in organizing demonstrations, lobbying the government, concluding collective agreements on different levels, and working with international union confederations.[34] Critics of the FNPR, however, spare few candid words, claiming that it is still a "Bolshevik union," a "Siamese twin" of management, colluding with management to prevent formation of new unions, that its membership is the result of automatic enrollment in unions, not workers' own choice, and that its prime concern is making money, not representing workers.[35] There was a pronounced change in interunion relations in 1999–2000, when the FNPR cooperated with its rivals in opposing a government draft of a new labor code that would have significantly stripped unions of some of the rights they enjoyed under the old system. However, by the spring of 2001, the FNPR and the independents were backing opposing drafts, with the FNPR working with the government on a proposal that the independents feel is aimed against them, as it would prohibit primary (*pervichnyi*) organizations from concluding agreements unless they were part of a union confederation, legally obligate the employer to negotiate only with unions representing the larger part of the workforce (in almost all cases, the FNPR union), and take the question of strikes away from unions and give it a vote of the entire work collective. This has led to a veritable war between the FNPR and some of its rivals, with the two sides publicly calling each other "traitors" and "Trotskyites."[36] Any goodwill generated by limited cooperation in the past may now be lost, especially since the government-FNPR version of the Labor Code became law at the end of 2001. While interunion squabbles are far from the most debilitating influence on the union movement, there is no doubt that it has undermined solidarity and has helped entangle unions in political conflicts.

Trade Unions and Politics

Russian trade unions have not been politicized nearly to the extent of their Polish counterparts. Indeed, there has been a palatable reluctance of many unions to enter the political arena, although the unions have not been able to—and could not be expected to—remain wholly apolitical. What is most interesting, perhaps, is the ambiguity of the unions' political role and their relations with the government, and the changes that have taken place in the last decade.

Early on, the FNPR, out of necessity, made a break with the Communist Party, declaring its political independence. Many of the independent unions, meanwhile, openly backed and courted Yeltsin as he began his ascension to power. Yeltsin, however, was wary of the potential role the FNPR could play in galvanizing opposition to his planned reforms, and thus in the fall of 1991, before the USSR was officially pronounced dead, Yeltsin promised consultation with the FNPR on social and economic questions and by executive decree established a national tripartite mechanism for social partnership, the Russian Tripartite Commission (RTK). Its practice, however, was (and still is) hampered by numerous problems, including the lack of employers' organizations, the state's economic troubles, government reshuffling, and disputes on the composition of the union side (the FNPR initially was given nine of fourteen seats reserved for unions, with three for Sotsprof, one for NPG, and one for the Pilots Union, but by 2001 the FNPR and its allies had twenty-eight of the thirty union seats). The first meeting of the Tripartite Commission was on January 2, 1992, ironically the very day shock therapy was launched. By March 1992, a General Agreement had been concluded, in which the unions promised to desist from strikes in return for job protection and state social support. In Burburlis's words, the unions thus became "co-authors"[37] of reforms; put differently, one could say that they were co-opted.

This would not last long. As the results of shock therapy began to be felt, unions demanded more government support. Although there were fewer strikes in 1992 than 1991, miners, oil and gas workers, teachers, medical workers, pilots, and air traffic controllers all went on strike and won wage increases. These increases, of course, did not make up for all that was lost in hyperinflation,[38] but they did serve to undermine the shock therapy reforms.[39] In retrospect, this period may be considered the apogee of the post-Soviet workers' movement in Russia: Yeltsin still took the threat of workers' movements seriously, and both the FNPR and the independents played an active and visible role. However, in many cases, the workers were working in consort with management, arguing for wage increases and state support for their sectors, and thus not all this workers' activity was truly autonomous.[40] This was also the period that saw the political ascendancy of Arkadii Volsky and his Russian Union of Industrialists and Entrepreneurs (RSPP), and the FNPR forged an alliance with Volsky under the banner of Civic Union, against radical reform efforts.[41] The independents, particularly Sotsprof and NPG, trod far more softly, not wanting to jeopardize their relations with state authorities, and while pressing claims on behalf of workers and leading strikes, in general argued for expediting reforms. Yeltsin was even awarded honorary NPG membership in 1993.

In the end, however, the FNPR overplayed its weak hand, and the independents would be cast aside as well. The critical event would be the standoff between Yeltsin and the Supreme Soviet in September–October 1993. The FNPR took the side of the latter and called for mass action in favor of parliament. This mass support failed to materialize, and when Yeltsin had crushed his opponents, the FNPR was left extremely vulnerable. Reports indicate that Yeltsin was ready to order the disbanding of the FNPR,[42] but he pulled back from this radical step. Instead, he forced a change in FNPR leadership, stripped the unions of the right of legislative initiative, and transferred control of various social funds to the government. The FNPR, realizing that another false step could mean its end and chastened by the results of its alliance with Volsky in the 1993 elections, in which the Civic Union garnered a mere eighteen seats, fell into line (as did the post-1993 Duma), signing an Accord on Social Peace in April 1994 and pulling back from its political involvement, focusing instead on solely economic questions. This policy of "treading softly" (albeit without a big stick) has been in place since then, even as wage arrears began to mount, workers' enterprise ownership was revealed as a chimera, and millions slid into poverty. Its essence is well captured by a comment from Mikhail Shmakov, president of FNPR: "Today it is clear that a decisive, open confrontation with the regime would throw our trade unions onto the backwaters of public life, would deprive them all of the constitutional means of defending the interests of the toilers, and would be a real threat to the existence of the Federation and of FNPR unions as a whole."[43] Given conditions in Russia, this position is hardly one of radical opposition. As one banner in a protest in Ekaterinburg in 1998 noted, "They don't pay slaves, but at least they feed them. We don't get either." The inability and unwillingness of the FNPR (and other unions as well) to harness such discontent—which was widely felt during this period—toward political action speaks volumes about the weaknesses of organized labor in Russia.[44]

In retrospect, the events of the fall of 1993 were a turning point, both for unions and for Russian politics more generally. It witnessed the creation of a "delegative democracy," with power concentrated in the hands of the president and his administration.[45] This phenomenon has been strengthened with the wars in Chechnya, the emergence of pro-Kremlin oligarchs, and the ascension of Putin. The problem is not only that unions lack power; the Duma, political parties, regional leaders, and the prime minister have all been marginalized by efforts to concentrate presidential power. Unions' weakness is thus symptomatic of the general pathology of post-Soviet political development in Russia.

It is in this context that Yeltsin backed away from the independent unions. He no longer needed them, and in fact they could become a threat if they were to be strengthened because they were both autonomous and had a proven capacity to mobilize society. From Yeltsin's point of view, it was better to deal with a declawed FNPR. Once the independents became political outsiders, they became demonstrably weaker, as they had pinned many of their hopes on their connections to political power. Observers have noted that they did not benefit at all from their proximity to power, that their willingness to back Yeltsin had benefited the FNPR, and that they had failed to build a solid organizational base while putting their hopes on political patronage.[46] Moreover, as the reforms backed by the independents did not bring the promised results, they saw their credibility diminish, and internecine battles over political questions emerged in the NPG, arguably the most important union.[47] Promises by the government to the miners were repeatedly broken, resulting in protests and strikes and culminating in the dramatic events of 1998, when the miners took the initiative themselves and blockaded railroads to force government concessions. These spontaneous actions, however, revealed the weakness of the independent unions, particularly the NPG, which was compelled to support them and at last demanded Yeltsin's resignation. Thus, unionization had come full circle: the FNPR had become more of a partner to the government than the independents.

Indeed, what has become most interesting is the relationship between the FNPR and the government. The FNPR has not been, and is not now, part of the "party of power"; it has, instead, chosen an ambiguous position. It cannot ally with communists, because such an action would undermine claims that it has broken with its past, although this might be the most logical position given the communists' backing for greater rights for workers and their collective bodies. The FNPR finds little sympathy with parties such as Yabloko or the Union of Right Wing Forces. It is thus forced toward the center, but it cannot logically enter into an alliance with the Kremlin. It has thus tried to add its support to center-leftist opponents of the Kremlin, allying with Volsky's RSPP and the state directors in 1993 and 1995 and working with the Fatherland-All-Russia of Yurii Luzhkov and Evgenii Primakov in the 1999 elections. None of these efforts have borne much fruit: Volsky's group, the Civic Union, won 1.9 percent of the vote in 1993, Trade Unions and Industrialists-Union of Labor a paltry 1.59 percent in 1995, and in 1999 Luzhkov's and Primakov's Fatherland-All Russia Party fared rather poorly, thanks to pressure from the Kremlin and emergence of the pro-Putin Unity Party. Still, the FNPR can note that fourteen of its own made it into the Duma in 1999 (the independents won two seats).[48] In 2000, the FNPR supported Putin's presidential run, although perhaps it did so because it knew the result was a foregone conclusion and did not want to alienate itself completely from the president. What is notable in all this is that the FNPR has been rather conservative since 1993, opposing the government, but not too vociferously or radically.

The reasons for this stance are not difficult to uncover. The FNPR's existence depends upon government benevolence. The government, if it so desired, could take away FNPR property, order inspections of union membership rolls, or take other measures that would seriously threaten the FNPR. The FNPR leadership is thus careful to maintain a discourse of social partnership, even while other unions previously close to the government have stepped up their criticism of the Kremlin and have even made some overtures to the communists. The ties between the government and the FNPR were made clear in 2001, when the FNPR broke with a united union opposition to the government's labor code proposal and, led by its deputy, Andrei Isasev, opted to work with the government on a compromise proposal. Many of the FNPR's suggestions (particularly those on overtime, expanded vacation time, unions' role in the dismissal of workers, and conclusion of collective agreements) were accepted in the proposal,[49] and this draft was passed in first reading through the Duma in July 2001 and became law that December. The independents, meanwhile, condemned this draft for provisions that allow employers to negotiate with only one union and prohibit purely local unions from concluding agreements.[50] Anatolii Ivanov, vice president of the VKT and a Duma member, confronted Isasev, asking, "If you are free to organize but de facto the law will refuse to recognize you to negotiate with the employer, what kind of freedom is that?"[51] Sergei Khramov of Sotsprof has been perhaps the most vehement opponent to the FNPR's version, suggesting that the provisions of this code will enable employers to create their own unions, and thus "in a year we will not exist, and in two—there will be no FNPR."[52] Why has the FNPR cooperated with the government on this issue? Aside from the ability to undercut its rivals, some also suggest Shmakov is trying to curry favor with the Kremlin so that he can better fend off challenges to his leadership of the FNPR.[53]

In addition to purely political battles, mention should also be made of the tripartite mechanisms in Russia ostensibly designed to promote social partnership, by providing another means of interaction between the government and trade unions. The RTK still exists, and it is supplemented by tripartite bodies at the regional, branch, and municipal levels. Labor thus has an institutionalized role in policy formation, and the FNPR attaches great importance to the fostering of social partnership in Russia.[54] However, it is questionable whether tripartism in Russia, at least at the national level, has much real importance. Walter Connor, who examined the initial period of the RTK's existence, walked away unimpressed, maintaining that democratic corporatism in Russia was virtually destined to fail given its authoritarian heritage, the underdevelopment of capitalist institutions, and the lack of consensus on basic policy among various groups.[55] The Commission's infirmities are well known and to date have not been adequately addressed: lack of laws on employers' organizations, the unrepresentativeness of employers' organizations,[56] no defined role for owners (as opposed to management), political instability, the indefinite legal standing of its decisions, lack of equality among ostensible partners, and government willingness to ignore its recommendations. Tripartism may exist de jure, but de facto "social partnership is no more than a hollow declaration, which has absolutely no legal basis."[57] Vadim Borisov notes that triparitism continues to work ineffectively under Putin, as reform plans are not subject to open discussion and the government typically uses the RTK as a mechanism to show society that it has ostensible social support for policies that will have negative social consequences. Genuine dialogue does not exist. One prominent example is the aforementioned new Labor Code, which was introduced into the RTK in 1998 and met serious objections. The government then turned around and introduced its original version—which took no account of the discussions with the RTK—to the Duma for consideration.[58]

National-level agreements cover only the broadest possible questions, such as a minimum wage (a paltry 300 rubles a month, or about $10, as of July 1, 2001) and general provisions of employment, but as in the case of the wage arrears crisis there is not an effective enforcement mechanism, even in cases of blatant and systematic violations. Valentin Presniakov of the (non-FNPR) Union of Flying Staff, who has attended many meetings of the Commission, was even more critical of its performance:

> It is merely a device to let off steam [klapan]. Say there's some tense situation. The commission meets, and the unions say, "Salaries are too low." Employers say, "Yes, but taxes are too high." The government says, "All right, guys, let's think of something." So each side works on its own plan, and in a few months later the commission meets again. By now, they may have already forgotten about the tense situation, and in any event the sides can agree on nothing but some banal generalities, usually calling upon the government to do more. Feeling satisfied with this, they go home, but all their work has done little to solve any real problems.[59]

Simply put, this forum is not where real policy making takes place. How could it be otherwise, given the centralization of the state and even the marginalization of the legislature?

However, critics (cynics?) might note that the Commission does serve a few purposes: it gives legitimacy to the FNPR and serves as a mechanism through which the FNPR looks to be actively protecting workers, even if it can claim few tangible results. In other words, it coopts the unions, as the unions become dependent on social partnership (which the government can always take away), and this dissuades them from promoting workers' mobilization or other forms of political and social action. Tripartite social partnership thus effectively replaces the Soviet-era troika of a fused party-director-union apparatus. The result, as before, is docile trade unions. And, in fact, given the blatant disregard by the government and employers of their promises made to unions in tripartite agreements, it is amazing that the discourse of social partnership survives at all. Obviously, this is the one notion that many unions can cling to for hope, and the only forum where they can point to "progress," however illusionary. In this respect, it is notable that in my interviews with union leaders there was palatably less enthusiasm for social partnership from non-FNPR unions, who are more willing to engage in protests in order to achieve their goals.

Trade Unions and Privatization

Of all the changes that have taken place in post–Soviet Russia, privatization must rank as one of the most fundamental, particularly for workers. Before, there was a single employer: the state. Now there are hundreds of thousands of independent firms and employers. Before, enterprises were integrated into the Plan and were supported by the state. Profitability was not a concern. Now, profits matter, and a competitive market has arisen in most spheres of the economy. Over 80 percent of Russian workers now work in the private sector, and the transformation from a communist system to a rudimentarily capitalist one cannot but affect Russian workers, labor relations, and trade unions.

It is worth noting a few basic facts about the processes of privatization in Russia. The first stages, which began during shock therapy in early 1992, allowed the creation of small private enterprises and facilitated privatization of existing small enterprises. These were rather uncontroversial measures. Far more heated, however, were discussions of privatization of large state enterprises, which was where the bulk of workers were employed and which constituted by far the largest amount of capital in the country. Polls indicated that the majority of Russians were against privatization of these enterprises.[60] Questions over privatization were prominent in the dispute between Yeltsin and the Supreme Soviet in 1992–1993. Ultimately, of course, Yeltsin prevailed in that struggle, and his economic team, led by Anatolii Chubais, lobbied hard for rapid privatization, arguing that such moves would create responsible, clear ownership, put a stop to the processes of "spontaneous privatization," help foster creation of a middle class of shareholders in Russia, and make a return to communism impossible.[61] Chubais originally envisioned privatization via auctioning the majority of shares to any buyer, with a nonvoting bloc of 25 percent of shares distributed free to managers and workers (called Option 1).

When this plan was originally unveiled in 1992, however, it ran into great resistance on the part of the Supreme Soviet, managers, and trade unions.[62] The latter two groups, which had close ties under the Soviet system, feared the displacements that would accompany the emergence of new, market-oriented owners who had no ties to the enterprise. Both also felt entitled to more ownership rights, given their years of work at the firm. On grounds of justice, therefore, they argued for more shares and rights for management and workers, as opposed to rich foreigners or nascent Russian capitalists. Thus, the directors' corps of the RSPP under Volsky and the FNPR (with other unions as well) lobbied the Supreme Soviet for an alternative privatization scheme that would support the rights of the "work collective" at a given enterprise. Ultimately, these arguments did prevail, and an additional option (Option 2) was made available, through which the management and workers could purchase 51 percent of the shares at a cost 1.7 times the determined value of the shares. However, given the hyperinflation of 1992 and the difficulties of estimating a firm's value, the shares were in effect sold at a nominal price. This option would be the choice of 73 percent of enterprises.[63] Remaining shares were then made available to other buyers, who could use their vouchers[64] or buy shares with cash at the market price. In many cases, the state kept a substantial packet of shares for itself as well.

Labor thus was envisioned to be a beneficiary in this process, and in addition organized labor—in the form of the work collective, *not* the trade union—was given the right to decide the form of privatization for the enterprise. It was probably naive to hope for the emergence of real workers' ownership and management. Certainly, there was some excitement generated by the prospect of true, legal ownership in the firm. However, as is well known, all did not work out as planned, both broadly speaking for Russia as a whole and for work collectives and individual workers. The story of privatization, as told to me in over forty interviews with trade union officials at the national, regional, and enterprise levels, varies little. An amalgam of the various tales would be something like this:

When privatization began, there was a lot of excitement. We would now receive both wages and dividends, and our voice would be heard in the enterprise. Initially, all was done in a legal manner. The work collective met, and there was some discussion, and we voted. However, to be honest, most workers did not really understand what was going on, and thus they tended to follow the suggestion of management. We used our vouchers to buy shares, and in some cases workers [often trade union officials] were appointed to the board of directors. However, things then began to change. Some workers began to lose jobs, and salaries were not raised. Management said it had to generate profits. We did not feel like we were owners of the enterprise, and besides, the enterprise was not generating any profits, so we saw no dividends. With inflation and wage arrears, we had to do what was necessary to get by, and thus many workers sold their shares. Workers lost seats on governing boards. Sometimes, new owners would take over the enterprise and remove the management, and usually this meant workers would be fired as well to increase profitability. In the end, we gained nothing from the process.[65]

This is, to be sure, a sad story, but one that should not be so surprising given how privatization was enacted.[66] In contrast with Poland, privatization of large enterprises in Russia was very rushed, in large part because of fears of a communist revanche and Western insistence on rapid reforms. Information was in short supply, so workers put their shares in their own enterprises, lacking knowledge about other options. Management was the beneficiary, using its access to information to its own advantage, misrepresenting the value of the enterprise to make purchase of additional shares easy, stripping firms of their assets, and frequently persuading or even coercing workers to turn over their shares in order to become not only de facto but also de jure owners. Having both capital of their own (which many had been accumulating since the Gorbachev period) and managerial control, managers were able to become the true owners without much difficulty. However, profitability would be difficult because there had been little enterprise-level restructuring and no new investment. Thus, privatization would be followed by still more economic decline and the emergence of unemployment, both official and hidden.

Hopes that labor markets would be flexible enough to respond to marketized conditions crashed against the realities of the housing market and the population's lack of savings, which had been wiped out during 1992's shock therapy. To be sure, privatization of housing stock may have meant that the worker now owned his apartment in Khamchatka, Khabarovsk, or Kursk, but he could not easily sell this and move to Moscow, St. Petersburg, or Nizhniy Novgorod where there might be better employment opportunities. Of course, some Russians—the younger, the better skilled, as well as those willing to work on the very margins of society—have moved, but predominantly their new jobs are nonunionized. Millions more work in the hidden economy.[67] Many Russians, however, have remained trapped in their localities and in their enterprises and have little choice but to endure forced administrative leaves, wage delays, and cutbacks in social services.

Privatization thus failed in its major economic aims: it has yet to produce clear, responsible ownership, it did not stop spontaneous privatization (in fact, privatization was accompanied by a visible increase in corruption and the emergence of an oligarchy), and it did not create a society of shareholders. The promises made to workers proved to be absolutely hollow. Some have attempted to argue that workers' ownership is still prevalent in Russian enterprises, but these data come from surveys of directors and reflect, at best, ownership of the work collective (which includes directors and workers), not workers.[68] Irina Stevenson, who has headed the U.S.-funded labor center Solidarity since 1996, maintains that there are no firms with majority workers' ownership, and in my own interviews only union leaders from the textile industry noted that a few firms were worker owned (and that these tended to be the best run from the workers' point of view).[69] Even if one were to find cases of de jure workers' ownership, it would be hard to argue that this means de facto workers' control. It is difficult for workers to obtain information about the company and even harder to vote their shares in a unified block against positions taken by management. Trade unions are also quite passive in this process. One study noted:

> Theoretically, groups of workers and their trade unions could have meaningful independent power on these company boards. . . . Yet we have not recorded one case in which they did so. These findings reflect the fact that Russian trade unions are heavily dominated by management. . . . In what free market economy could workers in most large factories belong to trade unions, own the majority of their companies' shares, yet never elect an independent representative to the board of directors?[70]

This lack of participation should not be construed exclusively as the fault of the trade unions. Rather, it is a reflection of how privatization proceeded in Russia, which resulted, due to a variety of reasons (some of which were foreseeable), in the economic disenfranchisement of workers in their own firms.

In addition, privatization has been accompanied by low wages, unemployment, wage arrears, breakdown of authority, benefit cuts, and a variety of other harmful effects on workers, although it cannot be said with certainty that privatization per se has been the cause of these phenomena, as the same problems were experienced in reform laggards such as Ukraine. Certainly, however, many union leaders perceive privatization to be, overall, detrimental for workers, a largely uncontrolled process, or at best "perhaps necessary, but not in the way it was done or in what it created."[71]

What is perhaps most surprising, however, is that most union leaders do not appear to be particularly concerned with the form of property in Russia today. Forgetting even the most basic precepts of Marxism, one union leader maintained that "questions of property, of ownership, these are not questions for trade unions, they have no bearing on labor relations."[72] The desire is primarily for effective, competent ownership—ironically an echo of Chubais—but the unions themselves largely eschew any role in management of the enterprise. Instead, even in well-known cases of labor militancy such as literal battles over ownership at Norilsk Nickel, the Kuznetsk Metallurgical Plant, and the Vyborg Paper Mill, the workers have mobilized against managers and owners that they view as incompetent and have lobbied for more effective ownership.[73] Invariably, they are pushed into this position out of desperation, as their enterprise teeters on bankruptcy and wage arrears have mounted. They are compelled to "sell" their support to a contending ownership group at a very low price. In general, however, organized labor has stood on the sidelines when major questions of reform are considered, thus belying claims about Russian corporatism or social partnership. Discussing the imminent restructuring of the aviation industry, a union leader noted, "For us, it's all the same how the sector is organized. Two companies, five, ten. What is important for us is that the parts work effectively enough that the integrity of the sector is preserved."[74] While many do lament the swindling of the workers, they are not fixated on this question. The hope (chimera?) of workers' ownership is long since past. Rather than fight a battle on this issue—a battle they will inevitably lose—unions look to the future, to a privatized economy where they can play an important role.

In discussing the effects of privatization on unions themselves, questions to ask are whether privatization has reformed industrial relations in such a way as to transform and invigorate the unions, or whether it has brought only negative results. Certainly, from the standpoint of union membership, the results have been harmful. Trade union membership has dropped by almost half and has fallen more rapidly since large-scale privatization was launched. In addition to workers who have retired or lost their jobs, certainly there has been significant movement to new enterprises and jobs in the private sector. These jobs—including those in banking, marketing, retail, petty trade, and sweatshops—are almost entirely nonunionized, and many of them (estimates are about ten million workers) are in small enterprises with fewer than fifty employees. There are some organizations in these smaller companies, but these "unions" were created on the initiative of owners of small cooperatives or businesses and these employers are granted membership in the union. The true status of these bodies was revealed in a comment by Anton Ziberov, the head of the Congress of Russian Trade Unions (KRP). According to him, "there are no contradictions between employers and hired workers. . . . If we divide our membership and ban the employers, then that in effect will be the end of union."[75] These organizations, however, are the exception: Ziberov himself concedes they are weak and that only 10 percent of workers in this sector are covered by collective agreement. Galina Strela of the FNPR acknowledged that the FNPR unions have made virtually no headway in this "new economy," save the creation of a million-member Union of Private Security Guards (and anyone who has encountered their members can testify that this union would not be a vanguard for democratization!).[76] Tatiana Sosnina, head of the Union of Textile and Light Industry workers, conceded that there are thousands of workers in her branch working at small, private enterprises, but that she has found it "pointless" to pursue unionization in such enterprises, as work stability is low, employers are hostile, and workers themselves express little demand for unionization.[77] Similarly, the head of the Oil and Gas Workers Union complained of a "nonunion zone" in small, new enterprises in his sector.[78] Boris Golovkin, vice chairman of the Nizhniy Novgorod FNPR, observed, "We have yet to create mechanisms to attract people from small, private, mainly service enterprises, to the unions. This has to become a priority, but we will have to find some way of attracting these people in order for us to preserve our strength."[79] However, when some union leaders in Samara attempted to create a department to coordinate efforts to attract workers from small businesses into the appropriate branch union, the organizers found that no one at the branch level wanted to conduct such "onerous work."[80]

In large, industrial enterprises, unionization rates remain high: 80–90 percent. Thus, unions continue to function where they did under Soviet times, and privatization has not been accompanied by union busting en masse, although several leaders would note that some new, nonstate owners do display a hostile attitude toward trade unions and new, independent unions are particularly difficult to form.[81] While most unions have survived pressure from management, there are still reasons to be concerned about the fate of these unions. Surveys by Leonid Gordon and his colleagues in 1993–1994 indicated that many of the socially active, "stronger" workers have left or simply quit the union, leaving a "weaker," more "passive" workforce.[82] Trade union leaders themselves acknowledge this trend continues to be a problem. Mikhail Tarasenko, head of the Miners and Metallurgists' Union, noted that unionization in his sector is roughly 85 percent and those who are not in the union typically are the better-qualified workers who have a high value on the market and do not think they need unions. He is doing little, however, to bring them back into the fold. "They don't need us? We don't need them. Let them fend for themselves. We will work with what we have."[83] This, however, does not augur well for union vitality and saps unions of some of their negotiating power if the best workers are not in the union. A comprehensive study of union membership in eight regions similarly found unions unable to coordinate efforts to recruit more members, as they lack the organizational and financial resources to do so. A further decline in membership thus seems "completely natural."[84]

Aside from possession of high skill levels (which render the minimums in the union-negotiated collective agreement often meaningless) why else leave the union? Oleg Lvov of Sotsprof provides a simple, direct answer: unions are simply unnecessary given how most enterprises work. His reasoning is as follows:

> As a rule, in our businesses, the employee receives salary in two ways. As an example, consider a worker who receives $300 a month. Officially, he receives only $50, maybe $70. The larger part of his salary is put in an envelope and given in cash, with no tax deductions for him or the employer. This situation makes it impossible for a union or worker to negotiate. If an employee or union leader complains about anything in the enterprise, the employer can in effect say goodbye to the employee by paying him only his "official" wage. The employee knows he cannot survive on this, so he is quiet.[85]

Some might dispute this claim, but given the well-established levels of corruption in Russia and the admission by the head of the tax inspectorate that

40 percent of the registered enterprises do not pay taxes,[86] a quid pro quo for payments *pod stolom* (under the table) is not out of the question.

Still, unions are in place in most large enterprises. However, it is important to ask whether and how their role has changed since Soviet times, when they were subordinated to the Party and the directors. This is perhaps the most complex question, and the obvious answer is that it depends on the enterprise, and a systematic review of the thousands of enterprises is simply logistically impossible. However, much evidence suggests that unions are still tied to management. Not only are there political linkages between the RSPP and the FNPR at the national level but also at the branch or enterprise level many unions cooperate with management to extract concessions and credits from the state. This state of affairs is similar to what existed under the USSR, and in many sectors not much has changed. It is true in the automobile industry, the aviation industry, the military-industrial complex, electricity, metallurgy, coal mining, textiles, and the public sector (teachers, doctors, etc.). Despite privatization in many of these sectors, state purchase of goods, state protection from foreign competition, or state investment is still desperately needed, and thus unions and directors lobby together.[87] Even strikes may be backed by management in order to pressure the state, and it is notable that strikes are far less common in the competitive sector. Moreover, in cases such as the Lomonosovsky Porcelain Factory in St. Petersburg and the Krasnaia Sornava plant in Nizhniy Novgorod, workers have mobilized in support of existing management who are threatened with dismissal or replacement by new owners.[88]

Some might explain this joint union-management action as a holdover from the collective mentality of Soviet times (*eto nash zavod*) or a residue of promises of workers' ownership. However, it is not simply a cultural artifact. In many ways, it makes sense, as the state must play a supportive role in order for many sectors to survive and profitability means wages and jobs. Unions need not be adversarial toward management all the time. However, as Gordon argues, "often joint action with the directors ends up with the factual loss of independence," as unions lose sight of workers' interests and become a tool of management, both in political lobbying and in ensuring discipline and workers' acquiescence on the shop floor.[89]

What this adds up to, of course, is that the unions have not substantially changed at the enterprise level, even in privatized companies. The party-state may be eliminated from enterprise governance, but all this has done is leave unions subordinate partners in a bilateral relationship with management. The result, a product of past heritage, desperate economic conditions, and form of ownership, is union passivity and workers' alienation from the unions. Surveys conducted among workers in eight sectors in the summer of 1997 are exceptionally telling. The results found that 33 percent of workers thought unions do not do anything, 18 percent credited them with supplying some social services, and under 10 percent thought they defended workers' interests on questions of wages, work conditions, and resolution of work conflicts. Coal miners judged their unions to be the most active, but even in this case only a minority credited unions with defending wages (34 percent) and helping workers in labor conflicts (29 percent). On overall satisfaction, only 5 percent thought unions defended workers well enough, with more (12 percent) saying the unions support only the directors. Last, and perhaps worst of all from a trade union perspective, when asked who defends their interests, the answers were no one (54 percent), immediate supervisors (24 percent), directors of the enterprise (11 percent), all higher than trade unions (9 percent). Only coal miners were more likely to name unions (23 percent) as their defenders compared to their bosses (16 percent).[90] These attitudes not only reinforce some points about the lack of internal reform of unions, but they demonstrate that privatization has not fundamentally changed labor relations in Russia.

Of course, it is unfair to make blanket statements. There are variations, and certainly some unions have undergone some change. One example is the union at the Tula Ferrous Metallurgical Plant (Tulachermet). The union chairman, Vasilii Filinov, acknowledges plenty of tension between the union and management, yet he claims that the threat of a strike and other forms of pressure have allowed the union to carve out an autonomous role for itself. He notes that trade unions cannot beg from the government, and he is very well informed about the financial status of the enterprise.[91] Contrast this with the union chief at the Tula Combine Factory who claims that "in principle there can be no conflict between the directors and the workers," the proud boast of the vice chairman of the trade union at the giant Gorky Automotive Plant (GAZ) that "in the last ten years, our relations with management have not changed at all," or the "accomplishment" at Kamsky Automotive Plant (KAMAZ) where the union managed to secure New Year's Day gifts for the children, even though wage arrears had mounted into the billions of rubles and the union clung to the promises of social partnership.[92]

What accounts for this difference? All are large enterprises that have downsized the workforce and are struggling with debts. While there are several possible factors (Filinov is part of a younger generation, his central union had broken with the FNPR for several years, management took a more hostile view of unions), I will call attention to two. One is the role of union-administered social facilities or various fringe benefits to union membership, a factor also identified by Stephen Crowley,[93] and one that helps explain why the newer unions, lacking such social property, have been far more vigorous in pressing claims against management. At Tulachermet, many of the social institutions (sanatoria, stadiums, etc.) have been sold off, and thus the union is no longer preoccupied with providing social services. In the other cases, high priority was set on maintaining these institutions, and at GAZ the union staff of 150 people is the social department of the enterprise, working primarily on this issue, caring far more about finding places for children at summer camps than what business strategies might be profitable. Whereas Filinov accepted the trade-off between higher salaries and fewer social services, the union at GAZ did not, claiming "money is not everything" and that "our traditions of the collective must be preserved," while conceding that the union must run subsidized food services because salaries for many workers are so low![94] The result is that state paternalism has been replaced by private paternalism, administered by unions in concert with management.[95] Significantly, Sarah Ashwin finds this phenomenon, what she calls "alienated collectivism," even among coal miners. She concludes that workers' organizations merely reproduce relations of domination-subordination, as workers continue to yearn for a leader, a boss (*khoiazin*) who will take care of them.[96]

However, it is not simply a matter of unchanged attitudes. Often, even in a privatized economy, there is a fusion of interests between management and the union, with the union interested in preserving its corporate interests and control in the social sphere and obviously unwilling to challenge management on many basic questions. On this score, it is interesting to note a small-scale survey of workers at three large enterprises in 1995, showing that workers tended to agree that a reduction in the unions' social role would be a prerequisite to the strengthening of the unions' role in defending their interests.[97] To date, however, reduction has not been common, even at one of the plants (the Zil factory in Moscow) in the above survey.

Reducing the unions' social role is connected to a second difference among these unions in our case study: the purchase of companies by outsiders, intent upon changing the existing practices at the firm. Tulachermet, for example, was owned by a Swiss holding company and now has been taken over by Siberian Metal. The first owner tried to cut costs and raise funds, and selling socially oriented property was part of the plan; the second owner is pursuing the same tactic. At GAZ, in contrast, the first postprivatization leadership included many who had risen through the trade union ranks (revealing again the operation of the Soviet system), and they were not inclined to shake things up. Now, GAZ has been taken over by Oleg Deripaska's Siberian Aluminum conglomerate, which has brought in its own management team. The union leadership notes that the new management team's business style appears to be far more pragmatic, but the union is nonetheless intent on holding on to its social programs (costing one billion rubles in the current collective agreement). However, viability of the social programs will be determined exclusively by profitability, which once again feeds into the commonality of interest between management and the trade unions. Ironically, the future of the unions, therefore, will in large part depend upon whether management wants to sacrifice some profitability and pay for the social institutions of the "collective" in order to preserve union dependence and docility. In the long run, it might be more rational to continue to buy off the union and let it have its social sphere. The result, as Gordon foresees it, is not the disappearance of unions, but the preservation of "pseudo-unions" engaged exclusively in social service functions, unable and unwilling to vigorously press claims against management.[98]

In some cases, this has taken on more direct forms, with large (and profitable) firms like Gazprom, Sibor, Yukos, Lukoil, and Norilsk Nickel recognizing a cross-sector "company" union. In other words, workers at one of these companies belong to a union that is established outside the normal branch, or territorial, structure. There are no alternative unions. This arrangement might make sense for these industrial behemoths, but critics would note that these unions can be understood as creatures of the directors.[99] At enterprises acquired by Lukoil (including those in Azerbaijan and Bulgaria), preexisting unions have even been dismantled or compelled to enter the "approved" Lukoil union. True, workers are well paid by Russian standards,[100] and the protests of the oil and gas workers in 1992 are now long past. In 2003, there were protests by the union at Norilsk Nickel over the company's refusal to grant the union exclusive representation on company works' councils, which was seen as a clear attack on the union because it was thought a bit too "independent."[101] However, lest this protest be considered solely explainable by workers' activism, at least one report suggested that the protests and work stoppages were actually convenient for management, by raising the global price for nickel and by raising the profile of the union leader, Valerii Mel'nikov, who has political ambitions to be mayor of Norilsk (which would require him to leave his union post).[102] At the same time, however, these unions conveniently do not ask questions in companies rife with corruption and mismanagement, and their isolation from the broader union movement weakens the political power of labor.[103] Moreover, if ownership changes, or if the company falls on hard times, these unions can find themselves in the lurch or sucked into a battle between competing ownership groups. These unions are thus not in a very strong position.[104]

These structures are also a symptom of another problem caused by economic reforms and privatization: the breakdown of union solidarity. True, workers' unity may have always been a bit of a myth and the Soviet system did serve to atomize workers,[105] but the construction of a post-Soviet workers' movement is complicated by the emerging economic system. Income inequality has markedly increased,[106] and many unions are in a competitive struggle over state funds. This competition has become pronounced between two of the more militant unions, those of coal miners and those in education. The latter believes that private industries should pay their own way and that they have no right to claim funds from the state budget.[107] Filinov from Tulachermet conceded it is hard to talk of much union cooperation at a local level when workers at his plant earn ten times as much as a teacher. With the wage arrears crisis abating, the unions' battle in Russia will turn to increasing salaries, and on this front there will be more interunion competition and less solidarity, as well as a shift in emphasis toward enterprise-specific action. These changes have already taken place among coal miners, where earlier (1989–1992) actions espoused nationwide demands but the more recent protests (1994–present) have tended to take on a more local character, with the workers' perspective and interest gradually narrowing from their branch, to their enterprise, to only those workers who are engaged in protest activity.[108] This localization trend is indicative of a more general decentralization and fragmentation of organized labor, and it is a crucial point in considering a workers' or union movement (which is most important from the perspective of political science) and not just individual unions. In short, "act locally" may become the norm, particularly as the system of collective bargaining in Russia is rather decentralized. However, the other half of the slogan—"think globally"—may well be forgotten.

Finally, looking ahead a bit, the future of organized labor looks highly uncertain due to one additional factor created by the "new economy": young people are not attracted to traditional working-class jobs, and institutes cannot afford to train workers. Many younger workers have already left the large industrial enterprises that used to compose the backbone of the economy. Reports indicate that the average age of a qualified worker in the defense industry is over sixty and that industries such as metallurgy and machine building cannot even fill vacancies for jobs. The worker (*rabochii*) is thus classified as a "disappearing phenomenon."[109] These jobs, with their harsh work conditions and paltry wages, are understandably unattractive, and it simply makes no economic sense to learn advanced industrial skills for them in a polytechnical school. This pending shortage is thus not simply a reflection of Russia's well-known demographic crisis, but instead a direct consequence of market forces at work in a privatized, marketized economy. True, a counterargument is that some industrial downsizing is economically rational and that eventually the market will correct itself (it only seems as if everyone can open a kiosk), but the problem of attracting youth to the spheres of work that are traditionally unionized is clearly a worry for many union leaders.[110] The point, though, is that a further fall in membership is likely, and with that, a loss in resources for Russian trade unions. Further disintegration, therefore, looms as more of a possibility than does dynamic transformation.

Trade Unions and Globalization

While there is at least some consensus that privatization has not been the boon that was sold to Russian workers, there is a greater range of views on globalization. Of course, globalization has not penetrated the political economy to the same extent as privatization, although it plays a crucial role in several sectors. As with privatization, globalization was presented as a positive development, "progress," a means for Russians to taste the fruits of world markets. That taste has been bitter for many, although, to be fair, some people interested in the development of trade unions welcome more foreign involvement in the economy.

We can look at different actors or spheres of globalization, including international financial institutions, trade, and direct foreign investment.

International financial institutions have played an important—some might say leading—role in the political economy of post-Soviet Russia. The IMF, backed by other international bodies and foreign governments, was an important source of advice and financing for those who aimed to make a capitalist Russia. The apparent success of shock therapy in Poland led Jeffrey Sachs and other leading international economists to recommend the same course for Russia, which was eagerly followed by Yeltsin and his team of reformers led by Yegor Gaidar and Anatolii Chubais. The results—economic disaster, corruption, and mass impoverishment of the population—are well known, although the story is very complex and interpretations differ as to who is at fault.[111] Some, such as Anders Aslund,[112] maintain that the Russian government, under pressure from the trade unions, among other actors, backed away from shock therapy and IMF advice and is responsible for the privatization plans that brought great corruption and inequality to Russia. Others hold the IMF accountable for dispensing bad advice, either ideologically flawed or simply not suited to Russian circumstances, leading, in the words of Sachs, to a "betrayal" of Russia.[113] Some go further and note the connivance between Western advisers and Russian reformers, with the advisers turning a blind eye to the problems of corruption that became increasingly obvious.[114]

At minimum, however, IMF involvement was, on balance, harmful to trade unions. Much of the problem, it appears in retrospect, was less what the IMF did than what it failed to do. In other words, there was a lack of oversight, which, when coupled with a focus on macroeconomic indicators at the expense of immediate living standards,[115] led to disaster for many Russians. For example, the IMF, putting top priority on balanced budgets and debt repayment, looked the other way as the Russian leadership failed to pay its obligations to its citizens in the form of wages and pensions, thus allowing the wage arrears crisis to occur.[116] The 1998 meltdown was caused, among other factors, by the IMF, which was beholden to a set of political interests, and turned a "blind eye to cronyism and systematic rule evasion"[117] and failed to make common cause with other groups (such as unions) that might have been able to produce a change in government policy. As for international assistance in the one sector most prone to labor militancy (coal mining), the World Bank, under pressure, admitted that many of the funds designed to help restructure the industry—and thereby presumably help save jobs—were misappropriated by state officials. Notably, however, the World Bank was hesitant to follow up its suspicion of the problem early in the process.[118] Clearly, of course, IMF advice was at times little different from diktat, as seen when recommendations from the IMF, published in a Russian newspaper, were included verbatim in draft legislation.[119] Obviously, trade unions—which claimed to represent millions of Russians—did not have such power, a fact that surely compromised the democratic nature of the polity.

However, beyond the general macroeconomic effects of reforms, were the explicit antiunion demands of the IMF. For example, in a memorandum drafted by the Russian government to the IMF on July 16, 1998, to qualify for IMF assistance, the government promised to pass a new labor code envisioning more flexible markets and individual labor contracts, removing "constraints on dissolving labor contracts."[120] Translation: trade union rights (particularly regarding collective agreements and dismissals of workers) would be curtailed. This memorandum became the impetus for the disputed labor code, although it was drafted in secret without consultation with any ostensible social partners.[121] As noted earlier, it was first submitted to the RTK in 1998 and rejected by the trade union side, but these basic notions continued to animate the government–FNPR "compromise" version, which became law over the objections of the independent trade unions, in 2001.

Another manifestation of globalization has been the opening to foreign trade. If Gorbachev's reforms let in a trickle of foreign products, it has now become a flood. This trade has helped spur a Westernization of sorts in Moscow and St. Petersburg, although the sheer availability of consumer goods ranging from Armani suits to French perfume to Japanese televisions has hardly promoted trade unions or democratization in any basic sense. Consumer trade, usually confined to rather small retail enterprises, has not offered much of an opportunity for trade unions.

Far more significant, from the trade union perspective, has been trade in industrial products and energy. However, it is important to recognize that a very clear division is appearing in the Russian economy between exporters—overwhelmingly from the energy and raw materials sector—and manufacturing.[122] Exporters profit, often handsomely, from globalization, and unions in these sectors, despite massive corruption in their companies, have not complained as workers are offered attractive wages by Russian standards while management takes home pay comparable with world standards. As mentioned, in many of the most successful export companies—including the leading three, Gazprom, Norilsk Nickel, and Lukoil—unions are formed on a company basis with potentially negative side effects.

However, the manufacturing sector has struggled, as Russia lacks the technology and infrastructure to compete globally. It is in these industries—automotive, aviation, machinery, chemicals, textiles—that wages are lower, wage arrears have been greater, and unemployment has been a real threat. One consequence is that unions in these sectors have found it difficult to articulate workers' interests as separate from that of management, as survival of the firm is at stake: thus, the often seen management-union alliance against the government and in favor of protection. In the automotive industry, this protectionism has taken the form of banning imports of used European cars;[123] in the aviation industry, calling for subsidies and preference in purchasing orders;[124] in textiles, demanding both tariffs and low-interest loans.[125]

Even where there is trade, it is often on unfavorable terms, and union leaders complain that it is harmful to their enterprises, the Russian economy as a whole, and ultimately to union members. Filinov at Tulachermet noted that much of the enterprise's production is in cheap cast iron for export and that the export niche is filled only because the firm is willing to accept the barest of profit margins. Trade is generating production and saving jobs, but it is not a source of revenue for investment.[126] Sosnina of the Textile Union noted that 70 percent of the work at sewing plants is done on order for export. Foreign firms supply the materials and Russians supply the labor. These agreements, she notes, generate little revenue or stability for the companies, most of which are just barely afloat.[127] Others note that Russians are being treated unfairly on international markets. Russian steel has been shut out of the U.S. market due to American protectionism and accusations of Russian "dumping." The results are losses up to $2.5 billion for Russian firms and workers' protests in front of the U.S. Embassy in Moscow.[128] Anatolii Breusov of the Aviation Industry Union complains of Western regulations against Russian flights and inveighs against a 1996 agreement in the Gore-Chernomyrdin Commission in which Western credit was provided for the purchase of both Boeing- and Russian-built aircraft. The Boeings were bought, with a tariff loss of over $1 billion to Russia, but the order for the Russian planes never materialized due to, among other things, complications resulting from the Yugoslav war.[129] Presniakov of the Pilots Unions agrees with this assessment, noting sardonically that in his sector "there is foreign influence, but no foreign investment."[130]

The third element of globalization is the one of most interest, impact, and perhaps threat to unions in Russia—the role of foreign direct investment

(FDI), which in some cases has meant foreign ownership of enterprises in Russia. While foreign investment in Russia in the 1990s was rather modest, was highly concentrated in Moscow, and had a minimal impact on the over- all economy[131] (and, of course, the crisis in 1998 led many investors to leave the market), by March 2003 accumulated foreign investment totaled $43 bil- lion, much of it in the energy sector and in retail trade.[132] While the growth in foreign investment is thus a relatively new phenomenon (and uncertain- ties sparked by the apparent attack on Yukos in 2003 make foreign investors nervous about Russia), there are still several issues to explore: whether for- eign investors respect Russian labor laws and Russian trade unions; whether they bring with them codes of conduct that may actually boost organized labor's position; and whether they are solely concerned with making a quick profit and act in a manner to harm or eliminate trade unions. As with priva- tized companies, there are examples of good relations with trade unions and examples of poor relations. Some companies—Danone, Nestle, Henkel— can claim to have generally sound relations with trade unions at their plants. Many more, however, have worked against union formation in plants that they have established or taken over. This list includes many of the most widely known MNCs: Caterpillar, BMW, Bosch, Phillips, Procter & Gamble, Coca- Cola, and McDonald's.

Generally speaking, if the foreign investor inherited a union, the union has survived, although in some cases relations have been quite poor. New enter- prises have not been fertile ground for unions, and owners are in no hurry to establish them. Moreover, because workers often enjoy higher salaries, they see little point in creating a union, at least until problems arise at the enterprise.[133]

This is not to say that there are no new unions in foreign-owned plants. An example of a new union is the well-known McDonald's case, in which union organizers endured almost two years of harassment, called in the Interna- tional Foodworkers Union, Shmakov of the FNPR, and Moscow mayor Yurii Luzhkov, eventually producing in 2000 a legally recognized union of fewer than twenty people out of a staff of 450 at its processing plant.[134] Gasoline station workers of the Finnish company Neste successfully organized in St. Petersburg, although the union activists also experienced various forms of harassment and the company is still hostile to the union.[135] In Primorskiy Krai, garment workers took a Korean company to court to establish their rights to form a union. One interesting case was in Novosibirsk, where work- ers struggled to create a union in the German-owned Westphalia Shoe Factory, eventually finding success only after lobbying together with management for subsidies from the regional government.[136]

In some cases, the transfer to foreign ownership has created frictions and union activation. This was the case at Tulachermet in 1996–2000, when the main shareholder was a Swiss company. ICN-Pharmaceuticals, a U.S.-based firm, has gained ownership of five plants in Russia, and there have been on-going labor disputes, particularly involving questions such as business transparency, wage delays, and conclusion of enterprise-level collective agreements. In the St. Petersburg plant, the negotiations for a collective agreement dragged on for over a year, with the workers eventually threatening a strike and finally securing agreement to most of their demands. In contrast, labor relations at Henkel, a German maker of detergents, also in St. Petersburg, are held up as a near model. Here the union is active, one of the strongest in the chemical sector, and salaries are relatively high and always paid on time. What is interesting is that in all of these cases involving an active, mobilized union, the union is not administering social enterprises—social provisions are given in cash, not through a union social department. Additionally, the head of the Henkel union consciously tries to use the workers' small shareholdings (6 percent) as a means to gain access to information and decision makers.[137] Also worth mentioning is the rather well known case of Procter & Gamble in Tula oblast'. Here, the union fought against management's blatantly anti-union policy by appealing to the Accounting Bureau to investigate irregularities in privatization, including special dispensations granted to the company by none other than Chubais himself. Using this information, the union has been able to conclude a collective agreement, and union-management relations at the plant are now reported to be better than those at many plants in the region.[138]

Another problem is that foreign owners often buy a company very cheaply, sell off productive assets or transfer them to a new firm, then run the company into bankruptcy, leaving workers unemployed. This practice is in part what precipitated the armed takeover by workers in 1999 of the Vyborg Paper Mill (although it is questionable whether the Cyprus-registered Altsem firm was really foreign). Other examples include the Achinsky Clay Factory in Krasnoyarsk and the Vladmirsky Tractor Factory.[139] Fear of a repetition of such action was one reason behind a strike by the independent union Unity at AvtoVAZ, which was negotiating with GM on joint production when rumors spread that GM intended to break AvtoVAZ up into several components.

This is not to say that all foreign owners are bad, of course. Tarasenko of the Metallurgists Union even went so far as to say that he views foreign owners as more civilized, experienced, and pragmatic than their Russian counterparts, who may have little experience with management, little respect for the law, and no concern about their employees.[140] This opinion, of course, may be more an indictment of Russian *byznesmeny* than praise for Western capitalists, but it is a valid point given business practices in Russia, where the local owner may have better wherewithal to evade the law.

In short, as many union leaders assert, the effects of globalization are not unequivocal (*neodnoznachny*). While globalization no doubt creates challenges for unions, in some cases these have been overcome and Russian workers benefit from foreign investment. No doubt, much depends on management, including both its national origin (Americans and Turks are often singled out as the worst) and its intentions for the long term in Russia. However, one clear lesson—one that Russian union leaders are just beginning to learn—is that adapting to global pressures will become an increasingly important priority and that unions in general must be stronger in order to assert their interests against international capital.

Organized Labor in Hungary

AT FIRST GLANCE, HUNGARY MAY SEEM like a peculiar case to include in a study of postcommunist labor. It has certainly witnessed nothing
like the dramatic events in Poland or even the occasional round of incidents
as in Russia. It therefore qualifies as a country with one of the least active—
or at least, the least visible—labor movements in the region. Extended strikes
have been extremely rare. Laszlo Bruszt, a well-known academic and former
leader of the LIGA, the largest noncommunist-successor union organization
in Hungary, contends that only the Vatican could boast of a more peaceful
system of industrial relations than Hungary.[1]

This is not to say that Hungary has no labor movement or that there has
not been concerted attention devoted to labor issues in the country. On the
contrary, unions in Hungary are numerous, and the country has more major
national union federations than any other postcommunist country. Many
unions have tried to play a prominent role in national politics, especially the
MSZOSZ (the main successor to the communist-era unions), through connections with the Socialist Party. Moreover, Hungary has created a highly

developed system of tripartite bodies that are designed to involve labor in decision making, so that Hungary, until recently at any rate, is the premier example of corporatist experiments in the region. Of course, whether these corporatist institutions actually work to empower labor is another matter. Critics suggest that they are largely paper creations, and virtually all reports on organized labor in Hungary concur that labor as a whole is weak and unable to accomplish much at the national level, through parliament or political parties, in enterprises, or in tripartite institutions.[2]

In part, perhaps, this can be explained because the Hungarian economy has performed rather well. True, unemployment has consistently hovered in the double digits, but this is not atypical by European standards. Real wages did take an initial beating, but they have rebounded (especially in 2002–2003), and there has been nothing like the wage arrears crisis in Russia. Privatization was pushed through without much heated controversy, and foreign investment has been courted more assiduously than anywhere else in the region. The drama of shock therapy (as well as some of the pain) was avoided, in part due to previous liberalization under communism but also because there was initially no neoliberal consensus on policy.[3] While there are depressed areas—particularly in rural areas in eastern Hungary—the economy as a whole has performed relatively well, people in general are optimistic about the future, and the political life of Hungary is a copy of Germany, with differentiated, democratic parties on the left, right, and center. Emblematic of its success, Hungary joined the European Union in May 2004.

Yet, amidst all of this, where are the trade unions? Their absence is conspicuous, which may lend credence to the contention that as a country becomes more "normal," "stable," or "Western," unions will find themselves with little role to play. In particular, Hungary is important to examine from the standpoint of labor relations because of the significant part played by foreign capital in the country's economy.

Union Issues in Hungary

When looking at organized labor in Hungary, what stands out most clearly is the plurality of organizations speaking for workers. There are numerous unions, both successors from the communist-dominated National Council of Trade Unions (SZOT), such as the National Confederation of Hungarian

Trade Unions (MSZOSZ), the Academic Employees Union (ESZT), the Federation of Autonomous Unions (ASZSZ), and the Trade Union Cooperative Forum (SZEF), and new unions, most notably the Democratic League of Independent Trade Unions (LIGA). There is also a Workers' Council organization (MOSZ), which both complements and competes with the trade unions for workers' support and government attention. Moreover, it is fair to say that both the former Communist Party and its trade union affiliates have reformed themselves into organizations of a social-democratic ilk. This reflects the results of a process that was begun under a liberalized communist regime.[4] Thus, there are fewer vestiges of an authoritarian past than in Russia or Ukraine.

This is not to say, of course, that the unions in Hungary are not without their problems. The most conspicuous internal problem for the unions has been their declining membership. The largest federation, the MSZOSZ (whose members tend to be in traditional manufacturing industries), has shrunk by over 75 percent; membership in the LIGA and the MOSZ has also fallen significantly from its earlier high. The reasons for this decline are not hard to ascertain: job loss, movement to nonunion jobs or sectors, and disillusionment with trade unions. In 1997, one the MSZOSZ official suggested the situation would improve, since "according to their own experience more and more workers realize that trade unions are necessary for enforcement of their individual and collective interests."[5] As in Russia and Poland, this remains largely wishful thinking. There has been no movement back to the unions in Hungary.

Moreover, unions are not doing much to activate their current membership. A survey of forty union leaders reported by Terry Cox and Laszlo Vass indicates that they much prefer official political channels of action instead of mobilizing public opinion or their membership.[6] Unions may prefer to maneuver this way because they recognize their inability to mobilize workers and the plethora of exit options for workers into nonunionized sectors. Indeed, industrial relations in Hungary have been largely peaceful despite blatant attacks on the unions and workers' rights by the government. Thus, with a shrinking and inactive membership, unions have difficulty in achieving many of their objectives.

In addition, union membership has been hampered by a lack of solidarity among workers. There has been no effort in Hungary, with the exception of a call for a general strike in 1999, to create any sense of a unified labor movement. This inactivity is not only a reflection of interunion conflict but also a carryover of individualistic strategies from communist times, as well as a result of a much decentralized bargaining system in Hungary.[7] Thus, even if unions are active at the enterprise level, this is not easily translated into mobilization or solidarity for general workers' issues. Arguably, this phenomenon has been exacerbated by marketization and privatization.

Problems of membership are but one handicap for Hungarian unions. Another difficulty has been interunion rivalries and competition, which has created a volatile situation described by some as "open warfare."[8] The basis for this competition is both ideological and economic. Ideologically, new unions such as the LIGA and the MOSZ claimed that the MSZOSZ and other successor unions were illegitimate due to their ties to the communist regime. The LIGA demanded all workers reregister with unions, obviously hoping that workers would not choose the MSZOSZ. For its part, the MSZOSZ considered the LIGA to be a front for political interests, not a labor union. The economic struggle was over union property, which the MSZOSZ claimed and the LIGA and the MOSZ wanted to see redistributed. Efforts to create a trade union roundtable failed due to the schism between the two groups, and the government became involved in the struggle as well. Needless to say, divisions among the unions were easily exploited by the government, complicated the work of the National Council for the Reconciliation of Interests (NCRI, reestablished in 1990), where the union side was required to vote as a single bloc, and also contributed to a loss of public confidence in the unions as they were seen to be squabbling over money rather than working to help their members.

These issues were eventually resolved through elections to social security boards and work councils in 1993 and again in 1995. The MSZOSZ dominated both, with the LIGA and the MOSZ garnering together less than half of the vote for the MSZOSZ.[9] These elections settled the issue of union legitimacy (which remains disputed in Russia) and helped the MSZOSZ join the International Confederation of Free Trade Unions (ICFTU). Moreover, the elections themselves were part of an interunion compromise, in which the MSZOSZ received 43 percent of the property. However, the final reason why interunion relations have been normalized in recent years has been the veritable collapse of the LIGA and the MOSZ, neither of which could overcome the dominance of the MSZOSZ and an environment not very conducive to unionization.[10] Tóth also adds that they were victims of their own efforts to politicize the labor movement, suggesting that by "turning most of their attention and efforts primarily to their political warfare, after reaching a peace [in 1993] they found themselves in a vacuum of missing social purpose for their existence."[11] However, splits began to emerge later between the SZOT successor unions, with those stronger in the public and state sectors (the ASZSZ, the SZEF, and the ESZT) taking an increasingly assertive position and the MSZOSZ, representing primarily workers in the manufacturing industries (mostly privatized in the 1990s), turning its back on any kind of labor militancy.

In sum, these rivalries seriously hampered the trade union movement, and the multiple fissures within the movement have prevented any sort of labor solidarity. This has affected unions both at the national and enterprise level. One can agree with Tóth that throughout the 1990s "there were only a few moments when unions were able to reach unity of action, and the lack of durable alliances seriously weakened unions' ability to promote a vision of a socially regulated society. In fact, just the opposite happened in most cases. When a union reached its peak of power, it was consumed with trying to achieve institutional changes that would weaken rival confederations. Thus rival unions blocked institutional changes which would have been favorable to all unions."[12]

Another internal issue to the workers' movement in Hungary was the occasionally competitive role played by workers' councils as an alternative to unions. The MOSZ had close ties to the ruling (1990–1994) Hungarian Democratic Forum (MDF), which in 1991 proposed a New Labor Code that would have stripped unions of the right to conclude collective agreements at the enterprise level and given this right to workers' councils. This plan was resisted by the unions, and the resulting 1992 Code was a compromise, giving the councils extensive consultative rights while giving unions the bargaining power, provided they could meet new thresholds for representativeness.[13] However, the result of this compromise was confusion and rivalry at the enterprise level, and managers were often able to play the unions and workers' councils off each other, using one to discredit or undermine the other.[14] Gradually, however, the workers' council movement found itself undermined by its failure to advance workers' self-management and by internal generational and ideological divisions. By 1993, it tried to reform itself into a "Christian" organization, but by then its membership had steeply declined.[15] Workers' councils, however, did not disappear, and in cases where there is no trade union they are the only forum for workers' representation at the enterprise. The new liberal-conservative government elected in 1998 has taken interest in workers' councils, amending the Labor Code to allow the councils to conclude agreements at the enterprise if there is no union. While in many ways this is a pragmatic step, it was resisted by unions, because it will make it even more difficult to extend union representation to currently nonunion enterprises.

Overall, the irony of the situation was that union pluralism did not prove to be helpful. In line with corporatist theory, it is possible that workers in Hungary would have been better off with one large "peak" organization to represent them. While the interunion squabbles largely subsided by 1994, they also produced an additional complication by bringing the government into the field of industrial relations, ironically just as the unions were proclaiming their independence.

Trade Unions and Politics

Hungary did not see the same degree of workers' mobilization and powerful political influence as in Poland or Russia. New trade unions, such as the LIGA (dominated by intellectuals) and *Szolidaritas* (more a blue-collar association), emerged, along with a virulently anticommunist work council movement. The LIGA became part of the opposition during the 1989 Roundtable and forged ties with the Alliance of Free Democrats (SZDSZ), and the leader of the MOSZ was elected to parliament as part of the MDF. There were workers' strikes in 1988–1989, but they were limited in scope and of short duration. In sum, these workers' organizations, although highly politicized, remained small and not influential, and their demonstrations rarely went beyond a token level. Tóth notes that Hungarian opposition leaders sought to "avoid the mobilization of the masses" and thus "did not create the opportunity for unions to assume a greater role in the transition process."[16] Labor and social issues were generally given only cursory attention in the negotiations leading to the end of one-party rule. There was no "breakthrough" for new unions,[17] and the old communist-dominated federation, which split into four different organizations and formally broke with the Socialist Party, remained the dominant representative organ for workers.

The government initially did little to interfere with the trade unions, adopting a more or less laissez-faire approach. It intended neither to hamper union development (on the contrary, the emerging labor pluralism was arguably very helpful to the government by dividing potential labor opposition), nor did it make a concerted effort to engage unions in dialogue. A law on associations and a law on strikes were duly passed in 1989, even before the holding of democratic elections. These measures did establish basic freedoms for unions. However, in the fall of 1990 a taxi strike in Budapest helped bring labor issues to the fore. The NCRI was revived by the government, and seven union confederations entered into this tripartite body.

By 1991, the interunion battle was in full swing, and the LIGA and the MOSZ began to push their allies in government to take action against the MSZOSZ, which in July of that year called for a two-hour warning strike and threatened a general strike in light of what it perceived to be antiworker actions on the part of the government. This confrontation alarmed the authorities, who passed two bills on trade unions. One (Act XXIX) required all union members to reregister with their unions. The goal here was to get those who belonged to the union only through sheer inertia (mainly in the MSZOSZ) off the membership rolls. The second (Act XXVIII) froze major union assets and ordered unions to redistribute their property on the basis of election results (the electorate was unspecified) that would determine the representativeness of each union. The LIGA and the MOSZ backed these measures, hoping the elections would reveal low workers' support for the MSZOSZ and allow the LIGA and the MOSZ to become the leading representatives of the workers. The MSZOSZ, predictably, vehemently protested these actions as antiunion and took the government to court. The court upheld the first measure, which no doubt contributed to some drop-off in union membership.[18] The second, however, was deemed in part unconstitutional. Ultimately, the unions worked out a compromise, agreeing to divide up property before elections to the social security boards and work councils. The result of these elections confirmed the dominance of the MSZOSZ and the other successor unions, and since 1993 the new unions have played but a marginal role. One former leader of the LIGA conceded in 1997 that the union had been moribund for some time and was highly unlikely to gain any new strength.[19]

The Labor Code of 1992 would also have lasting effects on the trade unions. This code mandated creation of work councils and divided representative, consultative, and bargaining functions between these bodies and unions. Moreover, it established a threshold of union representativeness, requiring that the union (or group of unions) receive 50 percent of the votes in work council elections in order to conclude agreements at the enterprise. While in some respects "democratic," one effect of this measure is to inhibit the development of new unions or unions at new enterprises that have no unions.[20] Moreover, the Code made radical cuts in unions' rights compared with the previous (1968) Code, which admittedly was simply a piece of paper. The new Code reconfirmed a previous court ruling prohibiting union codetermination of individual wages (hence institutionalizing wage decentralization), took away the unions' right to veto decisions of the employer, and stripped unions of an intermediate role in grievance procedures. Notably, the unions had "little influence" on these measures.[21] This code was supplemented with two others for workers in the public and state sectors, whose unions had even fewer rights on wage negotiations.[22] Notably, these documents and other pieces of legislation also envisioned no significant role for unions in privatization, since sale would be by competitive auction without any union veto or authorization.

The centerpiece of industrial relations in Hungary, however, would be the NCRI, and in 1992 the Economic and Social Agreement among the state, employers, and unions was reached. The aim of this body clearly was to establish a corporatist framework in Hungary, although it would be far more decentralized than in Germany.[23] Verdicts on its performance vary. Some assert that tripartism flourished during 1992–1994 and that the NCRI played a "historic" and "indispensable" role.[24] However, it was far from an unmitigated success, at least from the unions' perspective.[25] While there were intensive meetings, arguably the energy the unions put into this body in the effort to legitimize themselves on the basis of participation in tripartite forums hindered their work in building their organizations from the bottom up. In other words, the unions' "power" was granted to them by the government; it was not a product of their own actions. Interunion disputes also undermined the NCRI, as the union confederations had a collective vote and had to agree on policy. Moreover, it was politicized, with Sandor Nagy of the MSZOSZ complaining that the government favored its union allies while putting the MSZOSZ "in quarantine."[26] The government also took only marginal interest in it. Laszlo Neumann simply notes that, "It has been a widely held view among politicians of new parties in Hungary [including those in the 1990–1994 government] that economic reforms as well as privatization could be implemented more smoothly without unions having a meaningful say."[27] Last, the body itself had an uncertain legal basis, meaning decisions

were not binding on any of the partners and often had little effect on negotiations at the enterprise. The result, according to one observer, was an "un-
balanced structure" of both tripartism and bipartism (the latter reigning
supreme at the enterprise).[28]

The elections of 1994 were an important event for unions in Hungary, as
the Socialist Party, in clear alliance with the MSZOSZ, won overwhelmingly.
Now, perhaps, labor would have a more sincere partner in the NCRI. Gyula
Horn, the new prime minister, stated that social partnership with the unions
would be a key element of government policy, and one official even suggested
that the party seek means to institutionalize labor in the state or institutionalize the party itself, like the Labour Party in Britain.[29] The government said
it would seek to conclude a comprehensive, four-year social pact with labor,
an ambitious proposal in any situation, let alone one characterized by socioeconomic crisis and transition. Prospects for corporatism—meaning the creation of a powerful, institutionalized role for labor—arguably never looked
better in any postcommunist country.

However, matters did not turn out as labor had hoped. Even in the immediate wake of the elections, some observers detected government waver-
ing, arguing that the Socialists' decision to form a coalition (they did not need
to, having the majority of the seats in parliament by themselves) signaled an
effort to find a partner to balance the role of the MSZOSZ.[30] By February 1995,
talks in the NCRI had broken down. The reasons are several, including the
weakness of trade unions, the lack of a well-developed political strategy on
the part of the government, and little maneuverability on the part of the
government, this last factor the result of both "objective" economic factors as
well as pressure from the IMF to implement an austerity program. The result
was a "sorry spectacle," with the government essentially seeking approval of
a set of measures that it intended to implement regardless of labor's reaction.[31] In the end, as tripartism collapsed, the government announced an
austerity package that was harsher, in terms of social policy, than anything
proffered by the previous government. The unions, especially the MSZOSZ,
had been utterly defeated.

These events in 1995 would usher in a new stage for union-government
relations. The public and state sector unions (ASZSZ, ESZT, and SZEF),
whose members took the greatest beating from austerity, protested the government actions with strikes (the largest being among utility workers and
teachers), while the MSZOSZ remained on the sidelines. Union solidarity,

which previously had been oriented toward representing all "losers" of the reform process, broke down as each union confederation began to pursue a path more in line with the interests of its own members (in Russian parlance, "pulling the blanket over themselves"). The strikes did, however, soften government policy a bit and compelled the government to reestablish the NCRI framework. Fortunately, Hungary began to experience a bit of an economic turnaround (real wages began to grow and unemployment fell from its highs),[32] but this has not translated into a renewal of unions' power. The NCRI never became a meaningful venue for unions to assert any rights. The government continued to display a "contempt for deliberations" in which the finance minister would "invite comments about details" but present the program as "nonnegotiable."[33] Unions do not take tripartism "too seriously." According to David Ost, "Hungary may have had more than a decade's experience with tripartism but it certainly has not produced the concertation, much less the economic growth and security, that effective neocorporatism signifies in the West. Instead, the Hungarian experience is one of weak tripartites passing unenforceable agreements, treated instrumentally and imperiously by the government, impotent in defending workers' interests, and serving as cover for the onset of a neoliberal economy."[34]

The breakdown of Hungarian corporatism and social partnership, which had been occurring almost since their creation, would be finalized by the 1998 elections, which brought back into power a right-wing coalition that launched an assault on the unions.[35] The government was a throwback of sorts to the previous MDF government, treating the SZOT-successors with suspicion, while also lacking close ties with the LIGA or the MOSZ, both shadows of their former selves. The government disbanded the NCRI, replacing it with two new bodies designed to consult with social partners on social and labor policies. This move was obviously a step backward as far as the unions were concerned, for instead of strengthening the NCRI's legal base the government decided to push ahead a purely consultative system. The MSZOSZ issued a statement noting that interest in conciliation has "ceased to exist in effect" and that the exclusion of social partners from decision making is "leading in a dangerous direction."[36] In 2000, because tripartite bodies were not even meeting regularly, employers and unions concluded a bipartite wage recommendation to submit to the government. Clearly, any hope for corporatism à la Austria or Hungary has been dashed. Notably, health and pension funds, previously under tripartite control of state boards, are now under exclusive control of the state as well. As mentioned, the government has also amended the Labor Code, against union protests, to extend the powers of workers' councils, so that these bodies can conclude agreements that might supplant collective agreements. Moves such as these have "opened the way for employers to reformulate the industrial relations system to becoming a more company-specific and consultation-centered form of employee representation,"[37] a phenomenon that obviously erodes much union power. Public sector wage negotiations will also be decentralized, which will likely extend the process of deunionization into that sector, which has by far been the one with the most mobilized trade union membership.

Many unions have strongly condemned these measures, although Tóth notes that the MSZOSZ was rather silent, highlighting again how the lack of common policy among unions undermines their ability to press the government to take union concerns into account.[38] However, in late 1999 the Hungarian unions did, for the first time, launch a joint protest against government policy in the wake of a railroad workers' strike. Both the LIGA and the MSZOSZ noted their concerns about the handling of the strike, in which the government largely refused to negotiate with the unions, as well as amending the strike law and changing the check-off system for union membership, which had previously made union membership virtually automatic.[39] Thus, the hard line taken by the current government may allow the unions to focus their energies at a common "enemy," although it might now be a bit too late.

Overall, state–trade union relations have yet to be completely institutionalized, as the issue remains politicized and can change with each election. Nonetheless, given that unions have been unable to advance their cause under any government, the general picture is clear. Moreover, already by 1996–1997 much of the transition in Hungary was over. Property had been redistributed; legal frameworks for the market were in place; the economy was open to foreign trade and investment. Unions played little role in that transition. What remains to be seen is what, if anything, unions can make for themselves in the new conditions created by the move to a marketized, open economy.

Trade Unions and Privatization

The failures of organized labor in Hungary are generally well known and well documented. What is less clear is how labor has adapted to the new circumstances of a marketized and increasingly globalized economy. Indeed, given the prominent role of foreign investment in the Hungarian economy, it is often difficult to disentangle these two processes.

First, however, note how little a role Hungarian workers played in the process of privatization, even compared to their Russian counterparts. In general, the unions supported privatization as a necessary process, but they were largely unable to influence how this process was carried out. In 1988–1990, Hungary witnessed "vulture" or "spontaneous" privatization, and in some cases independent unions or work councils were formed to protect workers' positions. However, the 1990 Law on Privatization placed the state in the center of the privatization process by setting up a system of open auctions. Unions or work councils had no ability to block this privatization process initiated from above. The passage in 1992 of a law on employee stock ownership did help matters a bit by granting some concessions to workers in the bidding process, but this did not result in a major change of direction. Laszlo Neumann noted that employee-owned firms constitute only about 1 percent of the total in Hungary,[40] and János Lukács notes that most of these have been small enterprises with fewer than two hundred employees. Moreover, the law itself gives discretion to the State Property Agency (SPA) so that workers' voices were not always heard. Lukacs observes, "if pressure from the employers was not strong enough, the SPA staff never thought twice about ignoring it, especially if the investor objected to even minority ownership by employees."[41] One detailed case study noted how privatization could become a politicized question, hijacked by politicians and plant managers running roughshod over the workers, who even if they wanted to purchase their own enterprises lacked the funds to do so.[42]

Moreover, unions were often left in the dark on the main questions of ownership change, and binding contracts with unions were rare. Even a 1992 law that required outside buyers to present an employment plan, which was based on a German model, granted the unions only the right of consultation. These, however, had little effect, as privatization was accompanied by massive lay-offs, and only 18 percent of workers were covered by such agreements in any case.[43] A MSZOSZ report concludes that the government acted impetuously while pursuing privatization and that the various efforts to improve the legal position of workers and unions in the process had "not been effectuated" and that "privatization has intensified workers' defenselessness" by undermining the unions' role.[44]

What can be said of the consequences of privatization? The most obvious result of privatization has been deunionization. As in other countries, the causes are several: plants close or are down-sized; workers take positions in new firms where there are no unions; and unions are simply disbanded. Eöry Arpad of the MSZOSZ ranked the breakup of large enterprises as one of the chief reasons for deunionization, as unions cannot maintain themselves at smaller firms and, if it survives, the union committee invariably becomes very parochial, looking out only for its own narrow interests and having little to do with other trade unions.[45] Indeed, data reveal that there has been a significant shift to small- and medium-size enterprises in Hungary, with over 94 percent of enterprises in 1997 employing fewer than fifty workers, whereas in 1987 over 80 percent of firms had more than fifty workers.[46] While there is no comprehensive data on the precise costs of privatization on membership, it is clear by comparing the steep decline in membership in MSZOSZ unions (most of which are in the competitive sector now dominated by smaller businesses) with the relative stability of membership in the ESZT, the ASZSZ, and the SZEF, which still predominantly represent workers in the state sector. The MSZOSZ has lost over three-quarters of its membership; the others have not seen such a sharp drop. As in other cases, the unions exist almost exclusively in firms that date from the communist era; unions have made little headway in new firms created since 1990. Emergence of the service sector is also a relevant concern. The head of the Bank Employees Union noted that the company-specific nature of work in his sector, combined with the use of part-time or fixed-term employees, makes it much more difficult to attract workers to his union, which organizes only a small fraction of bank workers.[47]

One effect of privatization, which has been noted in earlier cases, is the differentiation of the workforce at the macrolevel. The result is a division in the economy, and even within union branches, between winners and losers, meaning workers at successful or potentially successful firms and those in less profitable or "prospective" branches. Unfortunately for unions, the winners, often in smaller, private enterprises, service industries, or in multinational corporations, are the least likely to be unionized. Unions are strongest in Hungary in the public sector, which corresponds with the situation in many developed economies of advanced industrialized states. To the extent that many of the high-growth sectors are nonunionized, one should not expect an economic turnaround to boost prospects for unions, who are stuck in the industrial dinosaurs of yesteryear.

Differentiation, however, is also occurring, and in fact may be more pronounced at the enterprise level where workers fall into two broad groups:

skilled workers who are highly valued by employers and constitute a sort of "labor aristocracy" and the less skilled who find themselves poorly protected in the market environment where they can be easily replaced. This phenomenon has been best identified by Neumann and is based upon years of study of various enterprises in Hungary.[48] He contends that this differentiation is in part a holdover of communist times, when labor shortages allowed some workers to reach profitable bargains with employers, but that privatization has brought a "new quality" to the situation. The national-level and branch-level tripartite agreements, he contends, are fundamentally unimportant, due to the decentralization of bargaining that has taken place, and only a small fraction (less than 20 percent) of the workforce in the private sector is covered by a local collective agreement.[49] Thus, management can exercise wide discretion at the enterprise level, and ad hoc arrangements are becoming more and more the norm. Through these mechanisms, favorable treatment can be extended to the privileged, less replaceable skilled workers and others can be given short shrift. In this fashion management can still uphold a median that meets basic minimum requirements. Unions are bypassed in this process, as the favored workers essentially have no need of them, relying upon their own market position and personal contacts with the employer. In fact, they may even resist unions as institutions attempting to strip them of their privileged status. Unions are thus, at this level as well as the macrolevel, left defending the position of the disadvantaged and in general have not had much success on this front. What is particularly notable is what occurs in firms with partial workers' ownership (a small minority in Hungary, totaling about two hundred firms). Here, the owner-workers are favored by the managers, and new hires or those who sold their shares find their positions often precarious. This is in part a logical outcome of the pattern of ownership, but it points to a fundamental obstacle in the way of any possible labor solidarity. The result is ultimately a largely paternalist pattern of labor relations and the minimization of the union role. This is, at the shop level, consonant with labor relations under communism.

Frege and Tóth's study of the workers in the Hungarian clothing industry highlights how these factors can be directly detrimental to trade unions. They found that Hungarian workers in this sector (as opposed to East German ones) do not strongly identify with or even trust their union, although they do identify with their work collective and are willing to act as "individualist activists." They argue that this is the result of the fragmented, decentralized union and bargaining structure in Hungary, which means that for workers "the union headquarters in Budapest is far away and has no real impact on their working lives."[50] Workers are thus left to themselves at their own enterprise, and the union, an organization that could link workers across enterprises and even across sectors, is not an important player. Tóth notes that unions are "being locked into the workplace" since decentralized collective bargaining—the norm in Hungary—"aims to regulate company-specific internal labour markets" resulting in "few efforts by unions to extend social regulation beyond companies by means of sectoral or industry-level bargaining."[51] Thus, although a particular union might survive or be successful, it is harder and harder to put faith in a revival of a union *movement*. The tentative conclusion here is that a turnaround in the economy—assumed by many to be necessary to increase unions' bargaining power—may not be enough to help Hungarian unions, given the structural difficulties they face in organizing themselves due to the existing system of decentralized labor relations.

This is not say that all unions have been failures. But, it is fair to say that the "successes" have not been unequivocal. Neumann documents the case of workers in the electrical complex. These utilities were privatized in 1994–1995, with many shares going to foreign companies. The trade unions (mainly in ASZSZ) and management objected to the government's proposal, which included, among other things, plans to privatize welfare facilities and did not include an agreement on employment. Unlike the Russian case, where the government pushed ahead with its privatization program over the objections of the unions, the lobbying effort in Hungary was fairly successful, and the unions' positions were incorporated into the final program. However, as Neumann notes, this union was successful in this unprecedented development for two main reasons: the workers occupied a strategic position in the economy, and they were allied with management.[52] However, Neumann notes some peculiarities as well. Promised welfare and employment funds have not been established, companies have been able to circumvent agreements with unions by buying out employees' contracts, and spin-off companies have been largely exempt from the previously made agreement. The net result is that even though the unions secured what they thought was a sound agreement, they found themselves helpless and paralyzed once privatization had occurred. Individual workers in this sector, it is true, may have received a good deal, but it was not due to trade unions' efforts. Neumann concludes his look at this case on a pessimistic note, suggesting, "Unions co-operating with the management cannot, maybe do not want to, fight downsizing and contracting out, which is leading to a great segmentation of the labour market and to the spread of atypical employment. Trade unions lose their members in units affected by the contracting-outs, and gradually become a strong interest representative organization for the insiders and renounce goals beyond company boundaries and day-to-day representation."[53]

Trade Unions and Globalization

Hungary has been by far the most successful country in postcommunist Europe in attracting foreign capital. On a per capita basis, the amount of foreign investment in Hungary by 2000 was equal to $1,762 per person, compared with a paltry $70 in Ukraine and Russia during the same time. Bela Greskovits and Dorothee Bohle thus call Hungary's capitalist project "foreign-led."[54] This investment takes on many forms, including thousands of joint ventures formed with companies from numerous European, North American, and Asian countries. Indeed, by the late 1990s foreign firms employed 40 percent of the Hungarian workforce and were responsible for 75 percent of the new jobs created in the 1990s.[55] However, by 1995 a mere thirty companies accounted for half of all investment in Hungary, and half of that money has been put into greenfield investments, which are usually subsidiaries of the MNCs.[56] Overwhelmingly, these firms are concentrated in the export sector (80 percent of exports are from firms with foreign investment or ownership), and trade has grown to over half the country's GDP.[57] Tóth even goes so far as to assert that there is a "globalisation-propelled, reindustrialisation" of the country.[58]

Given the scope of foreign investment in the country (over thirty-five thousand enterprises have some form of foreign participation[59]), it is difficult to make firm, systematic conclusions about the role of foreign capital at the firm level.[60] While some reports note the productivity and profitability of foreign subsidiaries in Hungary, claiming that the "evidence of positive impact of FDI firms is indeed overwhelming,"[61] this need not mean that FDI and MNCs have been wholeheartedly good for Hungarian unions, which is our concern here. Obviously, unions are very concerned about the potential impact of MNCs on labor relations and the unions themselves, and their fears and complaints echo many of those made by the ILO.[62] While comprehensive data are lacking, there is both anecdotal and some survey evidence to suggest that the influx of foreign capital has not led to a resurrection of trade unions in Hungary. For example, a survey of 165 joint ventures in 1993 found that 93 percent did not have any union representation.[63] Research by the union Vasas, representing iron, metal, and electrical energy workers, revealed widespread differences on multinationals' views of trade unions. However, the report notes that there has been much greater hostility at greenfield enterprises, where owners do not inherit a union, often work against the creation of a trade union, and have been more willing to use factory councils instead of trade unions, as the councils' area of jurisdiction extends only to the enterprise and can often be co-opted by management.[64] Tóth notes similar attitudes at the greenfield plants of GM-Opel and Suzuki.[65] At best, MNCs show some grudging acceptance of trade unions; at worst, they react with outright hostility and a willingness to disregard the law in an effort to prevent or undermine unionization. Ladó notes:

> Foreign partners regard already existing local union organizations as a *fait accompli* and only occasionally hamper them directly. In a great number of joint ventures and multi-nationals, however, there are no workers' organizations. According to empirical investigations, workers often do not see the necessity to organize a trade union as their wages are higher than in Hungarian enterprises, and they also receive a wide range of benefits. In other cases incomes and working conditions are not that favourable at all, but workers still refrain from organizing a trade union due to their defenselessness and disadvantageous position. Foreign employers profit from both situations and "buy" workers' loyalty relatively cheaply. [66]

A good deal of empirical evidence confirms this impression. At Suzuki, the workers tried to form a union, but they were pushed off-premises by management, and union organizers experienced direct harassment. They did, however, succeed in creating a union, although it was harassed by management, which eventually outmaneuvered the union through the creation of a workers' council and precipitated the closure of the union.[67] Other companies, such as General Electric (which purchased the giant Tungsram electrical facility) and Ford (another greenfield), have attempted to circumvent Hungarian law by "persuading" employees—through carrots of higher initial wages and various sticks—of giving up their rights to organize. They also contribute to the processes of differentiation by offering higher wages to key employees while at the same time downsizing the plant on a massive scale. One widespread problem is that management blatantly disregards the law by attempting to ban any union representatives on the premises, thus under-cutting workers' access to information and ability to join with a larger confederation.[68] Even where unions have organized, as they did eventually at General Motors, there is far less internal democracy (in terms of choosing team leaders), fewer opportunities to acquire additional skills compared to similar plants in Western Europe, and significant differentiation within the union based upon labor skills, which in turn weakens the power of the union.[69] Notably, the largest MNCs in the country have formed a lobbying group, the Hungarian Association of International Companies, which among other things has pushed for changes in the Labor Code that would further diminish the role of trade unions. Even before these changes, however, there was a connection between the existing laws and the role of foreign capital. Guglielmo Meardi suggests, "it does not appear coincidental that Hungary is both the Eastern European country which has attracted most foreign investment and that with the least labour-friendly legislation."[70]

One pattern that seems to have emerged is that foreign companies are more willing to work with workers' councils than trade unions. The reasons, suggested by Tóth and other observers, is that the workers' councils are easier for employers to manipulate and lack any sort of higher organs that could lead to workers' solidarity across enterprises.[71] Unions are concerned about this development because if employers prefer to recognize only workers' councils, then unions will become superfluous. They also fear that the workers' councils–employer relationship will be based on paternalist relations or other attributes specific to the enterprise, including management style, and thus workers' rights will not develop on a firm, institutionalized basis.

While the status of unions at greenfield plants is quite poor or even lacking, their role at preexisting firms that have attracted foreign capital does vary. J. E. M. Thirkell et al. examined two Hungarian firms with foreign capital, one which exported personal security equipment and the other Malev, the national airline. In the former case, a joint venture was established with minimal workers' input, and conflicts quickly arose between the foreign co-owner and the local general director over business strategy. The workers did not participate in these debates either, but they did experience a loss of social benefits and a general sense of disempowerment as they had "lost" their company.

Unionization rates fell precipitously, to around 25 percent of the workforce, and the foreign co-owner displayed a generally hostile attitude to the trade union, prohibiting union leaders from playing a real role in the enterprise even on basic questions such as wages. Eventually, the foreign owner sold his shares and the company became all-Hungarian, but the workers also did not participate in this. Thus, this case, according to Thirkell et al., demonstrates the "silent decay" of the trade unions, their marginalization and replacement by a paternalist and individualist model overseen by the management of the firm.[72]

The case of Malev is more complex, with a large number of different branch unions (pilots, mechanics, ground personnel, etc.) that were parts of different union confederations (mainly the LIGA and the MSZOSZ). Labor relations were very tense, as the airline pursued restructuring prior to privatization. However, intraunion disputes did hamper the ability of the unions to present a united front in the early stages of the process. While there was workers' activism to protest government and management proposals, much of it was spontaneous, not union led. A center of protest was in the maintenance division, which was to be turned into a separate joint venture with Lockheed. The deal with Lockheed was pursued secretly by management, and the mechanics union, once it discovered management's plans, acted to obstruct the privatization process. Its strategy, however, centered on political lobbying (the union was affiliated with the LIGA and thought it had good contacts with the then-MDF government). It lost this battle—the deal was closed—and also failed to gain a say in the restructuring of the enterprise, particularly on employment questions. The union leadership itself was not hired on by the new company, a one-time wage increase was offered to assuage remaining workers, and the union died within a few months of privatization. It would, however, be revived, facilitated by a generally prounion position of Lockheed-Malev management, and would lead a two-day strike in 1993 over wage increases. Notably, however, other unions within Malev did not express solidarity with the strikers, again revealing the differentiation occurring even within large enterprises. While this new union can be counted as relatively successful, that success was not easy to achieve and was heavily dependent upon some unique circumstances in this sector.[73] Moreover, had the unions not been undermined in the initial restructuring effort, a costly strike could have been averted.[74]

Turning briefly to a different issue, what can be said of international financial institutions in Hungary and their impact upon organized labor? In this case, there is a lot of criticism of the IMF, which Hungary joined in 1982 and which has had a major role in shaping government policy in the postcommunist period. Unionists and academics point to the IMF's concerns over falling budget deficits as factors that account for a decline in real wages in the 1990s and a decrease in funds for social programs and investments in human capital. Indeed, the austerity measures pushed through in the mid-1990s by the Socialist government are attributed to the IMF, which, according to the conventional wisdom of many Hungarians, forced such policies on a government that did not campaign with such a program. Karoly Lorant suggests that the government "could carry out its neoliberal policies only with strong support from the IMF" and that therefore "IMF policy has had a determining role in Hungarian economic policy."[75] Aside from questions about democratic governance, the pronounced role of the IMF also directly affected trade unions by limiting the ability of corporatist institutions to be effective, as the government—willingly or not—essentially had its hands tied by the IMF, and thus little could really be negotiated with organized labor. Of course, defenders of the IMF would argue that IMF advice was designed to correct structural problems in the economy and create conditions for long-term growth (and by the end of the 1990s there was a turnaround in the economy),[76] but clearly for the *unions*, IMF involvement in the economy weakened their power at the national level and certainly caused some dislocations in the less competitive sectors of the economy.

If the market-driven elements of globalization (MNCs and the IMF) have generally negative results for Hungarian labor unions, what can be said of the European Union? In the first place, as in Poland, there has been widespread support for the idea that Hungary should join the EU.[77] However, the quest for membership began to have notable repercussions in the domestic arena only recently, after accession talks with Brussels began in 1998. All along, Hungarian trade unions have been supporters of the membership bid, but they put great emphasis on the fact that the EU is a "community of values" above and beyond its aspects of financial or economic union.[78] They are attracted to the wealth of protections for workers and organized labor under the EU and view Hungarian membership as a means to reshape what they perceive to be the antiunion stance of the current government. In the words of the president of the LIGA, unions now need to ensure that their voices are heard "even as far as Brussels," especially given the reluctance of government to entertain union proposals.[79] Specifically, they envision schemes for wage equalization with the EU average (Hungarian wages are under half of EU average presently), amendments to the current Labor Code, adoption of the EU's Social Charter, and reanimation of tripartite bodies, which as discussed after 1998 have fallen into disuse.

To date, they can point to some progress on this front. Unions' complaints have been heard by the EU, and in turn, as accession talks have progressed, the EU has noted that "substantial further measures are required in order to promote social dialogue."[80] In the fall of 1999, the EU cautioned the government to back off changes in the labor law that would have infringed upon labor's rights, and the government heeded the advice of Brussels. Adoption of the Social Charter will no doubt force the government to adopt measures that will protect labor's interests, and unions may also benefit from the fact that European courts will have jurisdiction over a variety of social and economic questions. Transnational ties with European bodies such as the European Trade Union Confederation (ETUC) are also important, as Hungarian unions can use these groups to pressure both Budapest and Brussels. Indeed, during the railway strike in January 2000, the president of the ETUC wrote to the Hungarian prime minister, noting that the government was out of order for blithely dismissing union proposals to conclude a collective agreement.[81] While this did not result in an immediate settlement to the unions' liking, this could be a harbinger of the internationalization of labor disputes in Hungary. Given the weakness of Hungarian unions, such allies are quite important, and if anything would force the government to accede to some union demands, it would be EU pressure.

Of course, the precise effects of EU membership cannot be currently known. Unions complain that the government's European Integration Council, which was supposed to be a forum for civic groups to raise their concerns to the government over the accession process, has played only a minor role, effectively shutting the unions out of the bargaining process.[82] The government may try to use this to its own advantage, watering down changes in legislation demanded by Europe.

However, membership in the EU will likely reverse a steady tide of defeats suffered by the unions since 1990. True, the EU cannot solve all of the unions' problems. But, given the clear antiunion stance of successive governments,[83] with their efforts to modify items such as unemployment benefits, tripartite bodies, and the strike law, to the disadvantage of unions, it is understandable why Hungarian unions tend to welcome EU membership, hoping the institutions of Brussels can at least mitigate some of the more dire circumstances facing them.

In sum, what does this review of organized labor in Hungary demonstrate? First, labor's battle for political influence at the national level has been rather futile. Parties have been able to ignore labor without peril, and economic policies have by far been shaped more by the ideological predispositions of the political elites and the requirements of international markets (in terms of choices regarding privatization in 1990–1992 and the austerity package of 1995) than by union pressure from below. Corporatist efforts to integrate labor have led to few victories for labor; instead, they have been used to give legitimacy to neoliberal government policies. Organized labor itself has been markedly divided, due to both ideological reasons and market pressures. Union leaders also, by choice and by default, have with few exceptions not been able to mobilize members to put much pressure on the government or employers. Privatization has not been a boon to unions, and only in rare cases have they been able to exercise much control over the process. As in other cases, the effects of globalization are not clear-cut, although most observers and union officials concur that the massive inflow of foreign investment has not helped trade unions, insofar as most greenfield enterprises are non-unionized. In short, while Hungary can be gauged a "success" on a variety of fronts (particularly compared with its neighbors to the east and south), union leaders have been frozen out of many of the processes of socioeconomic and political change occurring throughout the country.

Organized Labor in Ukraine

UKRAINIAN TRADE UNIONS HAVE MUCH in common with their Russian counterparts. It could hardly be otherwise, given their common Soviet experience. For the most part, Ukrainian trade unions are the inheritors of the republic-level structures from Soviet times, although there are also some newer unions in a few sectors (mostly mining and transport) whose lineage can be traced to all-Union workers' organizations in the late 1980s. As in Russia, Ukrainian unions are attempting to overcome negative aspects of the Soviet period while at the same time adjusting to the still uncertain environment created by both economic dislocations and nascent marketization.

There are, however, some differences that are worth mentioning at the outset. The first is the general slower pace of economic reform in Ukraine. While Boris Yeltsin and Yegor Gaidar launched shock therapy in Russia in 1992, Ukrainian leaders in the first years of independence tended to dither on economic reform questions, with Leonid Kravchuk, the first post-Soviet president, at one point admitting that Ukraine lacked an individual with reform credentials such as Gaidar or Boris Fedorov.[1] While Russia encountered its own problems, the results of nonreform in Ukraine were arguably more disastrous, with the verb "to Ukrainianize" entering the Russian lexicon, meaning to bring to ruin. President Leonid Kuchma did push through an economic reform program in 1994–1995, and at the same time Ukraine began to receive substantial funds from Western states and organizations. However, on several significant measures (levels of privatization and marketization, foreign investment, trade, growth), Ukraine remains well behind most of her neighbors. Although economic reform has not brought ruin to Ukraine's trade unions (they were quite weak well before economic changes were launched), the impact on unions of the economic "reform" that has occurred in the country must be considered.

Moreover, political conflict in Ukraine has been much more subdued than in the Russian case. Regional and constitutional disputes have been settled peacefully, and political polarization has been much less pronounced. This is not to say that Ukraine has a stronger record on democratic reforms. Clans with roots in the Soviet *nomenklatura* dominate economic and political life in the country. The rule of law has yet to be established, and the president has resorted to political and electoral intimidation to push through measures to augment his powers. In 2000, matters reached a nadir when cassette tapes were aired with President Kuchma, apparently, openly ordering the intimidation of judges and regional officials, engaging in electoral fraud, accepting bribes, and advocating that a prominent opposition journalist, who was later found dead, be "dealt with" by the Chechens or the Ukrainian security service.[2] Kuchma was able to remain in power, a testament to the weakness of political opposition in the country. This broader political context is quite important from the perspective of civil society and trade unions, because there has yet to be any sort of "democratic breakthrough" that would thoroughly dismantle the structures of the old Soviet system.

Finally, Ukraine, arguably more so than in Russia, and certainly more so than in Hungary and Poland, has been occupied with nation- and state-building projects in addition to tasks of political and economic reform.[3] Neither of these concerns will be the focus of our discussion, but much of the state-building project in Ukraine is less from scratch and more from the ruins of the Soviet state, hence the presence of "residual corporatism" in the country.[4] Also, regional and ethnic disputes, particularly widely noted East-West, ethnic Russian-Ukrainian divides, manifest themselves in many of the broader political and economic debates in the country. These schisms have had some relevance as well in the trade union movement and at times have prevented workers' solidarity.

Union Issues in Ukraine

Ukrainian workers, like their Russian counterparts, are overwhelmingly represented by unions that are successors to the Soviet-era communist-dominated unions. Most of these unions belong to the Federation of Ukrainian Trade Unions (FPU), which occupies the old union building (still adorned with a hammer and sickle) on Kyiv's Maidan Nezalezhnosti and inherited most of the property of the old unions. The FPU is structured along both branch and regional lines, and its forty-one branch unions are for the most part the same unions that existed under Soviet times. Its membership has dwindled since the Soviet collapse, falling from twenty-five million in 1990 to twenty-one million in 1994 to under fourteen and a half million in 2001.[5] Hardest hit in terms of membership decline since 1994 have been those in the agroindustrial sector (−46 percent), auto construction (−48 percent), coal (−49 percent), textile and light industry (−53 percent), engineering (−57 percent), consumers' cooperatives (−68 percent), and radio electronics (−75 percent). Union membership has held steady in education and in oil and gas but has increased in no sizable sector. Union leaders attribute most of the decline to job loss from downsizing, and in most industrial sectors unions continue to represent upward of 95 percent of the current workforce. Thus, in Ukraine the problem has been workers moving from unionized jobs to jobs without trade unions rather than choosing not to belong to a union. Indeed, movement to nonunionized jobs in small businesses (legal or in the shadow economy) has been quite pronounced, given the official figures of deunionization together with officially quite low (4.2 percent at beginning of 2001) unemployment figures.[6]

There are some non-FPU alternative trade unions. Most are in the same sectors as in Russia (miners, air and rail transport workers, longshoremen), but there also are a handful of small, company-based regional trade unions that do not belong to the FPU. According to the ILO, many of these smaller unions have formed because the traditional, "official" unions "have been unable to reform themselves for work in a market economy and realize their stated goal of protecting workers."[7] While some of these unions claim highly inflated, impossible figures of hundreds of thousands, even millions, of members,[8] by far the most visible of these alternative unions is the Independent Miners' Union of Ukraine (NPGU), which claims 52,100 members, a mere 10 percent of the members of the FPU coal industry union. Independent unions for railway, air transport workers, and air traffic controllers count fewer than five thousand members each, and numerous others (e.g., longshoremen at Illichivsk, Kyiv metro drivers, female agroindustrial workers, workers at the Donetsk textile plant) are primarily local and far smaller in size.[9]

These groups, built from scratch, have had much trouble getting off the ground. Part of the problem is the simple collective action dilemma, along with fears among workers that joining a new union may jeopardize benefits such as housing, access to consumer goods, day care, and vacation packages. These newer unions lack such "selective incentives" to offer members, and given the realities of the labor market, workers appear to be loathe to rock the boat and leave their old unions, which enjoyed in the past a cozy relationship with management and distributed various goods at the enterprise. Of more concern, perhaps, are the widespread allegations of harassment and intimidation against would-be union organizers led by local authorities, plant management, and leaders of the established unions. In 1993, the leader of an independent pilots' union was defenestrated from his flat on the ninth floor; graffiti at the railway depot warned Semen Karikov, head of the Independent Railway Drivers Union, that he would be next.[10] Viktor Stepanov, deputy leader of the dockers' union outside of Odessa, noted that the enterprise management and existing unions, in collusion with the local administration, have refused to recognize his trade union and have attempted to intimidate and bribe him to stop his organizing efforts.[11] Mikhail Volynets, head of the NPGU, has noted threats against him and his family, which he attributes to enterprise management, rival unions, local officials, and members of the secret police that all work to protect a "coal mafia." He has also suggested that prominent officials have worked to intimidate NPGU members into voting against him as NPGU president.[12] A leader of the Capital-Regions union in Volyn oblast' noted that even though Ukrainian laws do offer rights to organize, "nothing really has changed. These laws exist for you [the United States], for Europe. They're just pieces of paper. If a manager wants to dismiss a leader of a union, it is illegal, but he can and does, and nothing can stop him."[13] This complaint was echoed by many, who noted that the general *bardak* into which Ukraine has descended has undermined the ability of unions to exercise their rights to organize workers.

Despite problems of falling membership, Ukrainian trade unions remain by far the largest organizations in civil society. Their more significant problem is the inability to mobilize the members they have to protect workers' interests. Indeed, as in other cases, workers' passivity in the wake of an assault on workers' living standards and job security has been the norm. There are numerous reasons for this: workers' fear of reprisals if they engage in protests or strikes; a belief, perhaps, that no action would do any good; unfavorable labor markets; and an unwillingness of union leaders, especially those from the FPU, to call for workers' action. However, one serious problem is the lack of trust in trade unions. Surveys in 1994–2000 show that confidence in both traditional trade unions (12–14 percent expressing full or some confidence) and new unions (7–9 percent) is markedly and consistently low. More telling, perhaps, is the fact that only 43 percent of employed respondents in a fall 2000 survey claimed membership in trade unions, a figure that does not jive with FPU claims of 94 percent representation of Ukrainian workers.[14] Obviously, either membership figures are inflated or many workers simply do not know they are members of a union. Membership is more assumed, a habit, a fact acknowledged and lamented by many union leaders.

What do workers think of unions? Unions could find some solace in the fact that in the above-mentioned survey from 2000 workers stated that they could appeal to unions on more localized issues such as work safety (34 percent), unfair dismissals (25 percent), and violation of labor contracts (26 percent). These, however, were the exact same issues that unions purported to serve in Soviet times, and few union leaders would claim that they are regularly effective in resolving such issues. On broader issues outside of the enterprise—on those factors that establish the general environment for Ukrainian workers—workers judged appeals to unions to be far less useful: only 11 percent mentioned an appeal to unions for wage arrears, 3 percent to protest price increases, and 2 percent to deal with utility cut-offs. And, not surprisingly, workers were more apt to think that local trade union organizations (33 percent) were best able to protect their interests (as opposed to 2 percent who cited the national union or 10 percent the branch level). Still, 52 percent did not know what union (if any) protected them, and 42 percent claimed management takes care of workers' interests, higher than the figure for the enterprise trade union.[15]

Part of the problem, at least for the top union leadership, is a widespread perception that unions have not shed their communist past and are still either too attached to management or too engaged with their own corporate interests separate from workers' interests. Ihor Kharchenko, a former head of the department of social and labor questions in the Cabinet of Ministers, had little good to say of the unions, especially the FPU, which he viewed as a commercial structure, concerned with managing and dipping into income from union property and control over the social insurance funds.[16] A Western adviser working with the newer unions accused the FPU of being little more than the "labor relations branch of the government . . . They have dotted their i's and crossed their t's to create the facade of a legitimate structure. However, this has never corresponded to reality."[17] Even the leader of the coal miners of the FPU accused the top leadership of being a "bunch of communists" for their passivity in the wake of economic depression, and the leader of the cultural workers lamented the continuation of democratic centralism that restricts union independence.[18] The leader of the L'viv FPU organization conceded that the FPU is the "most conservative social organization" in Ukraine.[19] Meanwhile, as might be expected, leaders of the new unions continue to refer to the FPU as a state or official union, and, indeed ties between its national and local leaders, enterprise directors, and government officials make many people question if it is an organization for workers.

The FPU is aware of these concerns and at the same time has undertaken efforts to preserve its unity against would-be internal dissidents. Valentin Pozhidayev, vice chairman of the FPU, reacting to some of the criticisms voiced above, noted that the "union organism is like a cloth," and little rips in it would soon result in "no cloth at all."[20] He later noted that "no one can be satisfied with the organizational structure of the unions," because they have become too amorphous, too divided, and need to remake themselves into a "powerful organism."[21] Local union officials noted in the main FPU newspaper that unions have lost their dynamism and unity and that they must "overcome the principle of pseudodemocracy" and maintain the "principle of democratic centralism" to maintain unity and financial strength.[22] While the hierarchy of the FPU complains that branch and regional unions are prone to "pull the blanket over themselves," many branch union leaders concede they have no choice, because they must fight for resources from the state budget and because the FPU as a whole may be incapable of defending workers in their sector.[23] Much of this fighting, however, is over union money, with the leadership demanding that more money be transferred to them and local or regional unions fighting to keep their union dues. In February of 2000, this split came to a head, as many regional FPU unions refused to participate in protests over social insurance funds that were organized by the central union leadership. Even leaders within the FPU were left wondering how the FPU can hope to be a major political player when it is constantly fighting internal battles to keep its members unified.[24]

The alternative unions outside the FPU have fared little better in terms of unity. A coalition, Free Trade Unions of Ukraine (VPU), under the leadership of Alexandr Mril' of the NPGU was created in 1994 but collapsed a year later due to personality disputes and endless debates on "trivial issues."[25] In 1998, a new Confederation of Ukrainian Free Trade Unions was formed (KVPU), and as of 2001 it unified seventeen different unions. However, it is dominated by the NPGU,[26] and several important unions (e.g., air transport, air traffic controllers, most of the interregional Capital-Regions union) are not part of it. The independent railway union, once one of the more active ones in Ukraine, is now split into two unions, only one of which belongs to the KVPU. However, even within the KVPU, there are notable divisions, with the coal miners being far more politicized and willing to mobilize members for protests and the remainder far more removed from the political arena. For example, in 2001 the NPGU was very active in the "Ukraine without Kuchma" movement and has forged an alliance with Yulia Tymoshenko's anti-Kuchma National Salvation Front. Other union leaders in the KVPU note with some condescension that such actions are in part political grandstanding and that they themselves prefer to eschew such political battles.[27]

In general, the alternative unions have been better able to mobilize their members to strike, both for political economic demands. Transport unions struck in September 1992 and won government recognition along with salary increases. A June 1993 miners' strike in eastern Ukraine, in which the NPGU and nonunion strike committees were very active, resulted in the government's making a host of concessions. However, in retrospect it is apparent that this event was the zenith for organized labor in Ukraine. Since that time, strikes (mainly by doctors, miners, and teachers) have been more spontaneous than organized by unions (mostly local) and have won only the most modest of gains for workers—typically the salaries that the government owed them. One NPGU leader noted that it took eighteen months of wage arrears to finally spark sustained action, and now, after back wages have been paid, workers go back to work, not thinking of their future or of rectifying the situation that led to wage arrears.[28] The alternative unions, despite sustained criticism of state policies and enterprise management, have been unable to lead anything close to a national- or sector-level strike since 1993. Mikhail Volnyets, head of the NPGU, noted in 2001 that efforts to generate sustained protests among miners failed, as miners at a given enterprise ceased actions after their mine had been temporarily bought off by authorities.[29]

Last, Ukrainian unions, in particular alternative ones, have also been hampered by the regional and ethnic divisions in the country. This was most apparent in the miners' strike of 1993, when coal miners in the Russified Donetsk region put forward a number of political and economic demands, including referendums of confidence in president and parliament and a referendum for regional economic autonomy for Donetsk and Luhansk in eastern Ukraine. Coal miners in the more nationalist western Ukraine, even those affiliated with the NPGU, looked upon such activity with suspicion, as they feared this event would benefit Russia and undermine Ukrainian statehood.[30] Some unions, such as VOST (All-Ukrainian Union of Workers' Solidarity) have aligned themselves with national-democratic parties such as Rukh, which are strong in western Ukraine but have little support in the more Russified eastern and southern regions. The acute regionalism that was manifested in 1994 and 1998 elections also undermined the ability of unions to organize workers across the country for political goals.[31]

In short, Ukrainian unions continue to suffer from a variety of organizational problems: maintaining membership, establishing their organizations, and creating unity within their respective blocs, not to speak of cooperation between the FPU and the alternative unions, which has been very rare.[32] These factors have contributed to their circumscribed political and economic role in the country.

Trade Unions and Politics

Ukrainian unions have been far more reticent to enter the political arena than their Polish or Russian counterparts. Russian unions, of course, are by no means politically powerful, but at least they do appear occasionally on the political radar screen. Since 1993, Ukrainian unions have not been visible, despite Ukrainians' widespread disappointment with the condition of their country.[33] Of course, unions are not the only passive group in Ukraine. Civil society in Ukraine today is a mere shadow of what it was in 1990–1991 during public movements for autonomy or independence from Moscow.[34]

While there are a variety of factors that might explain general Ukrainian passivity (political culture, focus on survival, widespread cynicism of politics), our question is more specific. Why have the unions been unable to channel immense public dissatisfaction into political protest? Some would claim that the answer is that unions—especially FPU unions—simply have no desire to do so. The lines of argument on this front are several. Some would note that Oleksandr Stoian, head of the FPU, was an adviser to then-President Leonid Kravchuk before he was named to his current post in 1992. Some might point to engrained habits from Soviet times—that union leaders thought of themselves more as agents of the state bureaucracy than as representatives of workers. The more likely reason, in my view, is that the state has held a strong hand and the unions a very weak one, especially on the question of union property. As in Russia, the threat to take away union property and control of social insurance funds (the latter was finally transferred to a tripartite body in 2001) prevented the union leadership from taking a hard line against the state, even as "Ukrainianization" of the economy devastated millions of workers.[35] Indeed, it is notable that symbolic one-day national protests aside, the FPU has yet to call for any nationwide or sectorwide strikes or protests. V. V. Postolatij notes, "The trade union elite is in no hurry to enter into opposition to the [current] regime and expend energy for the social defense of the population and interest of laborers, since that would require significant effort to remake the whole trade union movement, not the least of which would be to lose a sizable degree of their current comfort."[36] Unions thus restrain themselves, because they know it would be costly to push the envelope too far. Indeed, as one FPU leader in L'viv succinctly remarked, "Unions still exist only because they don't bother anyone."[37]

The FPU, as might be expected, offers different explanations. One widespread argument is that the FPU cannot assume a political role because it represents such a wide spectrum of society that if it takes a particular political position it would alienate many of its own members.[38] In all likelihood, this is a sober recognition of regional divisions in the country, but the argument seems rather specious given Stoian's ill-fated attempt to create a Ukrainian Workers Party in 1997 (it won less than 1 percent of the vote in the 1998 parliamentary elections), and taken to its logical conclusion, it would prevent the FPU from taking any position on any controversial question of public interest. More likely, as one adviser to Stoian conceded, is that the FPU has no political capital, and thus it would be foolish to stick out its neck when it cannot depend on societal support. In his words, "Trade unions today cannot afford to get into politics unless we know there will be some concrete achievement."[39] Of course, given the prevailing belief that any sort of popular political activity will fail, the unions become paralyzed in the political arena. Indeed, the silence of the FPU in the wake of the "Kuchmagate" tape scandal was deafening (and stood in stark contrast to the action of the NPGU), with the FPU education workers' union even calling off strikes so they would "not be used for political purposes."[40]

Rather than engage in protests or in overt political activity, the FPU—like the FNPR in Russia—emphasizes the need to pursue social partnership with the government and to conclude agreements to improve living standards for workers. Indeed, the FPU's newspaper, *Profsplikovi visti*, has printed numerous articles discussing the status of national and sectoral agreements and how the FPU has pushed issues such as wage and pension increases, unemployment insurance, payment of wage arrears, and work safety. Some of this work is centered in the *Verkhovna Rada* (parliament), to which Stoian and a handful of other union leaders have been elected, where they have tended to belong to centrist, propresidential blocs.[41] There, they have put forward bills on socioeconomic issues and on the tripartite National Committee for Social Partnership, which was established in 1993 and as of 2001 included twenty-two union representatives, ten of whom are from the FPU.[42]

However, it would be a mistake to deem the existence of this body as evidence that social partnership is alive and well. Part of the problem, as elsewhere, is that social partnership itself may be a chimera when two of the partners—business and the state—are in a much stronger position than the third, labor.[43] Fears of unemployment are very real, and the state budget ($5 billion) is minuscule compared to the numerous problems in the country. The FPU tries to put a positive spin on its efforts, but it is hard to cover up the vast failures of Ukrainian social partnership. General Agreements in 1993 and 1995 were violated by the government, but this engendered little protest from the FPU, with some officials stating that they were happy something had simply been signed.[44] By 1998, however, things were functioning so poorly that the FPU actually pulled out of the Social Partnership Committee briefly to protest its ineffectiveness. Since then, however, the FPU can point to few fruits of social partnership. Stoian, in an article entitled "Laws Are Passed . . . and Not Implemented. Why?" noted that as of early 2000 wage arrears totaled 6.5 billion hrivna (about $1.2 billion), a doubling since 1997. Moreover, according to him, 40 percent of workers failed to receive the established living minimum wage.[45] In the year 2000 itself—a year in which GDP rose by 6 percent and productivity rose 16 percent—the FPU noted that only 70 percent of the General Agreement was fulfilled, but the shortcomings were on the most important issues: minimum wage (118 hrivna a month, less than $25), pensions, unemployment, child care, and other social payments. Indeed, the average wage (296 hrivna) continued to be below the living minimum (311 hrivna), and real wages actually fell 0.9 percent in the year. The FPU also reported an incredible two million violations of the labor code by national, regional, and local governments and employers, which makes any claims about the utility of collective agreements at the enterprise level also ring rather hollow.[46]

FPU officials do concede disappointment with the progress of social partnership. They note that the Committee's recommendations often do not get authorization in the state budget, that the country has been hampered by political instability and unpredictability, and that follow-through on signed deals is weak. Economic conditions also weaken labor's hand. However, the government itself is not always a neutral arbiter. Grigorii Osovyj, an FPU official and cohead of the Social Partnership Committee, recognizes that there is a reticence to accept unions as partners: "Unfortunately, Ukrainian society is still not familiar with issues of the current trade union movement, and the attitude of the authorities and business toward unions is often based on obsolete ways of thinking that see unions exclusively in their former role in the command-administrative system and does not allow for the possibility of perceiving them as an equal partner."[47]

While few would haggle with this assessment, the more important question is what can the FPU do about this perception and make social partnership more effective. On this score, there are few answers, aside from the standard "it takes time" and "we must learn to adjust to new conditions," refrains that were as prevalent in 1992–1993 as they are today. Serhei Donkriuk, FPU specialist on protection of workers' economic interests, was more candid, if perhaps more pessimistic. He conceded that laws and agreements in Ukraine do not function very well, but he sees that the FPU has little choice but pursuit of social partnership: "What can we do? We really only have three choices. Rebellion and confrontation will lead to nothing but more chaos, maybe civil war. Doing nothing and giving up would obviously be no good, and many would accuse us of being bought off by the authorities. So we must work for a middle ground of social partnership, and try to do what we can. Yes, it doesn't always work, and there are lots of problems. But, what else can we do?"[48] Comments such as this one recall Evgen Golovakha's about the "Ukrainian way" of postcommunist development. It is worth quoting at length:

> The essence of the "Ukrainian model" of posttotalitarian development is found in the yearning of authority for social equilibrium, aided by minimum social change and preservation of old structures and mechanisms of social governance, in order to avoid social demand overload, which is an unfavorable result of fundamental changes of the social foundation. The result of this model, on the one hand, is the absence of widescale conflicts. On the other hand, it has also destroyed the economy and sociopolitical activism. Mass support for this social strategy is based on total fear of any sort of conflict, which is an unavoidable necessity of democratic development as conflict widens between the obsolete totalitarian structures and civil society. As a result of this fear of conflict, the population itself becomes a mechanism that restrains any sort of constructive action directed toward overcoming the socioeconomic crisis. Extremely afraid of possible social chaos from radical social changes, the majority of the population holds the same political line as the elite: support declarations of the idea of democratic society, market reform, and the construction of the rule of law, but do nothing to realize these aims. The final result is construction of a "bad peace," which may be better than a "good war."[49]

Although Golovakha wrote these words in 1993, they have much resonance today, as the FPU (and many other civic associations and political parties) have been unwilling or unable to generate much challenge from below to the existing power structure.

While the FPU, for the most part, may have settled for a "bad peace," not all unions or workers have. Not only have there been strikes (although the strike wave peaked in 1993) but also some attempts by organized labor to assert a stronger political role. Again, this has mainly been the work of the alternative unions (especially the miners), although others (including a few in the FPU itself) have aligned themselves with various political causes. Perhaps organized labor's most visible foray into politics was during the 1993 miners' strikes. Strike committees, the NPGU, and (to a lesser extent) the FPU coal-miners union put forward a number of demands, such as higher wages, state support for the coal industry, regional economic autonomy, and a referendum of confidence in the president and the parliament. This strike was highly controversial, not only because of regional tensions that it generated but also because many suspected that the mine directors themselves were behind the strike.[50] Indeed, this episode helped one of their own, Efim Zviagils'ky, to become acting prime minister. However, the threat of massive civil disobedience, coupled with the economic shock of the strike, forced the authorities to concede to a referendum of confidence in both the president and *Verkhovna Rada*.

Looking back, one can see that this was the apex of workers' political activism, and also the only time since 1991 that a movement from below was able to force concessions from above. This victory, however, would prove to be short-lived. The referendums were cancelled, replaced by elections for both branches in 1994. Workers' protest over this action was minimal, and Stoian and FPU echoed the official line that any referendum would be too disruptive. In early 1994, the NPGU tried to launch a strike to have a reformist politician, Volodymyr Lanovy, named prime minister, but this fizzled.[51] Afterward, union leaders such as Mril' and Karikov would castigate all political parties, claiming they have tried to turn unions into prostitutes and none represents the workers.[52] These accusations, while perhaps extreme, did hold a grain of truth. No party—save those on the left—could offer anything to the workers, and thus the alternative trade unions, which claimed a natural alliance with democratic political parties, could find no party to support workers' causes. Again, the problem here is a disjuncture between political reform and economic reform, the latter of which, at least in the short run, could promise nothing to the workers except more hardship and dislocation. Thus, appeals from proreform parties (whose support was mainly in western Ukraine) never received mass support, and it did not help that many were perceived as Ukrainian nationalists, that they muted their opposition to the political authorities, and that they could not unify even themselves—Rukh being a case in point, which suffered two schisms in less than five years.[53] Although there would be sporadic strikes 1994–1999, none of these gained any political momentum, and authorities dismissed them as provocations from rogue politicians or clan leaders.

The scandals of Kuchmagate in 2000–2001 would provide a pretext for a revival of civic activism. A grassroots movement, Ukraine without Kuchma, was formed, and tent cities were established for protestors in Kyiv. Some speculated that this would be Ukraine's real democratic revolution, leading to the overthrow of a Soviet-era *nomenklatura* that had plundered the country and shown mere lip service to democratic principles. The NPGU, under Volnyets, was active in this movement, and marches, sit-ins, and even clashes with security forces occurred in Kyiv in early 2001. However, efforts to open an independent probe on the tape scandal went nowhere (despite Kuchma's waffling on whether that was his voice on the tape), and security forces dealt with the protesters in an often brutal manner, à la Belarus's Lukhashenko or Serbia's Milosevic. What is notable is that the only union that was visible in this activity was the NPGU. The FPU stood entirely on the sidelines, and most other unions in the KVPU opted against openly political activity. As one leader said: "Yes, we have a police-bureaucratic, immoral dictatorship. Our leaders have forfeited the right to lead, and all political parties have sold out. . . . But, as for free trade unions, our political action must have a point. There must be a light at the end of the tunnel. If I don't see it, I worry about what might be out there in the darkness."[54]

In the end, of course, Kuchma prevailed. He held a far better hand than his opponents and played his cards skillfully. Nikolai Mitrov of the NPGU noted that in the Donetsk region municipal authorities restricted anti-Kuchma protests to certain times and places, and on the day of a major planned protest his mine organized buses to send pro-Kuchma people to the meeting. Meanwhile, because it was a Monday, many would-be protestors did not attend for fear of not getting paid or perhaps being fired from the mine.[55] This action speaks volumes about the current state of Ukrainian politics and the importance of business-government relations and how these two groups can work together to stifle voices from below. In case this be taken for an isolated incident, a certain letter will prove otherwise. Yurii Samoylenko, head of the Ukrainian security services for Donetsk oblast', writing during the period of protests, notes that the workers' movement is "the most dangerous force, capable of destabilizing the country," and that he "will not allow consolidation of various union structures."[56]

Actions undertaken by the authorities during Kuchmagate are indicative of a broader assault on trade unions, particularly the alternative unions which have not been as tamed as the FPU. One hotly contested issue has been the law on trade unions, passed in September 1999 with the support of the FPU. Two provisions of the law—one requiring registration to conclude collective agreements and one mandating only one national union per branch of the economy—flouted ILO conventions on freedom of association and were challenged in Ukrainian courts. Remarkably, perhaps, the court annulled these provisions, but as of late 2001 a new law has yet to be passed, and several unions, including the NPGU, remain unregistered and still are denied participation in social insurance programs. In February 2001, the government ignored the recommendations of the Social Partnership Committee and put forward a much more restrictive strike law, which would have prohibited strikes in fourteen different sectors of the economy, including mining, transport, and energy. Adoption of this measure would have crippled the unions. An ILO visit in spring 2001 forced the government to delay introduction of the bill, but it may yet be put up for a vote in parliament.[57] Ukraine's human rights ombudsman, Nina Karpachova, notes that in 1998–2001, of the 170,000 complaints her office received, 36 percent are violations of workers' rights, including the right to organize, which has been denied not only de facto by enterprise management but de jure by local officials.[58] While she did help win the case on the law on trade unions, it is uncertain how effective her office can be with these thousands of cases.

In sum, Ukrainian unions play at best a marginal role in politics, which has been the norm for all groups in civil society since Ukraine gained statehood. The FPU has explicitly refrained from playing a political role but in so doing of course bolsters the current authorities because there is less chance of workers' activism and protest. The rhetoric of social partnership has been upheld, even as the reality exposes social partnership to be rather hollow. The alternative unions, for their part, have fared little better, and only the NPGU can really be considered politically active. As in Russia, the alternative unions are viewed with suspicion by the authorities, and attempts have been made to essentially eradicate them. They have not yet succeeded, but nonetheless organized labor has found itself politically marginalized.

Trade Unions and Privatization

Looking beyond political questions, we can also ask how unions have been affected by economic changes in the country, particularly privatization. Again, as mentioned before, Ukraine is the reform laggard of all the countries considered in this study, and, indeed, of all countries (save Belarus) in Eastern Europe. While some early laws on business enterprises, foreign investment, and privatization were passed in 1991–1992, reform moved at a glacial pace for several years. Several problems can be considered—excessive taxation on private business, bureaucratic delays, lack of a clear law on property, political uncertainty—but what is striking about Ukraine is that there was no real timetable for privatization of any enterprise. Buyers' associations were free to choose when an enterprise should be privatized.[59] In fact, these buyers' associations were usually workers and managers at a given enterprise, and since they controlled the timetable for privatization, there was wide room for corruption, such as stripping the enterprise of its assets.

In 1994, under President Kuchma, privatization was stepped up a bit, but much of it was "leasing with buy-outs" (*arenda s vykupom*), an option that did little to promote capital investment or change in enterprise leadership.[60] Plans for voucher privatization were delayed, and this process began in earnest only in 1995, but by then inflation had eaten away the value of the certificates, whose face value was eventually pushed up to 1,050,000 *kupony* (about $4). However, as in Russia, vouchers were envisioned to be used for only a fraction of the total purchase of a firm, and multiple means of privatization (vouchers, insider purchasing, open auctions, renting with buy-out options) were eventually employed. By 1999, over sixty-nine thousand enterprises (mostly small enterprises) were in the nonstate sector of the economy, and this accounted for 55 percent of the GDP.[61] According to ILO surveys from 2000, insider ownership in Ukraine remains prevalent (47.9 percent of total equity in firms surveyed was held by managers and other employees).[62] However, this should be viewed as a victory from labor's perspective, as most shares are not held by ordinary workers.

Where then were the workers in this process? On paper, the workers were deemed to be important, privileged players. All else being equal, workers at an enterprise would be the preferred buyer, and they were given privileges such as the right to pay for shares in installments and the right to buy additional shares at book value for cash.[63] The problem, of course, was that by 1994–1995, when privatization finally did get off the ground, years of hyperinflation had destroyed personal savings and wage arrears problems also meant workers had little extra cash on hand to purchase shares. The value of privatization vouchers was also measly, so that workers really were given nothing in the process. On the other hand, directors of the enterprises, treated as "workers" under the law as they too were technically employees, did have resources on hand and were able to use privileges designed for workers to purchase shares and gain ownership of the enterprise. Kuchma, who prior to being elected president was the leader of the Ukrainian Union of Industrialists and Entrepreneurs, the largest industrial-business lobby, did nothing to stop this sort of takeover of enterprises, since, in the words of the organization's vice president, "yesterday's state directors are the most natural entrepreneurs."[64] Moreover, not all enterprises were subject to voucher privatization, which ended completely by 1998. Since then, privatization has been done by open bidding, and workers, still lacking resources, also do not have the privileges they had in the earlier stages of the process.

Where were the trade unions? According to one FPU official, the unions were extremely interested in the various aspects of economic reform, but "from the beginning of privatization unions were pushed away from participation in the process."[65] Unions had no legally defined role, as workers were empowered through their work collectives, not the unions. The work collectives, however, were usually poorly informed about their choices and easily manipulated by management. Although two-thirds of property was initially transferred to work collectives, "unfavorable economic conditions and the lack of experience working under new conditions did not give the workers the chance to take advantage of the results of privatization and become the real owners of their enterprises."[66] Inna Styrnyk, FPU expert on property reform questions, tries to paint a favorable portrait of the FPU in this process, claiming that the laws were adequate but that general ignorance and confusion led to workers selling their shares or being manipulated by management.[67]

Many, however, had more unkind assessments of the unions, particularly the FPU. An ILO official, at one time head of a non-FPU union, claimed that the unions had "slept through" (*prospali*) the privatization process, lacking a clear position and feeling rather naively happy with the various formal rights given to the work collective that were meaningless in practice.[68] One former FPU official responsible for questions of economic reform, now working for the FPU Seafarers' Union, opined, "The trade unions made a mistake during the privatization process. They stood for the rights of all to receive property. However, this ended up creating businesses without funds, and a bankrupt state. It would have been better just to sell the property to the highest bidder. As it was, privatization benefited neither the workers nor the state."[69] Indeed, in surveys in 2001 with over twenty-five union leaders (from the FPU and the alternatives), no one was happy with the results of privatization. "Privatization gave us nothing," "we were shut out," "our role was purely formal," and "nothing has really changed" were familiar refrains. At best, unions are resigned to the inevitability of privatization and know that they will not be setting the rules of the new economic environment, although they will be forced to play by them.

This story, of course, is well-known and shares much in common with that of Russia and other postcommunist countries. Styrnyk notes "that the train has left the station" and now the unions must work with the conditions they have, since the process cannot be undone.[70] This may be fair enough now, but there is little indication from her or others that Ukrainian unions learned anything from the experience of their neighbors (which marketized and privatized before Ukraine did). It is puzzling how union leaders in Ukraine can genuinely express surprise at the outcome of the process, given what occurred elsewhere, especially in Russia.

Above all else, one item is clear: the current economic conditions have dramatically hurt organized labor. Given the bankruptcy of the state, the weaknesses of the legal system, and employee dependence upon employers and fear of job loss, there is little that unions can do for their members. These circumstances obviously affect the popular view of unions as ineffective, bloated behemoths. While privatization is by itself not to blame for the crisis in Ukraine (although it is arguable whether it has made the preexisting crisis better or worse), it has led to much confusion and buck passing to and from companies and government officials. The head of the construction workers' union asked:

> What can we do? People come to us. They say, "Help us. We want our wages. They are not paying us." [Metallurgical] companies request work, and then refuse to pay. So we go the state, and the state says we have no money, and besides, it is not our business. We do not manage the firm. So we go to the managers, and they also say we have no money. Sure, we can take them to court, but this takes time and in the end, there is not a legal base in the country to enforce any decision. If the choice is between paying workers or bankruptcy, the state is not going to force a big company to go out of business. In the end, the worker sees how powerless we are, and of course we suffer for this.[71]

Economic conditions have caused other problems for union organizations in the country. Due to falling membership (and hence fewer union dues), union budgets have to be cut back. At the enterprise level, arguably the most important one, what this means is that the union can no longer offer full-time support to union representatives. These individuals now must work part-time at the enterprise as well, which limits their time for union work as well as creating dependency upon the owners.[72] Moreover, the shortage of state funds creates interunion battles as unions from various sectors attempt to "pull the blanket over themselves" and win benefits for their own members from the state budget.[73] In particular, divisions are being created among workers in the public sector with low salaries (e.g., doctors, teachers), those formerly in the state sector but still lobbying for state subsidies to boost production and salaries (e.g., miners, defense workers), and those fortunate few with high paying (by Ukrainian standards) jobs in sectors that do not need or want state support (oil and gas workers are the clearest case of this group). Thus, as elsewhere, organized labor as a whole is hampered in its ability to articulate a coherent strategy to deal with many of the common problems it faces.

The above are important and often mentioned concerns, but have privatization or private owners directly harmed unions in Ukraine? On this front the evidence is far sketchier. Inna Styrnyk does try to paint as rosy a picture as she can, noting that unions have representation on the State Property Board and on company boards, so that union voices are heard and the worst abuses can be prevented.[74] Again, however, most branch- and enterprise-level union leaders have little positive to report. The head of the Autoworkers' Union notes that privatization has yet to result in clear ownership or responsibility, as even today he is not sure who is the true owner of a given enterprise.[75] One common refrain is that state owners "knew" the trade unions and that channels of communication and responsibility were far clearer under the old system. Under the new system, unions must work harder, and given multiple owners and the fracturing of the command-administrative system, coordination among enterprise-level unions within a branch becomes much more difficult.[76] Another problem, as we have seen elsewhere, is that privatization has often meant the breakup of large firms into smaller ones and that this has presented a major obstacle to the organizational capacity of trade unions. One leader noted that in the past in his sector (textiles) the average size of an enterprise was four thousand workers. Now, the largest employ only four hundred workers, and employment also tends to be far more temporary than in the past; thus, it has been harder for him to maintain and coordinate union activity.[77]

For their part, private owners, many trade union leaders assert, either do not want trade unions or are unfamiliar with them. For example, one union leader noted problems at the Klemenchutsky Truck Factory in Poltava. There, the owners typically do not respect collective agreements and grant unions only the power to administer social programs, as they did in the past. "If we bring up wages or work safety issues or something like this, they push us aside and ignore us, and they know they can get away with this."[78] Svetlana Rodina of the Unions in the Agro-Industrial Sector, notes that her union—the largest branch union in the country—has had many problems with new, private owners. Not only do objective economic conditions give them the ability to control workers' activism by threatening to fire workers, but important subjective factors can matter as well. "These owners do not appear out of nowhere," she claims. "They do not become owners by accident and many are not, let's say, very principled. They know the local authorities, judges, etc. All of them are in their favor, and we have been rather defenseless against them."[79] This comment reveals one of the many problems with *nomenklatura* privatization: owners use their political connections to escape legal, social, and economic responsibility. It not only places workers in a worse position but is hardly economically efficient.

Of course, not all union leaders grouse about privatization. The leader of the oil and gas workers, for example, praised the management at Ukrnafta (the country's largest company by value), where wages are the highest in the country (1,000 hrivna a month, about $200) and benefits are of high quality.[80] However, among the industrial branch unions, his was the exception: that is, there is not much sectoral variation in the country, at least from the unions' perspective. The traditional unions are struggling to preserve what they can, and they have been unable to seize any potential advantages offered by privatization. In particular, they (meaning the FPU unions and the branch alternative unions) have little interest in making overtures to nonunionized workers in the nonstate sector (mostly at new firms, many of which, because they are unregistered or pay no taxes, could be considered in the shadow economy). For example, in construction, one of the sectors with the largest number of small, start-up businesses, attempts to form unions in such companies have gone nowhere, with the owners refusing to extend the contracts of workers who express interest in trade unions.[81]

Several "unions" in the nonstate sector, most of which were founded in the early 1990s, purport to represent the workers at new, small businesses, enterprises typically ignored by or unable to fit into the FPU. According to government data, as of 1999 there were 197,127 small businesses (generally with fewer than fifty employees) employing 1.68 million people, almost 10 percent of the nonagricultural workforce.[82] Many of these workers had lost their jobs in the industrial sector, in which employment has declined precipitously since 1990. Most of these enterprises have no trade union, but some do belong to "union" organizations, the largest of which is the Union of Workers in Innovative and Small Businesses, numbering eighty thousand members. However, these unions appear to be much more interested in facilitating small business development than in protecting the rights of workers in the sector. The president of the aforementioned union was emphatic that there could be no conflict of interest between employees and employers in small businesses. In his view, the employees should count themselves lucky to have a job. As for the suggestion that employers could exploit the current economic downturn to their advantage, he replied, "*C'est la vie.* That is the reality of the transition period."[83] Given this attitude, it would be fair to say that there are no true *workers'* unions in this sector.

However, while there have been some negative effects of privatization, it would be difficult to say that matters are that much, or any, better at state enterprises. Salaries tend to be lower, and chronic budget problems make wage arrears crises acute. True, workers such as teachers have shown a better capacity for organizing to put their salary demands to the state, and their protests do carry a certain amount of political resonance, but given their meager earnings, it would be hard to call the teachers privileged in any sense. Volnyets of the NPGU says that miners have suffered equally under private and state ownership, and in fact notes that he has been able to get along better with some (although by no means all) private owners than the state, which for political reasons has been openly hostile to his union.[84] Yan'shyn of the Construction Workers notes that the state will order work and then not pay and that given the multiple demands by the state, his union is near powerless to defend the workers.[85] Viktor Stepanov of the Longshoremen's Union notes that nothing has changed at his state-owned port, where the director and the city mayor (both stalwarts in the Communist Party under Soviet times) have close ties, and this obviously hampers his efforts to use local courts to win recognition for his union.[86] Indeed, given the state's general position toward the alternative unions, it is no surprise that they have tended to favor privatization. For the FPU's part, the struggles in the state sector help explain why it has continued to support, in principle, privatization and has generally eschewed the reactionary positions of the Communist Party.

It is interesting, however, to consider some of the cases praised as successes by union leaders. One case is the Bukhovina Pastry Factory in Chernovsti oblast'. It has bolstered its production in recent years and has been hiring more workers. Its average wage is a meager 297 hrivna per month (less than $40), but *Profspilkovi visti*, the FPU newspaper, praised management for giving birthday presents to workers and throwing evening parties on occasion.[87] The leader of the Aviation Workers' Union singled out Motor Sich in Zaporizhzhe as a very successful company, where production has grown in recent years and social activities have been preserved. However, according to his own data, the average salary at this "successful" enterprise is only 350 hrivna as of December 2000, 200 hrivna less than the minimum necessary salary according to the FPU estimates and thirty hrivna less than the average in his sector.[88]

These examples lead to questions of what constitutes a success and what role the unions envision for themselves. Clearly, the emphasis is on job security and production, which is perhaps understandable but means that the union is still playing part of its Soviet-era "dual role." However, there also continues to be an emphasis on the social sphere even if, as in the examples above, its maintenance may cut into workers' salaries. From the union perspective, various social activities—sanatoria, kindergartens, clubs, control over social insurance monies—are at minimum an important tool to motivate membership, and, at worst, as some critics charge, they constitute a slush fund from which unions can skim off the top. For employers, delegating social work to the unions keeps them quiescent and is probably cheaper than raising salaries. In this regard, the paternalist firm continues to be the norm in Ukraine (as opposed to a Western-style "flexible firm"), confirmed by a 2000 ILO survey of nearly seventeen hundred establishments employing over one million workers. The investigators suggest that this style of firm governance (indicated by variables such as extensive social benefits, nonmonetary payment of wages) is conditioned by insider ownership.[89]

Thus, at the firm level, there are fewer changes in Ukraine in management-labor relations than in our other cases, which is to be expected given Ukraine's slower pace of structural change. Most unions seemed satisfied with this arrangement, at least to the extent that they are working on familiar terrain and have not had to alter many of their most basic functions. However, a few union leaders are recognizing that emphasis on social aspects may be misplaced. Revealing were comments by Vasil Yan'shyn of the Construction Workers Union:

> When I went to Austria, I talked to union leaders about cooperation and exchanges, and I proposed to arrange sports competitions or send our children to each other's camps. These types of things, you understand, are traditionally what we have done. They had no idea what I was talking about. "We have nothing to do with such things," they said. . . . Then I saw the attention they gave to details of collective agreements, and how they were able to gain advantages for their workers, and how the average salary was so high. Now I think to myself, what the hell are we doing with these childrens' camps when we can't even get decent wages for our workers?[90]

In 2001, control of social insurance monies—including distribution of vacation accommodations—was stripped from the unions and put into the hands of a tripartite (government, business, labor) commission. Most alternative unions cheered this decision, as they saw FPU control of these funds as a means for the FPU to coerce workers into staying with their union. The FPU, for its part, is worried about the consequences of this action, with some leaders frankly fearful that this will harm motivation for membership.[91]

Clearly, Ukraine still has a long way to go before its transition is complete. Union leaders are quick to note that they still must learn how to function in a marketized system, but that with time they will become more successful in gaining workers' trust and defending their members' rights. This sounds optimistic, except that this refrain was equally commonplace in 1993–1994, when I first began examining labor issues in the country. The years of economic changes that have followed since my initial research have yielded little for unions, and I wonder if it is too late to hope for the resurgence of organized labor in Ukraine.

Trade Unions and Globalization

In issues of globalization, it is apparent once again how Ukraine lags behind most of its neighbors. For example, Ukraine's total exports in 1999 totaled $12.4 billion, compared to $21.8 billion for Hungary and $26.3 billion for Poland. This figure, it is worth mentioning, actually represents a drop from the value of exports in 1993, whereas the value of exports in the two Central European countries doubled in the same period.[92] While exports do amount to about 40 percent of GDP (higher than Poland's 25 percent), detailed studies show that Ukrainian firms have managed to gain few export markets outside the former Soviet republics.[93] For better or worse, Ukraine has also not been the most reliable candidate of the IMF and other international financial institutions, first winning substantial international support in 1994 after it signed the Non-Proliferation Treaty, but then subjected to repeated cut-offs due to political instability and failure to follow through on implementation guidelines. As for foreign investment, Ukraine attracted a mere $3.9 billion in its first nine years of independence (1992–2000), about $70 per capita, a pittance compared to Poland's $518 and Hungary's $1,764 per capita for the 1990s.[94] Part of the problem is geography and lack of natural resources, but other factors such as rapacious bureaucrats, unstable legislation, political uncertainty, the lack of a law on land ownership, and poor infrastructure have hampered the country's ability to attract the attention of investors.

How have the unions been affected by this? Given that trade patterns have not significantly altered in the past ten years and that Ukraine has been no slave to forceful dictates by the IMF,[95] it makes most sense to focus on foreign investment, which is a new variable for the unions. However, given its small volume, relative novelty, and concentration in just a few sectors (construction, food processing, and auto production), only tentative conclusions can be drawn. Indeed, the ILO representative in Kyiv noted that the Ukrainian government could not even produce a report on MNCs and labor practices in Ukraine for the ILO.[96]

That being said, what is striking in Ukraine is the generally favorable view of foreign companies held by union leaders. In part, this is easily understandable. Most branches are in desperate need of investment; foreigners can provide what domestic sources cannot. In those few sectors where there has been foreign investment, the general impression is that unions are happy to have it. The head of the Autoworkers' Union spoke about his experience with Daewoo, in 2001 the largest single foreign investor in Ukraine, which has put millions of dollars into a formerly idle plant now employing sixteen thousand workers in Zaporizhzhe. He claims wages are relatively high and are paid on time (this was before Daewoo announced its bankruptcy in late 2001), and he has far more complaints against "New Ukrainians" who have purchased enterprises in his sector. He noted, "For us, the situation is a bit paradoxical. We know about globalization and we know how Western unions are wary of it. However, if a factory is closed, and people are not working, and an investor comes in and puts in money, creates jobs, and production increases, how can we complain? The choice is obvious."[97] The president of the gas and oil workers echoed this sentiment, noting that for nationalistic reasons he may not be happy with Lukoil's prospective purchase of a refinery in Odessa and that he does have concerns about Lukoil's "company union" policy, but "Lukoil will buy the refinery, people will come back to work, and wages will be higher than they were before. As a union leader, I am in favor of this, of any owner or capital that can create jobs."[98] Yan'shyn of the Construction Workers' Union complained that Ukrainian laws are poor, and he wishes that Makoland, an Austrian firm that restored a building adjacent to Bezarabskyj Rynok, had been able to conclude more contracts in Kyiv.[99] Even in L'viv, often portrayed as a rabidly nationalist region, local union leaders conceded that they would support Russian efforts to buy the moribund L'viv Bus Factory, which has been unable to attract any domestic or Western investment.[100] In the agro-industrial sector, where there are many joint ventures in processing plants and breweries, investors have by and large been willing to work with the existing trade unions, and union leaders have a generally favorable view of foreign investors.[101]

There are, of course, exceptions, but most of these investments are at green-field sites where the foreign owners did not inherit a trade union. This has been true for Coca-Cola, as well as for the new joint ventures Ukraine International Airlines and Aerosvit, both of which (unlike the domestic air carriers in Ukraine) do not have trade unions. However, union leaders note that green-field investments in Ukraine have been the exception rather than the rule, as foreign investors have found it preferable to put money into an existing Ukrainian firm and find a Ukrainian partner to navigate the labyrinth of bureaucratic requirements.[102] The most divisive case—one mentioned on three separate occasions by parties not even involved in the dispute—has been at the Lutsk Ball Bearing Plant, which was purchased by the Swedish firm STF. Here, according to one trade union leader at the plant,[103] the owners have physically attacked would-be union organizers, engaged the militia to have them followed, and sued them for defamation of character. These activists are from the alternative Capital-Regions union; the FPU union present at the plant has not been harassed, although its critics accuse it of being a toady for management. However, a problem such as this—intimidation of union leaders, especially of those outside the FPU—is hardly unique to MNCs, and indeed it is questionable how important the variable of *foreign* ownership is here. In this case, as in some instances in the auto industry in L'viv, there has also been fear that the foreign owner is purchasing Ukrainian firms with the aim of destroying a potential competitor and thus ensuring the viability of the home country's firms. Unions have reported agreements with firms and local governments to ensure that this does not take place.[104]

There is one union in Ukraine, the Union of Workers in Joint Ventures, which is specifically designed to unify firms with foreign capital. This union purports to represent about one thousand enterprises (employing fifteen thousand people) out of the approximately four thousand joint ventures in the country.[105] It thus focuses on smaller businesses. Its leader notes that some companies are rabidly antiunion (he pointed to the Bila retail chain) and that workers in joint ventures often see little need for a union since they typically receive higher salaries and other benefits. However, as with the Union of Workers in Small and Medium Size Businesses, to call this organization a trade union would be a stretch. Much of its efforts are involved in lobbying for a better business climate, and its greatest accomplishment was going to court to gain access to social insurance funds. Its leader insists that workers and owners should be represented by a single organization—this is "natural," in his view. And, to top it off, the perks of membership include an on-site massage center and spa at union headquarters in Kyiv as well as access to a machine costing tens of thousands of dollars that can perform a complete chemical analysis of your body from examining a single hair (I would not believe this unless I had seen it!).[106]

Given the limited scope of foreign investment in the country, it is impossible to come up with comprehensive data or even a more comprehensive survey of union leaders, since so few of them have significant experience with foreign firms and investors. At present, it does not appear that globalization has really added any constraints or complications for trade unions, but this is because Ukraine is still very early in the process of opening up to the outside world. With time, then, globalization and its attendant challenges could present unions with more problems. However, now most union leaders would actually welcome more globalization—be it in the form of aid, more exports, or more investment. Its absence in most sectors of the economy helps maintain a grim predicament for most Ukrainian workers and their unions.

8

Conclusion

IN ORDER TO TIE TOGETHER in a more systemic and comparative fashion various strands of thoughts and arguments in this volume, my conclusion has three primary aims: to account for labor's weakness, particularly with respect to the effects of structural economic changes and global economic factors; to suggest if and how labor's weakness has explicit political consequences; and to postulate what developmental paths are open to unions in these states today.

Accounting for Unions' Decline in the East

Organized labor's weakness has been taken as a virtual given in this work, although the country studies provide plenty of reinforcement for this claim. More interesting, in my view, is identifying the factors that have put labor in this predicament. Others have tried to address this question by examining, among other variables, the role of discourse and ideology, the institutional and cultural heritage of the communist past, and the effects of economic crisis on unions. Certainly, these have played a role, but one aim of this work has been to link union weakness in postcommunist states with the decline of unions in Western democracies by suggesting how structural economic change and globalization (two factors that will not fade with time, as other variables might) are creating a new political economy that may permanently handicap unions.

Is this in fact the case? Before answering, let us back up a bit and identify the trends we are witnessing across the four countries examined in this book. True, as noted at the outset of this study, each country has its own particular features, whether related to the pace of reform and the results of economic changes or issues more specific to trade unions (e.g., union density, union political visibility, interunion competition, union activities and strategies). However, in broad strokes, the following trends can be identified, none of which is particularly encouraging from a trade unionist's standpoint:

Deunionization. Under communism, trade union density was nearly 100 percent. In just over a decade, union density has dropped markedly, and few think that the fall in membership has bottomed out today. It continues to fall, both in countries such as Poland that have longer experience with economic reform (union density in Poland today is under 20 percent), and in states like Ukraine, where union membership is roughly half what it was in 1991.

Competition among Trade Union Federations. The end of the party-state has also meant an end to a single, monopolistic trade union federation. All countries now have multiple trade union organizations, although in some countries such as Russia and Ukraine, alternative unions exist in only a few sectors, primarily coal mining and transport. While competition among unions corresponds with ideals of democratic pluralism, many unionists note that it hampers creation of a unified trade union movement, complicates the work of tripartite bodies, and allows governments and employers to play unions off each other.

Competition within Trade Union Federations. This issue is less obvious than the often politicized competition among different union federations, but it is nonetheless important. Unions are competing for resources from state budgets, and workers in the same branch are implicitly competing with workers at different enterprises, hoping that their enterprise will succeed and become more profitable than its competitors. Rhetoric of common interests aside, the interests of different branch- and enterprise-level unions will often diverge, and this hampers the emergence of a more unified labor movement.

Political Marginalization of Trade Unions. In all countries, trade unions have made alliances with political parties and coalitions. While trade unions have generally been ineffective in electoral politics in Russia and Ukraine (at best they have been minor players in large coalitions behind the president), they have backed winning parties in Poland and Hungary, and in these states trade union leaders played prominent roles in the government. However, for a variety of reasons, only rarely has this translated into substantial political power in terms of advancing policies that are explicitly proworker.

Ineffectiveness of Tripartite, Corporatist Bodies. All states have adopted tripartite bodies for social partnership or national reconciliation, and unions have placed great hope in these structures, being aware of the important roles that they have played in several countries in Western Europe. However, these bodies have rarely been effective in advancing union goals, as trade union leaders can point to modest accomplishments only, or can simply note that such a body exists and has the *potential* to give a voice to labor. To date, however, that voice has been frequently ignored.

Lack of Trust in Trade Unions. Unions do not enjoy high public standing in these states. True, most institutions of government suffer a crisis of confidence, but unions usually rank near the bottom. One could speculate as to why (they are seen as relics of the past, they are viewed as tainted by communism or corruption, they fail to deliver the goods), but there is little doubt that the lack of popular confidence in unions has weakened them both at the national and at the enterprise level.

Workers' Ownership Is a Chimera. Economic reform, particularly privatization, was sold to the population as an opportunity, specifically as an opportunity to become owners and shareholders. Workers, in particular, were granted rights to purchase shares of their enterprises at a discount, and this procedure was frequently used, especially in Poland and Russia. However, ordinary workers fared poorly in this bargain, as managers, classified as workers for purposes of these transactions, frequently were able to acquire real ownership of the firm. "Workers' self-management," a slogan popularized in the last decades of communism, proved to be illusionary. As a result, most industrial workers, a relatively privileged group under communism and the heart of any would-be labor movement, became one of several losers in the economic reforms in the region, losing their job security and high wages along with promises of a meaningful voice at their place of employment.

However, in accounting for union decline, what seems to stand out most clearly from this study is another trend.

Unions' Virtual Absence in New Sectors of the Economy. This finding is pretty clear. Unions have survived—certainly not thrived, but they are holding on—in the ever-shrinking state sector and in large (and mostly unprofitable) industrial enterprises that date from communist times. Unions are far rarer in new industrial plants (although there are some, to be sure), and they are almost entirely absent in the nascent service or white-collar sectors (e.g., banking, insurance, retail). They are also less likely to be found in small firms, most of which are in the service sector, but also in the smaller industrial plants that were created when giant conglomerates were broken up. In some cases, unions have died of atrophy or of employer hostility. In others, unions have not been formed, either because employees saw little need, the problem of collective action could not be overcome (e.g., organizing costs), or employers were hostile. In many cases, unions have survived or have been formed, but sizeable percentages of workers at the enterprise have chosen not to join, either because they do not like the union or choose to "free ride" on the collective agreements that will cover them regardless of union affiliation.

The question, however, is why unions are seen in some sectors and enterprises and not in others. One obvious suspect, certainly, is privatization, which has been a major subject of this study. Does privatization harm unions? Certainly, for many unionists, the answer to this question is an obvious yes, and there is a significant amount of data to suggest a correlation between privatization and deunionization (taking the latter as a variable for weak unions), insofar as workers at private firms, which tend to be newer, smaller, and in the service sector, are less likely to be unionized.

Does this correlation prove causality? While it is tempting to say yes and leave it at that, it should be recognized that the story is a bit more complex than simply Privatization = Weak Trade Unions. First, most trade unions have seen membership decline because of job loss in their sectors. This is true regardless of whether the sector has been privatized. As Boris Misnik of the Russian Mining and Metallurgical Workers' Union noted, "It is not privatization but rather obsolete production and uncompetitive products that are the reason for unemployment,"[1] and deunionization could easily be substituted for unemployment in this sentence. In other words, any sort of economic reform, even one that was not based upon private ownership, would have led to job losses and movement into different sectors of the economy less likely to be unionized. Communist economies were *over* unionized, and thus movement toward a more modern system of production and a more balanced economy (with more service sectors and smaller firms) would result in a loss of union membership. The massive erosion of trade unions in sectors such as coal mining, railroads, and defense industries (still state-owned for the most part) cannot be attributed to privatization by itself but rather is the result of economic restructuring that make profit and loss the basis of a firm's survivability.

Of course, this is not to say that private owners—whether those in new firms or in privatized ones—have done nothing to harm trade unions. In each country, we have seen that some owners are explicitly antiunion and get away with an array of activities that do not occur in state-owned firms or in the public sectors (e.g., among doctors, teachers, etc.). In some cases, this activity is relatively benign (e.g., pay higher wages or create superior working conditions so workers feel there is no need for a union), but in others it has included harassment, intimidation, and firing of would-be union members. Unfortunately, it is very difficult to quantify how often this occurs, although the Polish case surveys reported that 16 percent of nonunionized workers said that efforts to create a union were foiled by management.[2] Obviously, this is a problem, and in this way there is clearly a link between private ownership and weaker trade unions.

However, a couple of amendments should be considered. First, workers do enjoy strong legal rights to form trade unions. Harassment and intimidation by management are illegal. If the legal regime were stronger or if unions had more resources, especially legal staff, owners would be less able to get away with such behavior. Also, the tight labor market plays into this as well. If workers feel lucky just to have a job, even a nonunionized one with a hostile owner, they will be less likely to risk starting a union and will be more likely to back down when faced with threats from management if they do try to establish a union. Thus, while form of ownership does create some motivation for union busting (e.g., maximize profits), the opportunities are enhanced by some particular features of postcommunist states.

Moreover, other factors besides private ownership may inhibit unionization. As one Russian trade union official explained to me, it would be silly to think of forming a union in a barbershop in which there is the owner and a couple of employees.[3] True, there could be an interenterprise union of barbershop employees that would collect dues and mediate grievances between owners and their employees, but I would venture to guess that no such union exists anywhere in the world. In the past decade, a number of such micro-businesses have sprung up across the region, not to mention the millions who are now self-employed. These businesses will remain nonunion, and unions have given up efforts to organize workers in such enterprises.[4] Thus, it is not just privatization that has harmed unions, but problems of size and sector as well.

Another factor is unions' own shortcomings with respect to organizing new affiliates. Most unions, rightly or wrongly, have been forced on the defensive, holding on to what little they have. Few have the resources, skills, and access to recruit new union members or, harder still, start new union affiliates in nonunionized enterprises. Together with the most generic type of collective action problem—who will incur the costs of organizing?—this can go a long way to explain the lack of unionization in many firms.

Does this mean private owners should be let off the hook? No. But, it bears repeating, most trade union leaders were not hostile to privatization or private owners per se, and many could point to some positive experiences with private ownership (usually higher wages, but often more managerial competence, occasionally a better understanding of labor-management relations). Certainly, some owners are better than others, and thus to say private owners are always bad is impossible (no union leader I talked to said this, even though my line of questioning often may have encouraged such a response).

However, I would point to one structural factor about private ownership that does inhibit growth of a union movement (as opposed to individual, enterprise-level unions). Privatization brings with it a certain degree of decentralization. Before, there was one owner in the whole economy; now, there are several in each sector, and firms compete among each other. To date, owners in most sectors have eschewed the creation of strong employers' organizations. They value independence and flexibility and typically unite only to lobby the government for some type of industrywide subsidy or protection (e.g., car manufacturers in Russia). Given their decentralization, it is hard to create centralized union structures and make corporatist structures work. Collective agreements are rare in those sectors dominated by private employers, whereas they are relatively common in sectors in which the state remains the dominant employer. A decentralized system of industrial relations may allow unions to survive, and some workers can benefit under such arrangements, but it is questionable what this type of system means for trade union movements.

What of globalization, a bête noire of labor activists in much of the Western world? On this score, it is also difficult to make black-and-white arguments. On the one hand, there is little doubt that governments, businesses, and unions in the postcommunist world must take into account a global context. They must operate under constraints, lest profligate spending or passage of certain laws lead to loss of IMF credits, capital flight, or uncompetitive business. Postcommunist countries also do not have much clout in the international marketplace, and we have seen in several states that the IMF has more say in crafting government policy than workers or ordinary citizens. Whether this is justified by economic rationality is an important question, and as noted previously, Stone argues that IMF policies designed to limit inflation have been instrumental in securing economic stability.[5] This is no mean feat, and society as a whole can perhaps benefit from sage IMF advice, but it is also important to consider how IMF diktat is compatible with democracy and what such policies do to particular groups within society, especially industrial workers, who bore the brunt of IMF austerity measures when they were implemented.

The result has been a deindustrialization of most postcommunist countries, and job growth, to the extent it has existed (and even in the Polish case of high growth in the 1990s unemployment remained high), has been in sectors less conducive to unionization. From the perspective of the West, all of this may seem perfectly natural or rational (since this has been the trend in the West for years), but there is little doubt in the postcommunist context that it has weakened the position of organized labor, a key actor in the civil society that was supposed to be the catalyst and beneficiary of democratization. If and how this matters for democracy is a question that will be addressed later in the chapter, but surely there is a connection between the demands of an IMF-defined economic orthodoxy and the weakening of trade unions, as unions generally lack the resources to combat IMF-supported policies. As for the broader question of international trade, the argument about competitiveness can be employed by government and business to justify a host of policies (low wages, poor environmental standards, mass layoffs) harmful to workers in the aggregate (although, again, some workers may benefit). This result has occurred in a variety of postcommunist countries, although some workers in some competitive sectors have gained from engagement in the world economy.

One particular focus in this study has been on MNCs. Are they as harmful to unions as they are often accused of being? Certainly, negative examples abound, and greenfield MNC investments in the region are frequently nonunion, although whether this is because of MNC hostility or some other factors (e.g., collective action problems in creating new unions) is hard to say. However, many firms tolerate trade unions, and some (e.g., Volkswagen, Danone) encourage them. Certainly, trade unionists in the region are aware of the dangers of MNCs, and most can point to negative experiences in their own country.

However, what was interesting and in some ways surprising in my research is that I found little visceral hostility in principle to MNCs in the region. The typical response—encountered in all countries—was that yes, it would be better if Polish/Russian/Hungarian/Ukrainian capital could come and rejuvenate this particular business or branch, but, sadly, we don't have the money, so we need foreign investment and we, as unionists, want to see more of it in our sector in order to preserve jobs and decent wages and give our industry a real future. Of course, many would add that the government has to protect workers against abuses, but given the alternative between plant closures and foreign takeover, there really was not a choice—even for ostensible nationalists in western Ukraine. Moreover, many union leaders volunteered that local owners (or local managers of MNCs) were worse than foreign managers or owners, the latter usually having more experience with independent trade unions. This is an interesting finding, although it may say more about the bad behavior of Russian *biznesmeny* than the virtues of Western capitalists. Thus, for the general claim made by many opponents of globalization that MNCs harm trade unions and workers, the postcommunist world does not provide systemic evidence, although, of course, it does provide plenty of anecdotes of negative experiences with particular MNCs. However, an important point is that the presence of MNCs—which generally pay more and often strive to create work cultures that differentiate their enterprises from domestic ones—does appear to contribute to the discernible lack of union solidarity within countries in the region.

The more general convergence hypothesis, that globalization tends to produce a homogeneous type of labor relations system that generally does not empower labor, is not, strictly speaking, supported by the evidence, insofar as states have managed to pursue different strategies of reform. However, the general picture—that marketization and globalization have contributed to the weakening of labor laws, that regimes of all types have refused to engage unions systemically, that neocorporatist institutions are weak, that social welfare benefits have declined markedly—is quite negative for the unions. True, scholars of Western European systems have noted that globalization has not produced convergence, insofar as countries with strong unions and encompassing corporatist systems have managed, at least through the 1990s, to resist movement to Anglo-American variants of more laissez-faire capitalism.[6] However, the key point for our purposes is that the postcommunist countries did not enter the marketized, globalized world with strong unions or corporatist structures, and thus they have been unable to construct unions or prounion institutions given the demands of privatization and global markets. To the extent that weakness of labor tends to be the norm in much of the world (Sweden, Denmark, and Finland, commonly invoked by the anti-convergence group, are definitely outliers in this respect), this study would lend credence to arguments that tend to be downbeat about globalization's impact on organized labor.

Last, let me add a few words about the European Union, an international factor of increasing relevance to Poland and Hungary. Unions in both of these countries support EU accession, which finally occurred in May 2004. Union leaders believe EU accession will widen economic opportunities for their members through trade and labor mobility, although the latter will not come on the day of accession. EU laws may also offer protection to workers and encourage social dialogue (particularly provisions for the European Works Councils), but remember, the laws that were on the books (and in some cases are in the process of being dismantled) were very prolabor, so the gain in the legal regime may be marginal or even a net negative. Of more interest to me, however, is the open question of how the loss of sovereignty associated with EU membership will affect national-level bargaining. In other words, because of EU directives, certain items (e.g., tariffs) will be off the table—governments, employers, and unions cannot negotiate them. True, there will be a European forum for lobbying and negotiation, but it is uncertain how much of a role Eastern European labor will have in it. One concern is that of the various levels of social dialogue—European, national, branch, and enterprise—European Union membership, by adding a level even farther away from average citizens and workers and potentially taking many items off the national and even branch table, will give unions only one realistic option: focus on local, enterprise-level concerns, a trend that is already emerging. This may sound relatively benign, but something to consider is what happens to organized labor as a movement and as a political force in such a scenario.

What Are the Consequences?

This study has documented the weaknesses of trade unions in a number of states and across a number of dimensions. But a larger question looms over the changes in the industrial relations systems: does it matter *politically* that trade unions are so enfeebled? More broadly, what does their weakness say about postcommunist democratization and how does consideration of trade unions add to our understanding of processes of democratization?

As to the question of whether it matters, let us consider a hypothetical situation. Let us suppose that unions were strong, trusted by their members, mobilizing workers against abuses by management, lobbying the government on socioeconomic policies, and courted by political parties. Instead of workers' passivity in the face of severe economic crisis, there would be workers' activism. Instead of interunion bickering, imagine a situation in which unions could pool their resources and present a unified front on important issues. If the government failed to live up to its promises to workers, it would be held accountable, in the streets and at the ballot box. Reform measures would have to take into account the position of organized labor. Winners of elections would be beholden to trade unions, not oligarchs or the dictates of international financial institutions.

How different all of these countries would look! While recognizing the problems associated with hypothetical arguments, I think this line of reasoning makes it very clear that the weakness of organized labor *does* matter. In an important sense, it would turn the whole postcommunist transition experience upside down, with workers, not capital (to invoke the Marxist dichotomy), calling the shots. Of course, some would say this would be impossible—a social-democratic fantasy (or nightmare, depending upon your own political inclinations)—and further, as one observer of the Russian case added, "if the unions were effective in defending their members, the regime would try to repress them."[7] This, of course, speaks volumes about the existing political economy in these states if labor activism is written off as impossible or as something that no "democratic" government could countenance. However, the point is that a strong labor movement could have forced the government to pay more attention to social issues, implement a more civilized form of privatization, uphold the rule of law, and take action on problems such as the wage arrears crisis. While some economic problems were without question unavoidable, governments did have choices. In the Russian case, reform was rushed through despite public opposition to many policies and the lack of institutional development to ensure its success. In Ukraine, from 1992 to 1994 reform was minimal, despite the impact of economic depression on living standards. Reform, when it came, lacked both a well-developed social dimension and basic standards of transparency, producing generally the same results as in Russia. In Poland, despite the rhetoric that there was no alternative to shock therapy, the government, if pushed by the trade union components of Solidarity, could have designed a different program that would have paid more attention to the social costs of reforms.

Of course, while conceding that it *could* have been done differently, arguably strong organized labor would only have made matters worse. In other words, this hypothetical world would not necessarily be a better one, as unions would have had the capacity to undermine needed and economically rational reforms. For example, following Anders Aslund, Russia's problem was perhaps that it abandoned shock therapy too soon due to a variety of social pressures (mainly from enterprise directors, not unions)[8] and that, given labor's opposition to Yeltsin's program, a stronger labor movement would have made adoption of many "necessary reforms" impossible. This argument holds throughout the region, of course, given that unions did have a desire to defend many elements of the old system (e.g., job security, extensive labor rights, high levels of social spending) that were both impossible to sustain over the long haul and incompatible with a neoliberal economic order. Battles in all four countries over changes in the labor code—changes designed to create more flexibility for employers, changes that are argued to be necessary to alleviate chronic unemployment in countries such as France and Germany as well—would have multiplied several times over, and in this respect our hypothetical world (again, perhaps depending upon your political orientation) would not look so attractive. Moreover, a strong labor movement could have precipitated greater political instability, as protests would be rampant and democracy as government of the people could have become government by a mob.

However, on this score it is important to note a couple of points. First, the postcommunist country with the strongest labor movement, Slovenia, as measured by successful collective bargaining, enjoys both the highest wages and one of the most solid democracies and joined the EU in 2004.[9] This is not meant to imply that there is a cause and effect between the unions and the country's success, only to suggest that stronger unions need not lead to acute economic or political problems. More generally, however, the conclusions of the 1996 World Development Report of the World Bank stressed that in postcommunist countries "establishing a social consensus will be crucial for the long-term success of the transition," because "cross-country analyses suggest that societies that are very unequal in terms of income or assets tend to be politically and socially less stable and to have lower rates of investment and growth."[10] To the extent that unions strive for greater equality—and to the extent that weak unions were in many cases pushed aside in the redistribution of state property—union weakness matters and is detrimental to the country.

Antitrade union arguments are interesting for another reason. They reveal the disjuncture between the rhetoric of the importance of civil society and the consideration of real players in civil society. In other words, these arguments suggest that some actors in civil society—actors that represent millions and are recognized as legitimate political participants in Western democracies—are a danger to postcommunist democracy and marketization. Taken to its logical conclusion, marketization and democratization are incompatible, and only authoritarian systems can push through wide ranging reforms. Despite the belief of some that this contention is in fact true (witnessed by the admiration of the Chinese or Pinochet model by some in the region), it lacks empirical support.[11]

However, it is true that some labor movements, in the postcommunist context, while not necessarily wholly antireform, would have wanted to preserve many elements of the old system, particularly social guarantees. This need not mean, though, that the demands of marketization should have been or should be privileged over the demands of democratization. If democratization is to be pursued seriously, it may be necessary to abandon purely economic considerations of efficiency or sticking to a certain theoretically informed blueprint. While achieving social consensus on a reform program would have been difficult, it need not have been impossible, particularly if international financial agencies were not beholden to neoliberal dogmatism. The fact is, of course, that the reforms as adopted, resulting in the political marginalization of labor, served the interests of only a few, creating a political economy that few citizens see as particularly just. In Russia and Ukraine, the situation is even direr, producing a kleptocracy or oligarchic corporatism.[12] Strong groups in civil society such as trade unions could have mitigated the main problems in both of these states—overcentralization of authority and lack of checks on both political and economic power. More generally, the imposition of market reforms from above with little input from below flies in the face of what transitologists would recommend about social pacts to legitimate the new order. Of course, given thorny questions like property redistribution, it may have been difficult to forge such a pact, but there was no real effort to do so.

Some may still be unconvinced that union weakness has any strictly political consequences. Yes, economic reforms were distorted a bit (in some countries more than in others), but in many countries, particularly those like Poland and Hungary, now in the EU, democracy is secure, the "only game in town," Juan Linz and Alfred Stepan's criteria of a consolidated democracy.[13] However, before making this assertion it may be worthwhile to ask how citizens in postcommunist countries evaluate their current political system. Data from the European Values Survey, conducted among representative samples across thirty-one countries in 1999–2000, are presented in table 8.1.[14]

Several items are worth comment. First, predictably, the mean evaluation of the existing political system in postcommunist countries tends to be lower

Table 8.1 Dissatisfaction with Democracy in Various Countries

Country	Those not satisfied with how democracy is developing (%)	Those agreeing having democracy is very good (%)	Those agreeing democracies are too indecisive/lots of squabbling (%)	Mean evaluation of political system 1–10, (1 = very bad)
Poland	54.7	23.3	79.6	4.04
Hungary	67.1	35.7	62.4	4.00
Russia	92.9	8.0	72.2	2.59
Ukraine	84.3	21.7	54.3	3.39
Czech Republic	62.7	44.9	51.2	4.30
Romania	79.1	39.2	72.7	3.66
Germany	24.6	56.8	33.8	6.04
France	50.6	53.2	73.7	5.21
Great Britain	46.3	47.3	44.9	4.70
Sweden	40.1	71.4	47.8	5.20
Entire Sample	54.0	46.3	51.5	4.75

Source: Halman, Loek. *The European Values Study: A Third Wave*. Tilburg, Netherlands: Tilburg University, 2001.

than that in developed, Western democracies (although the figures for France are not so reassuring). Moreover, the figures tend to be much lower in Ukraine and in Russia, where the enthusiasm for the current political system is rather low. Longitudinal studies also confirm very poor evaluations of political institutions across the board—including a preference for how things were under communism—in these two states.[15] This is quite telling and should give pause to outsiders ready to lump these states in the democratic category. Beyond this, however, the raw scores themselves are worth noting: in successful countries such as Poland and Hungary, the majority of the people are not satisfied with how democracy is developing, and even here only a small fraction of those queried expressed great enthusiasm for democracy. Other surveys also show low degrees of trust in political institutions such as legislatures, governments, and political parties.

What can be said beyond presenting figures such as these? A more probing survey of Poles in June 2001, conducted by CBOS, sheds further light on the above findings. This survey asked about the understanding and acceptance of democracy, as well as an evaluation of the current political system in Poland.[16] The survey finds support for the contention that Polish democracy is a mere "facade" or a "fictional ritual." For example, it found little interest in participation (79 percent preferred to be "well governed" than to participate), and a plurality (35 percent) remarked that it made no difference if the government was democratic (34 percent preferred democracy, and 20 percent conceded that a nondemocratic system could be better). Asking about the pluses and minuses of democracy, the survey classified two-thirds of the respondents as prodemocratic but noted that two-thirds were also alienated from the current system, feeling confused about what to believe and uncertain on what or whom they can depend. One interesting finding related to our purposes was that low-qualified workers was the group most likely to have authoritarian tendencies (53 percent of such workers), meaning that class cleavages have hardly lost relevance, even if calls for class consciousness are derided as passé. The authors of the report suggest that the discrepancy between democracy in theory (supported) and democracy in practice (disdained by most) could lead to a breakdown in the existing democratic order, particularly if there is an ongoing economic or political crisis. Granted, these studies do not ask respondents to make a connection between union weakness and their perceptions of the political system, but given the multiple studies that suggest the public views unions as weak and wishes they were stronger, the statement that union weakness contributes to feelings of dissatisfaction and alienation (e.g., who represents *me*?) is not such a large jump.

Of course, such Cassandras have been heard before. In 1994, Lena Kolarska-Bobinska suggested in the Polish case that "If the government . . . quickly becomes alien, workers and farmers in particular will lose their last hope for political representation. This may lead to the eruption of dissatisfaction and the growth of radical movements."[17] David Ost and Stephen Crowley, writing more recently and with a focus on trade unions' problems, opine that union weakness "may have profound political implications, for it means that the anger that trade unions have traditionally funneled into class cleavages can get diverted into nationalist, fundamentalist, and other illiberal directions. If this is so, far from helping consolidate liberal capitalist democracy . . . labor weakness may threaten it."[18] Although Andzej Lepper's nationalist, anti-EU, and anti-Semitic *Samoobrona* polled about 10 percent of the vote in 2001 elections in Poland, radical movements have failed to galvanize the disgruntled citizens over the long haul. After a scare, Zhirinovsky has virtually disappeared from the Russian political scene, the main challenger to Ukraine's "party of power" at present is a national-democratic movement (not old-style communists or extreme nationalists), and Istvan Czurka's nationalist movement in Hungary is marginalized. True, those with questionable democratic credentials do remain on the scene in a number of countries, but the explosions predicted by some have not come to pass.

The failure of radical movements on either the left or the right is an interesting topic itself, one that deserves fuller treatment. Greskovits has suggested that radical movements fail to catch fire because discontented groups, such as workers, can exercise exit options and work in the informal economy. Moreover, he suggests that they do mobilize at the ballot box, not by voting in extremists, but by voting out incumbents.[19] Indeed, no incumbent party has held on to office in postcommunist Hungary and Bulgaria, and not in Poland since 1991. "Election cycling" is the norm throughout Central Europe (conditions in Russia and Ukraine have favored the existing "party of power"). This, of course, can be taken as a sign of healthy democracy (these countries pass a "two elections test," which means that government must change hands twice in order for the state to be a consolidated democracy), but the fact that incumbent governments cannot successfully appeal to voters may be a cause for worry.[20] How long can voters try one party and then the other, with neither able to satisfy them? Where, in particular, can workers go, since they remain largely unincorporated in the current regimes?

One should be careful not to push this argument too far. A counterargument is that deindustrialization and deunionization have been ongoing trends in Western countries for years, and even direct assaults on trade unions by Thatcher and Reagan have not dealt serious blows to democracy in Britain or the United States.[21] However, this sort of comparison misses a couple of key points. First, democratization and important socioeconomic reforms in many Western countries went hand-in-hand with strong labor movements. Such reforms included the expansion of suffrage in Britain, the New Deal in the United States, and the consolidation of democracy in postwar West Germany with the social market economy. Unions played an important role in aggregating and channeling interests and making authorities more accountable to electorates. To the extent that all the above reforms are consolidated, unions' political role may no longer be crucial for the maintenance of democracy.

Second, however, Western states today enjoy what might be called "diffuse support" for the democratic system. True, there may be a gap between democracy as an idea and democracy in practice, but years of experience with successful democratic governance give these states the wherewithal to adapt to structural economic changes. The decline of unions in the West has thus not been accompanied by dramatic or sudden political changes that threaten the democratic order. In postcommunist countries, of course, the new system does not have years of experience to fall back upon. Doubts about the effectiveness of democracy in practice could more easily lead to doubts about democracy in theory and precipitate more serious challenges to the existing democratic order. Moreover, with unions starting off weak or (as in the Polish case) undermined by the economic reform process that accompanied democratization, it is uncertain if and how the working class (to invoke a rather hoary term) will be represented in these states and if and how it will be able to demand and receive the various social protections (which have great political import) enjoyed by most citizens in Western states. To put it another way, Western states have less to worry about because of the past victories of labor movements; postcommunist states have no such advantage, and as they enter the world economy on its semiperiphery, they may be less able to build up the various protections and policies taken for granted in the West.

Let me say again to be careful not to push this argument too far. Democracy is not under immediate assault, at least in the Central European countries, and it has already survived economic crises that, if certain statistical findings are to be believed, should have led to democratic backsliding.[22]

Democracies, of course, can be resilient, and in postcommunist Europe extremist positions may be rejected for a variety of reasons (e.g., the desire to get into the European Union, the poor answers offered by extremists). However, I submit that the poor position of trade unions and the working class in the region does make the political environment more unsettled.

I would, however, push the relationship further between weak unions and low levels of consolidated democracy in countries such as Russia and Ukraine, which are obviously far behind countries such as Poland and Hungary in both economic and political development and where economic reform has left dire and obvious political consequences. In both post-Soviet cases, the weakness of civil society and the ability of economic and political elites to manipulate the situation to their advantage have led to the creation of an oligarchy. This situation need not have happened—consider our aforementioned hypothetical world or the more successful Central European countries, where unions were also weak (thus union weakness is *not* the only reason behind the rise of an oligarchy, but union strength could have prevented it). However, the reforms of the 1990s are part of the past, and it will be very difficult to undo them. Looking at the situation today then, it does not take a Marxist to wonder how a system of political economy based upon an oligarchy—where wealth and power are highly concentrated and the masses lack meaningful political and economic resources—can be transformed into a consolidated, liberal democracy. The results in these two cases are laced with irony: reforms designed to lay the groundwork for democracy were carried out in a very undemocratic manner for fears that some popular elements would undermine them. The results of these reforms, however, severely limit prospects for democratic consolidation. The window of opportunity for democratization today may be less open than before the reforms were launched, as witnessed by Ukrainian society's weakness in the face of growing authoritarianism, and popular support or at least acquiescence to Putin's strong-arm tendencies in Russia.[23]

Whither Trade Unions?

Despite their numerous problems, trade unions will not entirely vanish in the region. Even if they fail to find a foothold in the emergent private sector, they will continue to organize thousands of workers in the public sector and in large industrial enterprises, as in Western states. However, it is uncertain whether they will amount to more than just a part of the industrial relations system, a subject of study more relevant for economists and industrial sociologists than political scientists. Or, to echo Colin Crouch's words with respect to Western Europe, "Unions may have a long-term future, but do union *movements*?"[24]

Thus, to end this work, let us look at how unionists view their future in the region. In what institutions and strategies do they put their faith? One simple answer, often heard from trade unionists, especially in Russia and Ukraine, is that they need more time to adjust to the conditions of the market economy and marshal their resources to press claims against the government and employers. This may sound well and good, but the refrain has become tiresome. I submit that time has passed them by, and that instead of waiting for time to magically produce solutions for them, unionists will have to take more active stances. Alas, based upon my fieldwork in the region— especially in Russia and Ukraine—this has yet to occur, and few unions elsewhere can point to action that has led to *positive* change, as opposed to purely *defensive* action to preserve what little workers may have.

Some unionists hold on to that old dream (albeit stated in a different form) of international working-class solidarity, that the future of unions is international and that they must find ways to work together to solve common problems. This argument is also advanced in the context of EU integration, which unionists, especially in Poland and Hungary, hope will strengthen their already existing ties to European trade union movements. While this book certainly documents a number of problems common to unions East and West, sentiments for unity stand little chance to be realized. Suffice it to say that it is hard enough to create or maintain working-class consciousness and solidarity *within* postcommunist countries, let alone think that Polish, Ukrainian, Russian, German, American (and Brazilian and Korean, etc.) steelworkers or shipbuilders can somehow unify to press claims against national and global capital. One study looking closely at transnational action within firms that cross the East-West divide notes that to date it has been minimal,[25] and obviously workers in Western countries are less likely to view their counterparts in former communist countries as "comrades" than as people willing to work for less and thus "steal" their jobs.

Unionists do, however, have more concrete notions about how they may be able to survive and achieve success for their members. One path, usually given in response to the question of what unions have accomplished in the past decade, is that there are institutional mechanisms available for unions' voice to be heard and positions to be taken into account. In this case, unionists are referring to national tripartite or reconciliation boards that do give unions a formal role in the policy process. Many unionists continue to put their faith in such mechanisms, seeing this as a civilized development along the European model. However, as this work and others have shown,[26] these institutions are rarely effective. In most cases they do not have legal standing, interunion rivalries and weakness of employers' organizations have hampered their effectiveness, and on many important questions (e.g., changes in labor law or accession talks with the EU), governments have bypassed them entirely. These institutions, with rare exception, have been a facade, often giving predetermined government policy more legitimacy, allowing governments to claim that they did consult with unions. At best, they allow, as Crouch describes it in EU countries, a "shell" of a national union to play a "game" at the national level, but any agreement it reaches often has little importance at the factory level, where employers take advantage of a weak legal regime or the threat of unemployment to intimidate unions.[27]

Lacking dramatic success at the national level through such commissions and, more broadly, political involvement, some unions are trying to get back to basics at the local level by servicing members, organizing new affiliates, and pursuing more decentralized means of collective bargaining. Ost notes that this tactic is beginning to occur in Poland, especially in Solidarity, which is questioning its political-social movement approach and is trying to attend to basic needs of members at the shop level to achieve small, but meaningful, victories for members and win back union confidence. He refers to this as "economic unionism," which he suggests is simply representing the narrow economic interests of workers.[28] In Russia and Ukraine, there is also a realization among some union leaders that unions must make an effort to attract members and demonstrate that they can deliver goods to their members, but to date this form of servicing often takes its Soviet-era form, meaning the provision of social services and perks such as vacations, sport facilities, and subsidies for goods and apartments, not higher salaries or more job security extracted through tough negotiations with management. Laszlo Neumann notes that decentralization of collective bargaining is becoming more common in Hungary, as local unions try to bypass the national confederation and negotiate directly with the employer on more localized issues.[29] Notably, in the past couple of decades this has been the trend in a number of Western countries as well.[30]

More generally, in my fieldwork I noticed that the further I got away from union headquarters in the capital city, the more often I would hear arguments resembling economic unionism, as local union leaders claimed they and their members were skeptical of politicized approaches pursued from above. Ost claims that "old-fashioned, small-scale economic unionism" seems "quite vibrant," employing an adjective that could not be used about unions at the national level.[31] Sven Sterner of the ILO in Budapest agreed, noting that there is energy "from below" in certain unions and sectors, and he pointed to this as one of the few positive signs among the union movement in the region.[32]

From the unions' perspective, this strategy does make some degree of sense: they can focus on issues of most relevance to members, and local organizations are trusted more by members than the national leadership. Of course, this strategy runs counter to a national-level corporatist approach, which as noted is held out by some as a good mechanism for unions to reach agreements at a higher level with employers and governments.[33]

Despite its obvious appeal to pragmatism, I have several observations about this proposed strategy. First, it shows how far we have come from the heady days that celebrated the ethos of a civil society designed to defend society's interests—in general—against the state. Of course, it could be argued that civil society as a moral program had no chance of success in the postcommunist—or, for that matter, any—context.[34] Beyond this empirical claim, however, it is easy to see how consideration of actual elements of civil society runs up against well-propagated myths about civil society. Of course, this does not deny the validity of this strategy for unions, but it should make us think about civil society in more nuanced ways and help us appreciate its heterogeneous character composed of distinct interests (even within a single sector such as organized labor).

Also, real movement from below in terms of forming new organizations has been modest at best. True, there are unions in some Polish supermarkets and in McDonald's in Russia, but these higher profile cases deflect attention away from the fact that the most dynamic sector of the economy—small, private, service enterprises—are nonunion, and no unions have the organizational apparatus to really engage in union building on a large scale. Moreover, as a union official from Solidarity put it (and this has relevance across the region), "gaining a few thousand members in commerce [from the 'hypermarkets'] is no way to make significant progress because we continue to be on the downside in bigger industries due to downsizing, privatization, anti-union actions, etc."[35]

Moreover, proposals for decentralization and focus on local concerns can play into employers' demands for more flexibility and concern for firm survival in the competitive marketplace, as well as the desire to resist adoption of agreements negotiated "from above" by centralized union confederations. Of course, workers need to be concerned about the firm, but by focusing on themselves, they may surrender notions of labor solidarity. Neumann has done extensive work on this subject in Hungary, and he notes that decentralized negotiations allow employers to differentiate workers at the shop level, showering favors on a select few while ignoring demands of the larger stratum. In this context, individual defense strategies become more important, and the most skilled workers end up bypassing the unions entirely.[36] More generally, at the enterprise level unionists often talk about the need to preserve the competitiveness of the firm against foreign, domestic, and intracompany competition. Inter alia, of course, this implies they must defend themselves against competition from other workers, as what is good for Volkswagen workers in Poznan need not be good for Fiat workers in Tychy or Volkswagen workers in the Czech Republic.[37] This development reveals that the Marxist mantra of workers' solidarity has been replaced by one that argues what is good for business is good for workers. Prospects for union movements, to use Crouch's language, are minimal in such an environment, insofar as workers identify more and more with their own enterprise (and, implicitly, its management) and less with fellow workers in other firms. Last, employer concern for competitiveness, cost cutting, and flexibility—key concerns in the global marketplace—often involve subcontracting work, which is a growing phenomenon in postcommunist Europe, one that generally means that work is less likely to be done by a unionized worker.

The final question is by far the most serious and pragmatic: whether these strategies can pay off. "Think globally, act locally" is a nice slogan, but NIMBYism can result when people become so focused on local concerns and issues that they refuse to consider the common good or bigger picture. Local strategies necessarily narrow labor's concerns and prevent organized labor from going after the big issues that can make a significant difference to the economic and political well-being of the country as a whole. As Vadim Borisov noted with respect to miners in Russia, workers' demands have moved from the national level (e.g., Change the country!) to the enterprise level (e.g., Help *me*!) with no lasting result at either level.[38] Economic unionism may sound nice, but in union headquarters this is often referred to as "pulling the blanket over themselves," with the implicit notion that the union as a whole can suffer as a result. True, some workers can win and a few unions are successful, but it seems to me that the success of economic unionism is tied directly to the success of the firm in the marketplace. Again, this can lead to intraunion competition, and in many cases unions will fail simply because they are working in less successful firms, sectors, or national economies. Finally, the success of this strategy depends upon educated and skilled union leaders at all levels. Despite being optimistic about some union initiatives, Juliusz Gardawski notes in the Polish case (and many union leaders conceded this to me as well) that local union activists in the enterprises often are "ignorant" and union activity therefore suffers.[39] However, since unions lack funds for training, it is difficult to see a widespread turnaround in their ability to succeed at the enterprise level.

Echoing Crouch's language above, I maintain that parochialization of the labor unions leads to no labor *movement* at all. This does have political import. Discussing Poland and Hungary, Ost notes:

> [union] activity has been focused around narrow corporate interests—steel-workers seeking protection against imports, miners trying to avoid layoffs, nurses fighting for higher pay—rather than around the broad class interests that distinguished the west European neocorporatist development model. Neither of the two countries' labor movements nor the political parties with which they are allied, for example, have protested the decade-long state disinvestments in education, much less demanded improved chances for working class families —to take one example of an important class demand of postwar west European labor. By eschewing broad class concerns such as this, the weak labor movements contribute not just to a decline in social mobility that hurts their constituents but to a general weakening of the economy as well. . . . The point is that weak labor movements unable and unwilling to think or act in class terms are more likely a key factor stalling success than contributing to it.[40]

This assertion is meant to be provocative and of course links up with the earlier discussion of political consequences. Some maintain that class politics can no longer play (if it ever did), as the working class itself is being dismantled.[41] How unions can launch an offensive—given their decline in membership, low levels of public trust, and poor economic conditions for many of their members—is admittedly difficult to see, and to date big campaigns by unions for national political causes (admittedly campaigns that largely eschew class appeals) only brought more disillusionment. Many unionists in the region would call such an appeal "utopian," a "fantasy." The irony, sadly, is that this class consciousness was present in the region, years ago, during the birth of Solidarity.[42] To echo what some former Gdansk shipyard workers now say, after the shipyard barely avoided closure and many lost their jobs, "if we would have known what all these changes [as a result of Solidarity's success] would bring, we would not have started the movement."[43]

I would like to end on a hopeful note. However, the evidence presented in this study would make any optimistic conclusion disingenuous. Unions will survive, but mostly in the public sector or in redoubts of heavy industry that continue to be under economic assault. Unions are also graying, meaning that if present trends hold, the next generation of workers will be less likely to be unionized. Hopes for an economic turnaround in the region are not likely to be a boon to unions, given their virtual absence in the sectors of the economy best positioned for growth. They suffer from a wide variety of problems— declining membership and public trust, lack of unity, and political marginalization. For those who might think that these problems are temporary —the result of economic dislocation or of communist legacies—this study presents a bleaker picture by arguing that broad-based changes in the political economy are undermining the potential for any union comeback. In contrast to heady notions of "civil society" and all its trimmings (participation in politics, active exercise of citizenship, and openness of the political system to a wider public), to study organized labor is to perceive its enfeeblement, and likely union strategies in the future will undermine any remnant of solidarity.

While it need not produce deleterious results, the unions' predicament does reveal in important ways how the transitions in the region fall short in several important respects, most obviously in securing representation and voice for large numbers of people. In the final twist of irony, workers were able to organize to help overthrow a system that purportedly ruled in their name. However, they are poorly poised to do battle against governments and policies that make little pretense to serve their interests.

NOTES

Chapter 1: Civil Society, Trade Unions, and the Political Economy of Postcommunist Transformation

1. For works centering on civil society from Eastern Europeans themselves, see Vaclav Havel et al., *Power of the Powerless*, 1990; Adam Michnik, *Letters from Prison and Other Essays*, 1989; and George Konrad, *Antipolitics*, 1984. For two of the most celebratory works of civil society by academic observers, see Timothy Garton Ash, *The Magic Lantern*, 1990; and Vladimir Tismaneanu, *Reinventing Politics*, 1992.

2. Adam Przeworski, *Democracy and the Market*, 1991, 181–82. See also Bela Greskovits, *The Political Economy of Protest and Patience*, 1998.

3. Almost all works on postcommunist labor demonstrate severe infirmities for unions. For work that reviews labor's predicament in several states, see Michal Sewerynski, "Trade Unions in the Post-Communist Countries," 1995; Pekka Aro and Paula Repo, *Trade Union Experiences in Collective Bargaining in Central Europe*, 1997; J. E. M. Thirkell, K. Petrov, and S. A. Vickerstaff, *The Transformation of Labour Relations*, 1998; Paul Kubicek, "Organized Labor in Postcommunist States," 1999: 83–102; and Stephen Crowley and David Ost, eds., *Workers after Workers' States*, 2001. For country- or enterprise-specific studies, see Simon Clarke et al., *What about the Workers?* 1993; Linda Cook, "Russia's Labor Relations," 1994; Andras Tóth, *Labor Movements and Transition in Hungary from Socialism to Democracy*, 1994; Simon Clarke, Peter Fairbrother, and Vadim Borisov, *The Workers' Movement in Russia*, 1995; Mark Kramer, "Polish Workers and the Post-Communist Transition," 1995; Walter Conner, *Tattered Banners*, 1996; David Ost, "Polish Labor before and after Solidarity," 1996: 29–43; Stephen Crowley, *Hot Coal, Cold Steel*, 1997; Linda Cook, *Labor and Liberalization*, 1997; Sarah Ashwin, *Russian Workers*, 1999; Paul T. Christensen, *Russia's Workers in Transition*, 1999; Paul Kubicek, *Unbroken Ties*, 2000; Rick Simon, *Labour and Political Transformation in Russia and Ukraine*, 2000; Sue Davis, *Trade Unions in Russia and Ukraine, 1985–1995*, 2001; and Debra Javeline, *Protest and the Politics of Blame*, 2003. In addition, numerous articles can be found in the journals *Labor Focus on Eastern Europe* and *European Journal of Industrial Relations*.

4. *Izvestiia*, March 21, 1995.

5. See interview with Balcerowicz in Mario Blejer and Fabrizio Coricelli, eds., *The Making of Economic Reform in Eastern Europe*, 1995.

6. Ost and Crowley, "Making Sense of Labor Weakness in Postcommunism," 2001, 219.

7. Philippe Schmitter, "The Consolidation of Democracy and Representation of Social Groups," 1992: 422–49.

8. Nancy Bermeo, "Civil Society after Democracy," 2000, 244.

9. David Ost, "The Politics of Interest in Post-Communist Europe," 1993: 453–85.

10. Richard Rose, "A Divided Europe," 2001: 93–106.

11. By labor activism, I am referring to the ability of labor to mobilize its members for protests, strikes, and political activities. For a study of protests in Poland in the postcommunist period, see Grzegorz Ekiert and Jan Kubik, *Rebellious Civil Society*, 1999.

12. Giovanni Baglioni and Colin Crouch, eds., *European Industrial Relations*, 1990; Lowell Turner, *Democracy at Work*, 1991; Kathleen Thelen, "West European Labor in Transition," 1993: 23–49; Jeremy Rifkin, *The End of Work*, 1994; Jonas Pontusson, "Explaining the Decline of European Social Democracy, 1995: 495–533; Jeremy Waddington, ed., *Globalization and Patterns of Labour Resistance*, 1999.

13. Central Europe is defined as Poland, Hungary, Czech Republic, and Slovakia. The distinctiveness of this region, in both government performance and public acceptance of democracy and the market, as opposed to that prevailing in most post-Soviet countries, is well documented. For recent data see Rose, 2001.

14. Ost and Crowley, "The Surprise of Labor Weakness in Postcommunist Society,"2001, 5.

15. Bermeo, 2000, 249.

16. The literature on civil society is vast and ever expanding. For general works that discuss the concept's origin, evolution, and various uses, see Adam Seligman, *The Idea of Civil Society*, 1992; Ernest Gellner, *Conditions of Liberty*, 1994; and John A. Hall, ed., *Civil Society*, 1995. For application by East European dissidents and academics, see Vaclav Havel et al., 1985; Adam Michnik, 1985; Konrad, 1984; and Jadwiga Staniszkis, *Poland's Self-Limiting Revolution*, 1984. Academic works on civil society in postcommunist Europe are legion. Some book-length treatments include Zbigniew Rau, ed., *The Reemergence of Civil Society in Eastern Europe and the Soviet Union*, 1991; Paul G. Lewis, ed., *Democracy and Civil Society in Eastern Europe*, 1992; M. Steven Fish, *Democracy from Scratch*, 1995; Vladimir Tismaneanu, *Fantasies of Salvation*, 1998; Ekiert and Kubik, 1999; and Kubicek, 2000.

17. Thomas Carothers, *Aiding Democracy Abroad*, 1999, 248.

18. Electoral democracy refers exclusively to the existence of competitive elections in a state. It does not address other elements, such as civic freedoms, the rule of law, and protection of minority rights, that are necessary to make a full-fledged democracy. For more on this notion, see Larry Diamond, "Is the Third Wave Over?" 1996: 20–37.

19. Alexis de Tocqueville, *Democracy in America*, 1951. For modern takes on Tocqueville, see a special issue of the *Journal of Democracy* (volume 11, no. 1, 2000) devoted to a consideration of Tocqueville's ideas. For a notable book that applies Tocqueville's ideas to contemporary Italy, see Robert Putnam, *Making Democracy Work*, 1993.

20. For more on the Tocquevillian role played by civic groups, see Gerald Clarke, "NGOs and Politics in the Developing World," 1998: 36–52.

21. See Lewis, 1992; Gellner, 1994; Ekiert and Kubik, 1999; and Juan Linz and Alfred Stepan, *Problems of Democratic Transition and Consolidation*, 1996.

22. Carothers, 1999, 248.

23. Samuel Huntington, *Political Order in Changing Societies*, 1968. See Sheri Berman, "Civil Society and the Collapse of the Weimar Republic," 1997: 401–29; and Stephen Hanson and Jeffrey Kopstein, "The Weimar/Russia Comparison," 1997: 252–83.

24. Margaret Levi, "Social and Unsocial Capital," 1996: 45–55.

25. Jan Kubik, "Between the State and Networks of 'Cousins,'" 2000, 182.

26. James Madison, "Federalist X," 1987.

27. Ost, 1993.

28. Corporatist theory would argue that the larger the unions are and the more inclusive their membership, the more unions will have to take responsibility for the general good of society. This may be true in the sense that one, overarching union federation will be more universal than particular branchs or local unions, but it does not entirely remove the notion of a particular interest from that federation's raison d'être.

29. Samuel Valenzuela, "Labor Movements in Transitions to Democracy," 1989: 445–72.

30. David Collier and Ruth B. Collier, *Shaping the Political Arena*, 1991; and Dietrich Rueschemeyer, Evelyne Huber, and John D. Stephens, *Capitalist Development and Democracy*, 1992.

31. Valenzuela 1989; Przeworski, 1991; and Barbara Geddes, "Challenging the Conventional Wisdom," 1995.

32. Philippe Schmitter, Guillermo O'Donnell, and Laurence Whitehead, eds., *Transitions from Authoritarian Rule*, 1986.

33. See Guiseppe Di Palma, *To Craft Democracies*, 1990; Przeworski, 1991; John Higley and Robert Gunther, eds., *Elites and Democratic Consolidation in Latin America and Southern Europe*, 1992; Linz and Stepan, 1996; and Jon Elster, Claus Offe, and U. K. Preuss, *Institutional Design in Post-Communist Democracies*, 1998.

34. Philippe Schmitter and Terry Lynn Karl, "The Conceptual Travels of Transitologists and Consolidologists," 1994, 184.

35. Ken Jowitt, *New World Disorder*, 1992, 285.

36. The well-known debate was between Schmitter and Karl, on one side, and Valerie Bunce, on the other. See Schmitter and Karl, 1994, 173–85; Bunce, "Should Transitologists Be Grounded?" 1995: 111–27; Schmitter with Karl, "From an Iron Curtain to a Paper Curtain," 1995: 965–78; and Bunce, "Paper Curtains and Paper Tigers,"1995: 979–87.

37. Przeworski, 1991, 62–63.

38. Barbara Geddes, "What Do We Know about Democratization after Twenty Years?" 1999: 115–44.

39. Charles King, "Post-Postcommunism," 2000, 143.

40. Stephen Cohen, *Failed Crusade*, 2000.

41. Guillermo O'Donnell, "On the State, Democratization, and Some Conceptual Problems," 1993, 1356.

42. Przeworski, 1991, xii.

43. See Bunce, "Should Transitologists," 1995; Linz and Stepan, 1996; and David Stark and Laszlo Bruszt, *Postsocialist Pathways*, 1998.

44. Linz and Stepan, 1996.

45. Rasma Karklins, "Explaining Regime Change in the Soviet Union," 1994: 29–45.

46. Some scholars have identified over a dozen factors that differentiate postcommunism. See Leslie Holmes, *Postcommunism*, 1997, 15; and Richard Sakwa, *Postcommunism*, 1999, 5–6.

47. Bunce, "Should Transitologists," 1995.

48. Bunce, "Should Transitologists," 1995; and Claus Offe, "Capitalism by Democratic Design?" 1991: 865–902.

49. Bunce, "Should Transitologists," 1995, 120–21.

50. Much of this section borrows from Christensen, 1999, 5–14.

51. Schmitter et al., 1986.

52. Przeworski, 1991; Di Palma, 1990; and A. Schedler, "What Is Democratic Consolidation?" 1998: 91–107.

53. Joseph Schumpeter, *Capitalism, Socialism, and Democracy,* 1976; Robert Dahl, *Polyarchy,* 1971.

54. Petr Kopecky and Cas Mudde, "What Has Eastern Europe Taught Us about the Democratization Literature (and Vice Versa)?" 2000, 524.

55. Christensen, 1999, 6.

56. Terry Lynn Karl, "Dilemmas of Democratization in Latin America," 1990, 14–15.

57. Christensen, 1999, 6.

Chapter 2: The Postcommunist Inheritance

1. In Poland, the ruling party's moniker was the Polish United Workers Party. In Hungary, it was called the Hungarian Socialist Workers' Party.

2. Quoted in Robert Conquest, *Industrial Workers in the U.S.S.R.,* 1967, 8.

3. Milan Djilas, *The New Class,* 1957.

4. See Blair Ruble, *Soviet Trade Unions,* 1981; Jan Triska and Charles Gati, *Blue Collar Workers in Eastern Europe,* 1981; and Ivan Suhij and Vladimir Lepekhin, "Evolution of Interest Representation and Development of Labour Relations in Russia," 1994.

5. *Spravochnik Profsoiuznogo Rabotnika* (1962), quoted in Conquest, 187.

6. See Viktor Zaslavsky, *The Neo-Stalinist State,* 1982; and Donald Filtzer, *Soviet Workers and De-Stalinization,* 1992.

7. Valerie Bunce and John Echols, "Soviet Politics in the Brezhnev Era, 1980; and Blair Ruble, *The Applicability of Corporatist Models to the Study of Soviet Politics,* 1983. For a recent effort to revive corporatist theory in the Russian case, see Sergei P. Peregudov, *Gruppy interecov I Rossiiskoe gosudarstvo,* 1999.

8. Jerry Hough, "Policy-Making and the Worker," 1979, 375.

9. There are many scholars who make this argument. See David Lane, *Soviet Labour and the Ethic of Communism,* 1987; Ed Hewett, *Reforming the Soviet Economy,* 1988; and Walter Connor, *The Accidental Proletariat,* 1991. For a critical review of this thesis in light of the collapse of the USSR, see Linda Cook, *The Soviet Social Contract and Why It Failed,* 1993.

10. David Mandel, *Rabotyagi,* 1994, 8.

11. Alex Pravda, "Political Attitudes and Activity," 1981, 57.

12. Vadim Borisov, Simon Clarke, and Peter Fairbrother, "Does Trade Unionism Have a Future in Russia?" 1994: 15–25; and Ashwin, 1999.

13. This factor is also central to the analysis of Crowley, 1997; and Thirkell et al., 1998.

14. Ashwin, 1999, 27.

15. Andras Tóth, "Labor Movements and Transition in Hungary from Socialism to Democracy," 1994; and Thirkell et al., 1998.

16. See the following essays: Daniel Nelson, "Romania," 1981; Jan B. de Weydenthal, "Poland," 1981; and Jack Bielasiak, "Workers and Mass Participation in 'Socialist Democracy,'" 1981.

17. See discussion in Thirkell et al., 1998, especially chapter 4.

18. Mandel, 1994, 9.

19. Ashwin, 1999.

20. Sources that stress the role of intellectuals in giving Solidarity its basic ethos include David Ost, *Solidarity and the Politics of Anti-Politics*, 1990; Leszek Kolakowski, "The Intelligentsia," 1983; and Stanszkis, 1984. For an alternative view of Solidarity's "workers' roots," see Roman Laba, *The Roots of Solidarity*, 1991; and Lawrence Goodwyn, *Breaking the Barrier*, 1991.

21. See Ost, 1990.

22. On this point, see David Ost and Marc Weinstein, "Unionists against Unions," 1999: 1–33.

23. For in-depth coverage of state–labor relations in the Gorbachev period, see Connor, 1991; Mandel, 1994; Mandel, *Perestroika and the Soviet People*, 1991; Cook, 1993; Clarke et al., 1993; Crowley, 1997; and Christensen, 1999.

24. See Theodore Friedgut and Lewis Siegelbaum, "Perestroika from Below, 1990: 5–32.

25. Surveys reported by Clarke et al. indicate that in 1989, only 4 percent of workers respected their unions, and 1990 surveys in the strike regions of the Kuzbass and Donbass found small fractions of workers (14 percent and 6 percent, respectively) satisfied with their unions. See Clarke et al., 1993, 94–95, 114–15.

26. Clarke et al., 1993, 158.

27. For more on the positions of the NPG, see Clarke et al., 1993; and Crowley, 1997.

28. Clarke et al., 1993, 158. For the higher figure as well as self-reported figures for other unions, see Cook, 1997, 25; and Peregudov, 1999, 167.

29. Aleksandr Tarasov, "Soviet Trade Unions on the Road to a Shameful Fall," 1993, 14.

30. See Kubicek, 2000.

31. By the end of the 1990s, major unions within the SZEF include the Trade Union of Teachers, the Democratic Trade Union of Workers in Public Health, and the Union of Hungarian Public Employees and Civil Servants. Major unions in the ASZSZ include the Association of Hungarian Chemical Workers Union, Association of Gas Industry Unions, Association of Electrical Industry Trade Unions, and the Association of City Transport Employees Union. The MSZOSZ comprised many of the manufacturing workers, including those in the textile, mining, metallurgical, food processing, and construction industries. For a more complete list, see Andras Tóth, "Attempts to Reform a Workers' Movement without Mass Participation," 2000, 337–38.

32. Grigor Gradev, "Bulgarian Trade Unions in Transition," 2001; and Charles Rock, "Employment and Privatization in Bulgaria's Reform," 1994.

33. Gradev, 202.

34. See Jonathan Stein, "Neocorporatism in Slovakia," 2001.

35. Ost and Crowley, 2001, 1.

36. M. Chorna in *Post-Postup* (L'viv), December 30, 1993, A5.

37. For various attempts to measure union strength, see Neil Mitchell, "Theoretical and Empirical Issues in the Comparative Measurement of Union Power and Corporatism," 1996: 419–28; and Miriam Golden, Michael Wallerstein, and Peter Lange, "Unions, Employers' Associations and Wage-Setting Institutions in North and Central Europe, 1950–1992," 1997: 379–401.

38. *World Employment Report, 1996–1997*, 1997.

39. Sources include T. Chetvernina, P. Smirnov, N. Dunaeva, "Mesto profsoiuza na predpriiatii," 1995: 83–89; Mark Cramer, "Polish Workers and the Post-Communist Transition, 1989–1993," 1995: 71–114; Irena Panków, "The Main Actors on the Political Scene in Poland," 1996; Anna Pollert, "Trade Unionism in the Czech Republic," 1996: 6–37; Anna Pollert, "Labor and Trade Unions in the Czech Republic, 1989–1999," 2001; Richard Rose, Stephen White, and Ian McAllister, *How Russia Votes*, 1997; David Blanchflower and Richard Freeman, "Attitudinal Legacies of Communist Labor Relations," 1997: 438–59, 455; and *Politychny portret Ukrainy* 20, 1998.

40. See in particular Chetvernina et al., 1995; Pollert, 1996 and 2001; Ashwin 1999; and Ost and Weinstein, 1999.

41. William Mishler and Richard Rose, "Trust, Distrust, and Skepticism," 1997: 418–51.

42. Carola Frege and Andras Tóth, "Institutions Matter," 1999: 117–40.

43. Ost, 2000.

44. Pollert, 2001, 28.

45. Kubicek, 2000.

46. In Hungary, 1999 is an anomaly. In 1997, 853 strikers missed 1,923 days of work, and in 1998, 1,447 strikers missed 392 days.

47. Ost, 2001.

48. See Ekiert and Kubik, 1999; and Maryjane Osa, "Contention and Democracy," 1998: 29–42.

49. David Kideckel, "Winning the Battles, Losing the War," 2001, 99.

50. Andras Tóth, "The Failure of Social-Democratic Industrial Relations Model in Hungary," 2001, 45

51. Andras Tóth, "Invention of Works Councils in Hungary," 1997: 161–82.

52. Pollert, 2001.

53. Kubicek, 2000.

54. G. Rakitskaia, editor's note in *Profsoiuzy i problemy demokratii v Rossii*, 1997, 9.

55. Discussions on this issue were prominent in my interviews with trade union officials in May–June 2001. See details in *Rabochaia sila*, 2001; and *Za rabochee delo*, 2001.

56. Ost, 2001, 80.

57. V. G. Rupets, *Profsoiuzy i problemy demokratii*, 1997, 24.

58. Ost and Weinstein, 1999.

59. For a generally positive review of collective bargaining, see Aro and Repo, 1997. For a critical view, see Pollert, 2001; and Laszlo Neumann, "Circumventing Trade Unions in Hungary," 1997: 183–202.

60. By corporatist institutions, I am referring to the "democratic," "societal," or "neo" corporatist arrangements, in contrast to "state corporatist" institutions of

authoritarian systems in Latin America and Southern Europe. For the difference between the two, see Philippe Schmitter, "Still the Century of Corporatism?" 1974: 85–131.

61. See David Cameron, "Social Democracy, Corporatism, Labor Quiescence and the Representation of Economic Interests in Advanced Capitalist Society," 1984; and Miriam Golden, "The Dynamics of Trade Unionism and National Economic Performance," 1993: 439–54.

62. Kubicek, *Unbroken Ties*, 2000; and David Ost, "Illusory Corporatism in Eastern Europe," 2000: 503–30.

63. Ost, 2000, 504.

64. Suhij and Lepekhin, 1994.

65. Connor, 1996, 166–67, 187.

66. Mitchell Orenstein, "The Czech Tripartite Council and Its Contribution to Social Peace," 1996, 184.

67. Foreign Broadcast Information Service (FBIS), *Eastern Europe*, February 9, 1994, 5.

68. Vladislav Flek, quoted in Ost, 2000, 512. See also Pollert, 1996 and 2001.

69. Orenstein, 1996, 180.

70. Laszlo Bruszt, "Workers, Managers, and State Bureaucrats and the Economic Transformation in Hungary," 1993.

71. See Tóth, 2001.

72. Ost, 2000, 515.

73. Kubicek, 2000.

74. Tarasov, 1993, 15. See also Sarah Ashwin, "Russia's Official Trade Unions," 1995: 192–203.

75. Pollert, 1996, 15.

76. Crowley, 1997.

77. Ashwin, 1999, 14–15.

78. Javeline, 2003.

79. Ashwin, 1999.

80. See Crowley and Ost, 2001, especially chapter 11. See also Ost, 1993, 1996, 2000, and 2001.

81. Mandel, 1994, 184, 195.

82. See the case study in Ashwin, 1999, for details on coal mines in Russia.

83. Galina Ratitskaia, "What the Workers Are Demanding in Terms of Social and Economic Policy," 1994: 15–18.

84. Tóth, 1994.

85. Pollert, 2001, 36.

86. Crowley and Ost, 2001, 230.

87. Vera Lashch, former cochairman of Union of Work Collectives, in Mandel, 1994, 110.

88. These theories, it is worth noting, apply better to the independent, "noncommunist" trade unions. The communist-successor unions formed different alliances and were under fewer illusions about marketization

89. Tadeusz Kowalik, "From 'Self-Governing Republic' to Capitalism," 1995. See also Laba, 1991; and Goodwyn, 1991.

90. ILO-CEET (International Labour Organisation Central and East European

Team), "Report on ILO Seminar on Collective Bargaining in Central and Eastern Europe," 1996.

91. Clarke et al., 1995.

92. Mandel, 1994, 180–95, quotations from 180–81.

93. Ost and Crowley, 2001.

94. Greg Bamber and Valentin Peschanski, "Transforming Industrial Relations in Russia," 1996: 74–88.

95. Colin Crouch, *Industrial Relations and European State Traditions*, 1993.

96. Thirkell et al., 1998, 10.

Chapter 3: East Meets West

1. For a skeptical view of the notion of convergence with the West, see Andrew Herod, "Theorising Trade Unions in Transition," 1998.

2. Some have made the argument that a unique form of postcommunist capitalism is developing in Eastern Europe. See for example David Stark, "Recombinant Property in East European Capitalism," 1996: 993–1027. While it is true that starting points differ and the specific manifestations of capitalism will not be the same, I would focus the reader's attention here on the broad parameters of the emerging system, which is clearly capitalist in orientation.

3. David Peetz, *Unions in a Contrary World*, 1998, 1.

4. Some sources would include Philippe Schmitter, "Corporatism Is Dead!" 1989; Baglioni and Crouch, 1990; Turner, 1991; Kathleen Thelen, "Beyond Corporatism," 1994: 107–24; Pontusson, 1995; and Peetz, 1998. These sources form the basis of many claims below about union decline in the West.

5. George Ross and Andrew Martin, "European Unions Face the Millennium," 1999, 6–15.

6. Bo Rothstein, "Labor Market Institutions and Working-Class Strength," 1992.

7. Jon Elster, *The Cement of Society*, 1989.

8. Michael Wallerstein, "Union Growth in Advanced Industrial Democracies," 1989: 481–501. This argument, of course, suffers from a chicken-and-egg problem.

9. Martin and Ross, 1999, 9.

10. Peetz, 1998, identifies both structural change and policy shift, but given that the latter follows the former, structural change could make a policy shift of employers and governments far more likely.

11. This is the language used by Polish labor sociologist Juliusz Gardawski in *Zwiazki zawodowe na rozdrozu*, 2001, 44–53.

12. Pontusson, 1995.

13. V. Egorov, "Privatisation and Labour Relations in the Countries of Central and Eastern Europe," 1996: 89–100.

14. See Pontusson, 1995; Barry Hirsch and John Addison, *Analysis of Unions*, 1986; and Bruce Western, *Between Class and Market*, 1997.

15. Peter Katzenstein, *Small States in World Markets*, 1985.

16. Gardawski, 2001, 49.

17. A good review of many of the arguments presented here can be found in Kim Moody, *Workers in a Lean World*, 1997; and Jeremy Waddington, "Situating Labour within the Globalization Debate," 1999.

18. See Charles Tilly, "Globalization Hurts Organized Labor," 1995: 1–23; and Martin and Ross, 1999. For more on the erosion of the state, see Susan Strange, *The Retreat of the State*, 1996.

19. For more on this concept, see Richard Freeman, "Are Your Wages Set in Beijing?" 1995: 15–32; Ethan Kapstein, "Workers and the World Economy," 1996: 16–37; Dani Rodrik, *Has Globalization Gone Too Far?* 1997; Geoffrey Garnett, *Partisan Politics in the Global Economy*, 1998; and Paul Hirst and Graham Thompson, *Globalization in Question*, 1999.

20. See testimony of Doug Hellinger, executive director of Development Gap, before Hearings of International Financial Institutions Advisory Commission on Civil Society Perspectives, October 1999, at www.developmentgap.org/ifitestimony .html.

21. Turner, 1991.

22. Peetz, 1998.

23. Ross and Martin, 1999, 8.

24. Philip Cerny, "Paradoxes of the Competition State," 1997: 251–74.

25. See Colin Crouch, *Industrial Relations and European State Traditions*, 1993.

26. Henk Thomas, "The Erosion of Trade Unions," 1995, 3.

27. Thomas Friedman, *The Lexus and the Olive Tree*, 1999; Daniel Drezner, "Globalization and Policy Convergence," 2001: 53–78. Rodrik, 1997, debates aspects of this as well, presenting arguments on both sides.

28. Garnett, 1998; and Peter Lange and Lyle Scruggs, "Globalization and National Labor Market Institutions," 2002: 126–53.

29. ILO-CEET, "Dealing with Multinationals," 1996.

30. Randall Stone, *Lending Credibility*, 2002.

31. Eddy Lee, "Globalization and Labour Standards," 1997: 173–89.

32. David Bartlett and Anna Seleny, "The Political Enforcement of Liberalism," 1998: 319–38.

33. Overall, the effects of the European Union and statutes such as the Social Charter are debatable. Many observers in the West would not find them a boon for labor. See Stephen Silvia, "The Social Charter of the European Community," 1991: 626–43; Lloyd Ulman et al., eds., *Labor and an Integrated Europe*, 1993; and John Addison and W. Stanley Siebert, "Recent Developments in Social Policy in the New European Union," 1994: 5–27.

34. For a review of many points, see Crouch, 1993, chapter 1.

35. Bela Greskovits and Dorothee Bohle, "Development Paths on Europe's Periphery," 2001, 20. See also David Ost's review of their piece, "Labor Weakness Is No Condition for Success," in the same issue, 45–49.

36. The EBRD (European Bank of Reconstruction and Development) reported that the average size of an enterprise under communism was two thousand workers. There is no systematic evidence on plant size in the postcommunist period, but the EBRD noted as early as 1995 that small and medium enterprises (under 250 workers) are growing in all countries, accounting for 37 percent of workers in the Czech Republic, and roughly a quarter in Hungary, Poland, and Slovakia. In Russia, the figure was only 10 percent, but this has surely grown as reforms have been pushed through. See EBRD, *EBRD Transition Report, 1995*, 1995. In Poland, the OECD reports that by 1999 there were 1.8 million microenterprises (fewer than five employees

—not an auspicious place for unionization) and an additional 3.5 million Poles employed in small- and medium-size enterprises (under 250 employees). Together, these types of firms employ 62 percent of the corporate workforce. See OECD, *OECD Economic Surveys, 2000–2001*, 2001, 75. In Hungary, data reveal that there has been a significant shift to small- and medium-size enterprises, with over 94 percent of enterprises in 1997 employing fewer than fifty workers, whereas in 1987 over 80 percent of firms had more than fifty workers. See Bartlomiej Kaminski and Michelle Riboud, *Foreign Involvement in Restructuring*, 2003, 11.

37. There is an extensive literature from economists, experts on industrial relations, and political scientists on ownership change in the region. Sources include Cook, 1997, chapter 4; Thirkell et al., 1998, chapter 4; Stark and Bruszt, 1998; Saul Estrin, *Privatization in Central and Eastern Europe*, 1994; Michael McFaul and Tova Perlmutter, eds., *Privatization, Conversion, and Enterprise Reform in Russia*, 1995; Anders Aslund, *How Russia Became a Market Economy*, 1995; Maurice Ernst, Michael Alexeev, and Paul Marer, *Transforming the Core*, 1995; and Joseph Blasi, Maya Kroumova, and Douglas Kruse, *Kremlin Capitalism*, 1997.

38. Thirkell et al., 1998, 62.

39. A review of IMF activities in Russia, one of the most controversial cases of IMF assistance, can be found in Nigel Gould-Davies and Ngarie Woods, "Russia and the IMF," 1999: 1–22; and Stepan Hedlund, "Russia and the IMF," 2001: 104–43.

40. Stone, 2002.

41. *EBRD Transition Report 2001*, 2001. All figures are from 2000.

42. In the Russian case, foreign investment, especially in the energy sector, increased significantly in 2003.

43. *EBRD Transition Report 2001*, 2001. All figures are from 2000.

44. See Bamber and Peschanski, 1996.

45. Clarke et al., 1995, 408.

46. Mandel, 1994, 14.

Chapter 4: Organized Labor in Poland

1. Ost, 1996, 29. That workers were that passive can be disputed. However, there is little doubt that the union leadership played a key role in keeping workers' concerns in check.

2. *The New York Times*, June 15, 2002.

3. Mariusz Konicki, "Zwiazkokracja," *Polityka*, December 12, 1998.

4. See Ekiert and Kubik, 1999; and Osa, 1998.

5. See David Ost, "The Weakness of Symbolic Strength," 2001; and Carol Timko, "The 1992–93 Strike Wave and the Disorganization of Worker Interests in Poland," 1996.

6. Tomasz Inglot, "Between High Politics and Civil Society," 1998, 148.

7. See Michal Wenzel, "Polacy o zwiazkach zawodowych," reported by Public Opinion Research Center (CBOS), July 2001, from the survey "Actual Problems and Events," based upon a representative sample of 1,015 Poles. This particular survey is used by other authors in CBOS reports. All CBOS reports can be found at www.cbos.org.pl. Wenzel reports data from 1993 to 2001, and those surveyed who said unions had too little influence varied from a low of 42 percent in December 1999 to a high of 65 percent in July 2001.

8. These issues have been well explored by others. In particular, see Ost, 1993, 1996, 2001; Lena Kolarska-Bobinska, *Aspirations, Values and Interests*, 1994; Al Rainnie and Jane Hardy, "Desperately Seeking Capitalism," 1995: 267–79; Kramer, 1995; and Marc Weinstein, "Solidarity's Abandonment of Worker Councils," 2000: 49–73.

9. For a profile of union members 1991–1994, see Juliusz Gardawski, *Poland's Industrial Workers on the Return to Democracy and Market Economy*, 1996, 102–3. In surveys from July 2001 (mentioned above with Wenzel, 2001), 55 percent of Solidarity members classified themselves as *robotnik*, either skilled (41 percent) or unskilled (14 percent). OPZZ figures were 21 percent and 10 percent, respectively. See Gardawski, *Zwiazki zawodowe*, 2001, 79.

10. Interview, "Od destrukcji do wspolpracy," *Rzeczpospolita*, March 20, 2002.

11. Gardawski, *Zwiazki zawodowe*, 2001, 79.

12. Gardawski, *Zwiazki zawodowe*, 2001, 78; and information from Solidarity, "Trade Union Membership in Poland," 1999.

13. Gardawski, *Zwiazki zawodowe*, 2001, 78; and Michal Wenzel, "Opinie o zwiazkach zawodowych," report by CBOS, 2000, www.cbos.org.pl.

14. Solidarity 80 claimed as many as 500,000 members, but its importance faded after the strike wave of 1992–1993. Gardawski finds that only 0.1 percent of workers in 2001 claimed membership in this union. See *Zwiazki zawodowe*, 2001, 78.

15. Gardawski, *Zwiazki zawodowe*, 2001, 71.

16. Juliusz Gardawski, "Zasieg zwiazkow zawodowych w wybranych dzialach przemyslu i sekcjach uslug publicznych," 1999, 79.

17. Ost, "The Weakness of Strong Social Movements," 2002. Solidarity activists at the Poznan Volkswagen plant, in a roundtable with the author (July 5, 2002), made this point as well, attributing their success in part to their abstention from political activities and concentration on shop issues.

18. Gardawski, *Zwiazki zawodowe*, 2001, 230–34; and interview with Gardawski, Warsaw, June 27, 2002.

19. These points were emphasized by Frank Hantke, an officer with the Friedrich Ebert Foundation's Warsaw Office responsible for trade union issues, interview, Warsaw, June 26, 2002; and by Andrzej Matla, coordinator of International Department of Solidarity, interview, Gdansk, July 8, 2002.

20. The best source on this is Weinstein, 2000.

21. Matla, 2002.

22. Pankow, 1996, 144. See also Kramer, 1995.

23. Gardawski, 1996, 108–9.

24. Wenzel, "Polacy o zwiazkach zawodowych," 2001.

25. Wlodzimierz Pankow and Barbara Gaciarz, "Industrial Relations in Poland," manuscript, no date.

26. Pankow and Gaciarz, "Industrial Relations"; and W. Pankow, "Funkcje zwiazkow zwodowych w zakladach pracy," 1999, 163–208.

27. Bernadeta Waskielewicz, "Dinozaury dostaja druga szanse," *Rzeczpospolita*, December 27, 2001.

28. Pankow, 1999. Chapter 1 of Pankow's volume details the methodology of the survey "Trade Unions 1998." It covered 202 enterprises and 1,225 workers.

29. All figures from Waskielewicz, 2001; and Gardawski, *Zwiazki zawodowe*, 2001.

30. Roundtable at Volkswagen Poznan, 2002; and interview with Robert Szewczyk of Solidarity International Department, Gdansk, July 8, 2002.

31. Quoted in Rainnie and Hardy, 1995, 271.

32. *Rzeczpospolita*, March 2, 2002, and January 24, 2002.

33. In addition to numerous sources cited above, see Kazimierz Kloc, "Polish Labor in Transition," 1992: 139–48; Irena Jackiewicz, "Solidairity in a Double Role," 1996; Marc Weinstein, "From Co-Governance to Ungovernability," 1996, 38–58.

34. Steven Levitsky and Lucan Way, "Between a Shock and a Hard Place," 1998: 171–92.

35. Quotation in Kolarska-Bobinska, 1994, 68.

36. Ost and Weinstein, 1999, 12. Of Solidarity activists surveyed, 57 percent cited market reform, 53 percent noted speeding privatization, and 19 percent mentioned fighting the Balcerowicz plan. For OPZZ, the respective figures were 36 percent, 42 percent, and 14 percent.

37. Leszek Balcerowicz, "Understanding Post-Communist Transitions," 1994: 75–89.

38. In 1991, there were 305 reported strikes, compared with 6,351 in 1992 and 7,443 in 1993. See Timko, 1996, for details on these actions.

39. Timko, 1996.

40. Gardawski, 1996, 101.

41. Julian Bartosz, 1996, 43–44.

42. Bartosz, 1996, 44.

43. See in particular OPZZ statements in "The Black Paper of the Social Dialogue in Poland," 1998; and "Resolution of the Board of the All-Poland Alliance of Trade Unions, 27 April 1999," available at www.opzz.org.pl.

44. Ewa Tomaszewska, quoted in Ost, 2000, 515.

45. Membership data supplied by Adam Ditmer, head of Solidarity Metallurgy Branch in Katowice, and Eugeniusz Sommer, head of the OPZZ Steelworkers Union, Katowice.

46. *The Economist*, "Limping towards Normality: A Survey of Poland," October 27, 2001, 6.

47. Tomasz Jasinski, organizational department of OPZZ in Warsaw, interview, June 24, 2002.

48. Walesa's discussion with me at Oakland University, Rochester, Michigan, October 26, 2001.

49. *Rzeczpospolita*, "Cuda sa mozliwe," January 24, 2002.

50. According to Arkadiusz Sliwinski, vice chairman of the Warsaw region Solidarity organization, Solidarity and the OPZZ did reach agreement at the regional meeting on a joint stance against the government proposal, but it was the OPZZ national leadership that broke with the unions' position and reached agreement with the employers' confederation. From interview, Warsaw, June 25, 2002.

51. In a January 2002 survey of 973 Poles, only 3 percent rated the general economic condition of the country as good, whereas 56 percent said it was bad, and 19 percent said it was very bad—scores that were lower compared to Czechs, Hungarians, and even Russians, who were queried at the same time. See Michal Wenzel, "Opinie o sytuacji gospodarczej i materialnych warunkach zycia w niektorych krajach Europy srodkowej i wshodniej," CBOS, 2002, www.cbos.org.pl.

52. Gardawski, *Zwiazki zawodowe*, 2001, 70.

53. Andrzej Mokrzyszewski, "Zaufanie pracownikow do zwiazkow zawodowych," reported by CBOS, August 2001, www.cbos.org.pl.

54. For a detailed study of the labor force, based upon surveys from workers in Lublin, see Mary Winter, Earl Morris, and Krystyna Gutkowska, "Polish Workers during Economic Transformation," 1998: 61–80.

55. Kolarska-Bobinska, 1994, 109–11. Solidarity/OPZZ figures from 1990 survey only.

56. Kolarska-Bobinska, 1994, 107.

57. Greskovits and Bohle, 2001, 22.

58. Ryszard Rapacki, "Privatization in Poland," 1995, 62.

59. Rainnie and Hardy, 1995, 274.

60. Solidarity Economic Department, "Privatisation in Poland—1990/1999," mimeo., September 20, 2000; and Kolarska-Bobinska, who reports that in 1994 only 2 percent of the population was well informed about the mass privatization program (1994, 120).

61. Juliusz Gardawski, "Forms and Structure of Ownership," 1999, 92. This work contains much useful data on the subject. In addition, consult R. Schliwa, "Enterprise Privatization and Employee Buy-Outs in Poland," 1996.

62. Interview with Wlodzimierz Pankow, a leading expert on Polish industrial relations, Warsaw, June 26, 2002; and Barbara Morosz, testimony to Polish Senate, "Direct Privatization in Poland," found on Polish Treasury Department website, www.mst.gov.pl.

63. Rapacki, 1995, 63.

64. Solidarity, "Privatisation in Poland 1990/1999," 2000.

65. Henryk Nakonieczny, President of Solidarity's National Coal Mining Division, interview, Katowice, July 3, 2002.

66. Rapacki reports that by 1995 there were 1.9 million individual private proprietorships employing 2.7 million people, a quarter of the nonagricultural labor force. See Rapacki, 1995, 59.

67. Solidarity Economic Policy Department, "Privatisation in Poland," mimeo., September 20, 2000.

68. Kolarska-Bobinska, 1994, 114.

69. Mokrzyszewski, "Zaufanie," 2001. For results of earlier surveys, see Ost and Weinstein, 1999.

70. Rainnie and Hardy, 1995, 275.

71. Ost and Weinstein, 1999, quotations 3, 20.

72. Solidarity Economic Department, "Annual Survey on violation of trade union rights in Poland, 2001," mimeo., 2001.

73. Information supplied by Slawomir Adamczyk, head of Solidarity Liaison Office with Branch Structures, Gdansk, July 9, 2002.

74. Interview, Warsaw, June 25, 2002.

75. Adam Ditmer, chair of the Solidarity Metallurgical branch, interview, Katowice, July 1, 2002.

76. Ditmer, 2002; and interview with Ryszard Lepik, vice chairman of OPZZ, Warsaw, June 27, 2002.

77. This is based upon remarks made by several union leaders on the shop level, particularly in Huta Katowice, about efforts to reform or sell their enterprises. These remarks were delivered during a roundtable at Slanski (Silesian) University in Katowice, July 2, 2002.

78. *OECD Economic Surveys*, 2001, 68.

79. Ost, 2002. See also Gardawski, *Zwiazki zawodowe*, 2001, 200–225.

80. Best coverage is Gardawski, *Zwiazki zawodowe*, 2001, 226–49.

81. Pankow, 1999.

82. Gardawski, "Zwiazki zawodowe w zakladach pracy," 2001, from CBOS, www.cbos.org.pl.

83. This strike captured the attention of the *New York Times*, June 12, 2002.

84. Walesa's discussion with me, Oakland University, October 26, 2001.

85. For analysis by Sachs himself, see his *Poland's Jump to the Market Economy*, 1993.

86. Carol Graham, "Safety Nets and Market Transitions," 1994: 36–40.

87. Stanislaw Gomulka, "The IMF-Supported Programs of Poland and Russia, 1990–1994," 1995: 316–46; and Erwin Tiongson, "Poland and IMF Conditionality Programs," 1997: 55–68.

88. Katarzyna Sobon, coordinator of Solidarity European Integration Commission, interview, Gdansk, July 8, 2002.

89. See report at www.paiz.pl/main/kraje2000.html.

90. See Philip Cooke et al., "Inward Investment and Economic Development in Poland," 1997, 692; claim made by the Central and Eastern Europe Business Information Center (US) at www.mac.doc.gov/eebic/country/poland/market/growth1 .htm; and Arjun Bedi and Andrzej Cieslik, "Foreign Direct Investment and Host Country Regional Export Performance," 2000.

91. Gardawski, *Zwiazki zawodowe*, 2001, 327.

92. Interview, Warsaw, June 27, 2002.

93. Frank Hantke, interview, Warsaw, July 26, 2002.

94. Examples from Guglielmo Meardi, *Trade Union Activists, East and West*, 2000, 195.

95. See discussion of the campaign to organize unions in these stores in Gardawski, *Zwiazki zawodowe*, 2001, 219–26.

96. From Matla, 2002. For the Danone case, see Meardi, 2000, 199–203.

97. Matla, 2002.

98. Interviews with Adam Ditmer of Solidarity Metallurgy Branch in Katowice, July 1, 2001; and his counterpart at the OPZZ Steelworkers Union, Eugeniusz Sommer, Katowice, July 3, 2002.

99. Nakonieczny, interview, Katowice, July 3, 2002.

100. *Tygodnik Solidarnosc*, May 24, 2002, 1.

101. This is based upon a roundtable with me and four representatives of the Volkswagen Poznan Solidarity union, held July 5, 2002.

102. Jerzy Wozniak, in *Tygodnik Solidarnosc*, May 24, 2002, 11. See reports on Daewoo here and in the May 31, 2002 issue, 3.

103. See Barbara Gaciarz and Wlodzimierz Pankow, *Przeksztalcenia przedsiebiorstw przemyslowych*, 1997. For an opposing view, see Meardi, 2000.

104. By far the best study of Fiat in Poland is that of Meardi, 2000. Basic background on the plants can be found on pp. 77–81.

105. Based upon conversations at Volkswagen in Poznan and in Gdansk with Slawomir Adamczk of Solidarity.

106. Sobon, interview, 2002.

107. See Statement of National Commission of Solidarity on Integration of Poland with the European Union, mimeo., no date.

108. Report from European Union, found on www.gla.ac.uk/ecohse/poland2.pdf.
109. Magdalena Kusmierz, "Unions versus Union," 2001.
110. See T. Schulten, "European Works Councils," 1996: 303–24.
111. Kusmierz, 2001.

Chapter 5: Organized Labor in Russia

1. David Mandel, "Russia," 1996, 41.
2. According to the ILO, in 1992–1999 Russia, on average, had 7,455 strikes each year involving 430,363 people. From ILO, *Yearbook of Labor Statistics*, 2000.
3. Outside observers noted, however, that the 2004 presidential elections could not be called free and fair.
4. Javeline, 2003, reports that in the spring of 1998 over twenty million Russians were owed back wages of $10 billion, with over 70 percent of workers claiming they were not paid regularly. By 2001, the total had been brought down to just over 30 billion (new) rubles, just over $1 billion. See government data in *Solidarnost'* (newspaper of the FNPR) 19 (314), May 2001, 2.
5. This is captured in nationwide surveys of VTsIOM reported in *Monitoring obshchestvennovo nneniia*, various issues. For example, the number of those expecting economic improvement has grown from 16.5 percent in September 1998 and 12.3 percent in September 1999 to 31.7 percent in September 2000. Similarly, 32.6 percent in 2000 expect improvement in the political situation, compared to 11.7 percent in 1999 and 19.9 percent in 1998.
6. A survey by VTsIOM in January 2000 found that 75 percent preferred order to democracy, even if the establishment of order is harmful to democratic principles. More disturbing, perhaps, in June 2000, a survey found 40 percent in favor of creation of a dictatorship, as opposed to 43 percent against. Reported in VTsIOM, *Obshchestvenoe mnenie—2000* (Moscow: VTsIOM, 2000, 68–69.
7. All these figures are self-reported. There is no independent confirmation of any membership figures for any unions.
8. This is based on conversations with several branch union leaders. Interestingly, the FNPR itself refused to provide comprehensive membership data by sector, claiming that they could not give this out (?!).
9. *Kommersant*, May 24, 2001.
10. See reports in *Russkaia msyl'*, February 22, 2001; and *Kommersant*, March 1, 2001, and May 24, 2001.
11. This point was particularly stressed by Aleksandr Dolgorybin, head of the FNPR organizational department. Interview, Moscow, May 24, 2001. Survey data from 1,500 union members in Moscow also reveal the high importance members place on union sports facilities (61 percent), medicine (66 percent), a place to live (48 percent), and day care (32 percent). See V. Naumov and S. Tatarnikova, *Motivatsiia profsoiuznovo chlenestva*, 1996. Moreover, fully 35 percent of respondents in 1996, and 50 percent in 1992, claimed they joined "out of habit."
12. See comments of Mikhail Shmakov, president of FNPR, in *Solidarnost'* 13 (308), April 2001.
13. Simon Clarke, "Russian Trade Unions in the 1999 Duma Election," 2001.
14. Comments in *Solidarnost'* 18 (313), May 2001, 3.
15. *Izvestiia*, May 24, 2001, 1.

16. Surveys in *Monitoring* have consistently shown low trust in trade unions. In 1994, 8 percent expressed complete trust in them, 17 percent partial trust. Figures for September 1999 are 9 percent and 22.3 percent, and figures from September 2000 are 11.4 percent and 28.3 percent. Trust is not appreciably higher for those self-described as workers, and overall in the September 2000 survey, trade unions were second from the bottom in terms of trust of all institutions, ranking below the parliament, the courts, the militia, and lawyers (!), and above political parties only.

17. *Trud*, December 10, 1996.

18. One report claimed that of the eleven thousand strikes in 1998, in only one hundred cases did employers take the workers to court for striking illegally. Of these one hundred cases, three-quarters involved non-FNPR unions. The conclusion would be that many FNPR "strikes" are blessed by management. See report of the chairman of Sotsprof to the 4th Congress of Sotsprof, March 1999, in D. Semenov and S. Khramov, *Profsoiuznoe remeslo*, 2000, 195.

19. Petr Biziukov, "Al'ternativnye profsoiuzy na puti osvoeniia sotsial'novo prostranstva," 2001, 34–36; and Vadim Borisov, *Zabastovki v ugol'oi promyshlenosti*, 2001.

20. Clarke, 2001, 51.

21. The best source on worker protests is Javeline, 2003.

22. For a report on views of one campaign by the FNPR, see Peter Rutland, "Russian Workers' Protest Carries a Mixed Message," *OMRI Analytical Brief* #444, November 1997.

23. Tatiana Mizguireva, "Between Voice and Exit," 2001, 77.

24. Formed in February 1991, Sotsprof (Social Trade Unions) claims to unite a variety of unions in different professions (metallurgy, teaching, television, writers, light industry) and have twenty-six territorial organizations.

25. Formed in August 1995, leading members of this confederation include the Independent Miners' Union (NPG), the Union of Norilsk Nickel workers, the Kuzbass Confederation of Labor, the Interregional Association "Solidarity," the Union of Workers of Social Service Enterprises, and the Union of Drivers of City and Passenger Transport.

26. Formed in April 1995, its leading members are the Union of Dockers, the Seafarers' Union, and the Union of Locomotive Drivers.

27. Self-reported, and, I should add, disputed, figures include 440,000 for Sotsprof, 180,000 for the NPG, 63,000 for the dockers, and a few thousand for most of the remaining unions.

28. Bliziukov, 2001, 32.

29. This was a prevalent theme of the ILO-cosponsored Conference on Freedom of Association, Moscow, May 25–26, 2001, with many union leaders reporting harassment and difficulty in forming a union. Consult issues of the Sotsprof paper, *Rabochaia sila*, for numerous actions taken by these parties against new unions. In 2000–2001, the leading case was that of an independent Sotsprof union at the massive AvtoVAZ factory in Tol'iatti, a union which primarily attracted workers who repaired the assembly line. In September 2000, this union conducted a brief strike, after which its leaders were cajoled and coerced by management to leave the union. Reports in issues 6(56), August–September 2000, and 2(60), March 2001.

30. See surveys in Rose, White, and McAllister, 1997; and report in *Nezavisimaia gazeta*, May 5, 2000.

31. Interview in *Russian Labor Review*, 2, 1993, 14.

32. This was an early demand of the independents, especially Sotsprof. See *Nezavisimaia gazeta*, February 29, 1992.

33. Viktor Gorenkov, member of the Central Committee, Union of Automobile and Agricultural Machinery Workers, interview, Moscow, May 24, 2001. The context of this discussion was the above strike at AvtoVAZ, which the FNPR union dismissed as a nonevent.

34. Boris Kravchenko, Head of International Relations Department of BKT, interview, Moscow, June 6, 2001; Nikolai Shtirnov, vice president of both NPG and BKT, interview, May 28, 2001.

35. Resolution of 4th Congress of Sotsprof, March 31, 1999, in Semenov and Khramov, 2000, 191–93; and Rupets, 1997.

36. For a description of differences between the drafts, see *Za rabochnee delo* (St. Petersburg) 6 (99), 2001; and *Solidarnost'* 22–23 (317–18), June 2001. For the polemic battles, see *Kommersant*, June 6, 2001, 2; and *Nezavisimaia gazeta*, June 7, 2001, 3.

37. Quoted in Elizabeth Teague, "Pluralism versus Corporatism," 1994, 116.

38. Data on real wages show a drop of 33 percent in 1992, with wages falling to under half of 1990 levels by 1995. See Leonid Gordon et al., *Kpytoy plast*, 1999, 27.

39. Cook, 1994. Connor, 1996, offers perhaps the most comprehensive picture of this period, including the battles in the tripartite institutions.

40. This is noted in the case of the miners by Borisov, 2001.

41. For more on the RSPP during this period, see Eric Lohr, "Arkadii Volsky's Political Base," 1993: 811–29.

42. Mandel, 1996, 46.

43. Quoted in Mandel, 1996, 58–59.

44. Surveys from September 1998 in *Monitoring* 6 (38), and November–December 1998, show that 78.6 percent rated the economic situation very bad and 47.9 percent thought protests were likely.

45. Paul Kubicek, "Delegative Democracy in Russia and Ukraine," 1994: 443–61.

46. Rupets, 1997; and Biziukov, 2001.

47. Christensen, 1999, 112.

48. Compare this with eight trade unionists from the FNPR in the 1995–1999 Duma. Of the fourteen, four entered from the Fatherland-All Russia list, three from the Communist Party's, one from Unity, and six as independents. The multiplicity of parties reflects some of the fractures within the FNPR. See Clarke, 2001.

49. *Kommersant*, May 2, 2001, 2.

50. According to the new Labor Code, if multiple unions cannot agree on a position, workers will be represented by the union representing the majority in a given sector—invariably an FNPR union. Moreover, only affiliates of a nationwide trade union will be allowed to negotiate branch-level collective agreements, which will exclude many locally based, non-FNPR unions.

51. Discussion at a round table at the ILO Conference on Freedom of Association, Moscow, May 27, 2001.

52. *Nevavisimaia gazeta*, June 7, 2001, 3.

53. *Kommersant* June 5, 2001, 2; and *Nezavisimaia gazeta*, June 7, 2001, 3.

54. Time and time again, this emerged as an important goal for the unions in my discussions with union leaders from the FNPR. For a classic statement from the

FNPR on social partnership, see Mikhail Shmakov, "Profsoiuzy Rossii na poroge XXI veka," 2000.

55. Connor, 1996.

56. As Viktor Gorenkov, head of the department for social and economic questions for the Union of Workers in Automobile and Agricultural Machinery, rhetorically asked, "Who is up there representing the employers? Volsky. And, tell me, who does he represent? Volsky." Interview, Moscow, May 24, 2001.

57. Aleksandr Sitnov, deputy chairman of the Union of Chemical Workers, interview, Moscow, May 21, 2001.

58. Vadim Borisov, "Sotsial'noe partnerstvo v Rossii," 2001: 56–66.

59. Interview, Moscow, June 4, 2001.

60. One survey in the fall of 1993 found 72 percent of Russians opposed to privatization of large-scale enterprises. See *Financial Times*, October 6–7, 1993, quoted in Mandel, 1996, 43.

61. The basic story of Russian privatization is rather well known. See McFaul and Perlmutter, 1994; Aslund, 1995; Blasi et al., 1997; and Chrystia Freeland, *Sale of the Century*, 2000.

62. Cook, 1997, 67–68.

63. Christensen, 1999, 107. A third option, which provided for sale conditional on an economic strategy plan, was also available, but chosen by a mere 3 percent of firms.

64. Each Russian citizen was given a voucher of 10,000 RR (Russian rubles) to buy shares. This was roughly equal to $86.

65. This is based on interviews with over forty trade union representatives from over a dozen sectors of the economy, conducted May–June 2001.

66. Interestingly, most Russians foresaw what would happen, even if Western advisers or Chubais did not. According to survey results from April 1993, over half of the respondents thought the real owner of their enterprises would be the current administration (31.7 percent) or the current director (18.5 percent), whereas only 15.4 percent thought it would be the work collective. However, over 40.3 percent wanted the owner to be the collective, as opposed to 12.7 percent for the two groups of management. Reported in *Monitoring*, no. 8, December 1993.

67. For an effort to account for this sector, see Leonid Gordon, "Massovoe rasprostranenie skrytykh zarabotkov," 2000, 3–63.

68. See Blasi et al., 1997.

69. Irina Stevenson, interview, Moscow, June 5, 2001. Interviews also with Tatiana Sosnina, chairman of the Unions in Textile and Light Industry, Moscow, May 29, 2001; and Valentina Stepanova, chairman of Tula branch of the same union, Tula, June 1, 2001.

70. Blasi et al., 1997, 107.

71. Comment of Nikolai Shtirnov, vice president of NPG, interview, Moscow, May 28, 2001.

72. Petr Sudakov, head of Nizhniy Novgorod Sotsprof affiliate, interview, June 8, 2001.

73. The Vyborg case of summer–fall 1999 may appear to be an exception, given that the workers forcefully seized the plant, barred the owners from entering its premises, and declared the factory a "popular" *(narodnoe)* enterprise. Surveys among workers, however, reveal that this was more a tactic and that the eventual goal was to transfer

ownership to an owner who would preserve jobs and invest in the plant. The former director and the chief of security at the enterprise were also involved in this takeover, leading some to hypothesize about mafia connections, and the episode was tied up in regional politics as well. See B. I. Maksimov, "Klasovyi konflikt na Vyborgskom TBK," 2001: 35–47. Also informative were interviews with Mikhail Tarasenko, chairman of the Union of Miners and Metallurgy Workers, Moscow, May 18, 2001; and Sitnov. For some information on Norilsk Nickel, see Christensen, 1999, 137–38.

74. Interview with Anatolii Bresov, head of the Union of Aviation Industry Workers, Moscow, June 13, 2001.

75. Interview, Moscow, June 19, 2001. The KRP is a coalition of seven unions representing workers and employers in small, nonstate enterprises. Ziberov claims a total membership of two million workers, but this cannot be confirmed and at best may reflect the number of workers who have joined, at the employers' initiative, this trade organization.

76. Interview, Moscow, May 16, 2001.

77. Interview, Moscow, May 29, 2001.

78. Lev Mironov, interview, Moscow, June 6, 2001.

79. Interview, Nizhniy Novgorod, June 8, 2001.

80. Marina Karelina, "Tendentsii izmeneniia chislennocti professional'nykh soiuzov," 2001, 46.

81. Union–employer conflicts were prominent at the aforementioned ILO Conference, Moscow, May 26–27, 2001; and were mentioned in several discussions with union leaders, including Tarasenko, Sitnov, Stepanova, Oleg Lvov of Sotsprof, Moscow, May 23, 2001; and Boris Kremnev, head of the Civil Aviation Workers Union, Moscow, June 5, 2001.

82. Gordon, 1995, 47.

83. Interview, Moscow, May 18, 2001.

84. Karelina, 2001, 46.

85. Interview, Moscow, May 23, 2001.

86. *Nezavisimaia gazeta*, May 31, 2001, 1.

87. This observation is based upon numerous interviews with union heads. The one exception to this was the oil and gas industry, which has no trouble selling its product and gets plenty of foreign investment.

88. Interview with Oleg Lvov, 2001.

89. Gordon, 1995, 46.

90. Sample of 1,442 workers, results found in Natalia Kovaleva, "Konflikty, profsoiuzy, sotsial'naia zashchita," 1997: 26–32.

91. Interview, Tula, May 31, 2001. Also see his interview in *Solidarnost'* 20 (315), June 2001 (Tula Region Supplement), 4.

92. Interview with Evgenii Akimov, Tula, June 1, 2001; and Nikolai Kamanev, vice chairman of the GAZ Union, Nizhniy Novgorod, June 7, 2001. On KAMAZ, see statement of G. Nuretdinov, union committee head, in *Profsoiuzy i ekonomika* 7, 2001, 38–41.

93. Crowley, 1997.

94. According to Valentina Leonova, vice chairman of the regional autoworkers union in Nizhniy Novgorod, "We care about the humanitarian side of things. Business questions are for the managers." Interview, June 7, 2001.

95. Gordon, 1995, 46.

96. Ashwin, 1999.

97. Karin Klement, "Predposylki kollektubhykh aktsii protests ha predpriiatiiakh," 1996, 73. Unfortunately, he does not provide the figures upon which this conclusion is based.

98. Gordon, 1995, 46.

99. For comments on this problem, see Mikhail Golovanets, head of the Krasnoyarsk regional Miners' and Metallurgists' Union, in *10 Let GMPR Budushchee Profsoiuza—za molodezh'iu*, 2001, 63; and Andrii Mrost, regional head of the International Federation of Chemical, Energy, and Mine Workers (ICEM), "Praktika raboty mezhdunarodnykh profsoiuznykh organizatsii i TNK," 1999, 121–28.

100. Boris Kravchenko of the BKT (interview, 2001), of which Norilsk Nickel (NN) is a member, reports that at NN the average salary is 19,000 RR a month (about $700). However, given the hard currency earnings of this company, these wages are quite paltry.

101. The director of one Norilsk Nickel affiliate, dismissing trade union "extremism," noted that, "We will establish an effective system of social partnership with the [work] collective." *Kommersant-Daily*, March 13, 2003.

102. *Nezavisimaia gazeta*, January 22, 2003.

103. All but Norilsk Nickel are still formally part of the FNPR, but there have been discussions about exiting the FNPR and forming a separate federation among these company-based unions.

104. This misgiving was a concern of Sitnov, which noted that many "company" unions are being formed in the chemical sector. Interview, 2001. See also Mrost, 1999.

105. Filtzer, 1992.

106. Government data show that wages of the top 10 percent of the population are fourteen times the wages of the bottom 10 percent. By sector, as of 2001, agricultural workers earn 863 rubles (on average); cultural workers 1,226; light industry 1,252; ferrous metals 6,163; and energy 7,375 (28 RR = $1). Reported in *Izvestiia*, May 24, 2001, 1.

107. Interview with Nikolai Kolobshkin, international secretary of the Union of Education Workers, Moscow, May 24, 2001.

108. Borisov, *Zabastovki*, 2001, 389–90.

109. See reports in *Nezavisimaia gazeta*, May 22, 2000, 5; and *Trud*, June 9, 2001, 1.

110. This was the theme of the publication *10 letGMPR*. It also figured prominently in discussions with Dolgorybin of the FNPR organizational bureau.

111. See Gould-Davies and Woods, 1999; and Hedlund, 2001.

112. Aslund, 1995.

113. Jeffrey Sachs, "Betrayal," 1994, 15.

114. Janine Wedel, 1998; and Cohen, 2000.

115. Michel Camdessus, then managing director of the IMF, was quoted as saying in 1997 that IMF-backed structural adjustment policies might require that Russia "sacrifice a generation," something more akin to Stalinist discourse on constructing socialism than that of a democratic politician. See Soren Ambrose, "IMF Bailouts: Familiar, Failed Medicine for Asian 'Tigers,'" January 1998, at www.igc.org/trac/corner/worldnews/other/other83.html.

116. Hedlund, 2001.

117. Hedlund, 2001, 123.

118. *Moscow Tribune*, October 22, 1999.

119. *Nezavisimaia gazeta*, December 18, 1997.

120. This memorandum can be found at www.imf.org/external/np/loi/071698 .htm.

121. See also Borisov, "Sotsial'noe partnerstvo," 2001, 58.

122. For example, a list of Russia's top exporters in 1999 found twenty-three out of the top twenty-five exporters engaged in extraction or transportation of oil, gas, or metallic ores. Gazprom alone accounted for the value of the next five largest exporters. See *Russia Journal*, November 18–24, 2000.

123. *Kommersant*, June 6, 2001; *Trud*, June 8, 2001.

124. Anatolii Breusov, president of the Workers in Aviation Industry, interview, Moscow, June 13, 2001; and interview in *Profsoiuzy i ekonomika* no. 2, 2000, 22–31.

125. Sosnina, interview, May 29, 2001; and in *Izvestiia*, May 24, 2001.

126. My interview with Filinov at Tulachermet, Tula, May 31, 2001.

127. Interview, 2001.

128. *Nevavisimaia gazeta*, June 5, 2001.

129. Breusov, interview, 2000.

130. Interview, June 4, 2001.

131. According to the EBRD, cumulative FDI inflows for 1994–1999 amounted to $10.3 billion, about half the amount put into Poland, a much smaller country. See *EBRD Transition Report 2000*, 2000, 74. For details on foreign investment in Russia during the 1990s, see Paul Fischer, *Foreign Direct Investment in Russia*, 2000. Quotation from Fischer, 2000, 311.

132. Interfax, May 19, 2003. See also report in *The Times* (London), May 18, 2003.

133. Grigorii Miakishev, vice chairman of the Union of Workers in Joint Ventures, interview, Moscow, June 21, 2001.

134. *Moscow Times*, August 11, 2000.

135. Angelika Pastrenina, head of the Neste Petrol Station Workers Union, interview, St. Petersburg, June 22, 2001.

136. Interview with Sosnina, 2001.

137. Interviews in St. Petersburg, June 22, 2001; and Anatolii Shadrin, head of the Henkel Union, "Uporstvo i natisk," 1999, 104.

138. Aleksandr Alekseev, head of the Procter & Gamble Union in Novomoskovsk, "Opyt organizatsii profsoiuznoy raboty v novykh usoloviiakh," 1999, 83–86; and interview, Tula, June 1, 2001.

139. Golovets, 2001; and Gorenkov, interview, May 24, 2001.

140. Interview, 2001.

Chapter 6: Organized Labor in Hungary

1. Quoted in Tóth, 1994, 27.

2. Previously cited material in earlier chapters includes Tóth, 1994, 1997, and 2001; Frege and Tóth, 1999; and Neumann, 1997. Other sources include Maria Ladó, "Workers' and Employers' Interests," 1994; Ladó, "Continuity and Changes in Tripartism in Hungary," 1996; Lajos Héthy, "Negotiated Social Peace?" 1996; and Neumann, "Privatisation As a Challenge for Hungarian Trade Unions," 1999. For a view that

argues that unions have been relatively effective based upon survey responses from union officials, see Terry Cox and Laszlo Vas, "Hungary," 1998.

3. Stark and Bruszt, 1998.

4. For unions in the late communist period, see Stephen Nott, "The Shifting Position of Hungarian Trade Unions amidst Social and Economic Reforms," 1987: 63–87; Tóth, 1994; and Joe C. Davis, "The Splintering of the Hungarian Labor Movement," 1995: 371–88.

5. Karoly Gyorgy, chairman of the MSZOSZ international department, correspondence with me, October 29, 1997.

6. Cox and Vass, 1998. Perhaps this is an artifact of the survey itself, which may have been directed more to national leaders who operate at a political level and less to the grassroots leaders.

7. The best work on this topic is Neumann, 1997.

8. The MSZOSZ Newsletter, June 1996. Excellent sources on this period are Tóth, 1994; and Ladó, 1994.

9. The 1993 health care board election results were 45.22 percent the MSZOSZ, 19.13 percent LIGA, 12.8 percent the MOSZ, and 8.39 percent SZEF. For the pension board, the results were (respectively) 50.1 percent, 10.1 percent, 10.9 percent, and 10.6 percent. Workers' councils results were (respectively) 71.7 percent, 5.7 percent, 2.2 percent, and .02 percent (SZET garnered 49 percent in the public service councils, the relevant bodies for its members).

10. One report noted that by 1993 there were only three hundred workers' councils in Hungary with a total membership of twenty-four thousand and that hopes pinned on them to reshape labor relations have gone unrealized. See Mihaly Laki, "Opportunities for Workers' Participation in Privatization in Hungary," 1995, 317.

11. Tóth, 1994, 19.

12. Tóth, 2001, 88.

13. Tóth, 1997.

14. For examples of work councils being manipulated by management in individual firms, see Laki, 1995, 317–35; and the Suzuki case in Csaba Makó and Péter Novoszáth, "Employment Relations in Multinational Companies," 1995.

15. Cox and Vass, 1998.

16. Tóth, 2000, 306.

17. Tóth, 1994, suggests that new unions had branches at only 3–5 percent of all enterprises and often were able to attract only a small fraction of the workforce at a given enterprise.

18. Ladó, 1994, notes that from 1990 to 1991, after the reregistration, the MSZOSZ membership dropped from 2.7 million to 2 million.

19. Interview with Laszlo Bruszt, January 1997, Budapest.

20. Tóth, 1994.

21. Laszlo Andor, "Trade Unions in Hungary," 1996, 73.

22. See Cory Fine, "Public Sector Unionism and Strikes in Developing Countries," 1999: 1–15.

23. Tripartite bodies also existed in the public and state sectors, and at the regional level.

24. Ladó, 1996, 158, 166, 167.

25. Bruszt 1993; Tóth, 1997; and Héthy, 1996.

26. Foreign Broadcast Information Service (FBIS), June 1, 1994, 20.

27. Neumann, 1997, 6.

28. Ladó, 1994, 38.

29. FBIS, June 13, 1994, 12, and June 10, 1994, 12, respectively.

30. Judith Pataki, "Trade Unions' Role in Victory of Former Communists in Hungary," 1994, 1.

31. Lajos Héthy, "Anatomy of a Tripartite Experiment," 1995: 361–76, 371.

32. According to the ILO, by 1997 real wages in manufacturing had reached their 1992 levels. See ILO, *Key Indicators of the Labour Market, 1999*, 1999.

33. Stark and Bruszt, 1998, 174.

34. Ost, 2000, 511.

35. Tóth, 2000, 336.

36. Statement of MSZOSZ, "Evaluation of the Economic, Social Situation in Hungary," March 28, 2000, at www.mszosz.hu/news.htm.

37. Tóth, 2000, 334.

38. Tóth, 2001.

39. MSZOSZ, "Evaluation," 2000; and statement of István Gaskó, president of LIGA, "The Day They Broke the Camel's Back," 1999, at liga.telnet.hu.

40. Neumann, 1999, 5.

41. János Lukács, "Privatization and Employee Ownership in Hungary," 1995, 136.

42. Laki, 1995.

43. Neumann, 1999, 4.

44. "Report by the Confederate Council of MSZOSZ to the 3rd Congress of MSZOSZ," March 16, 1995, 16–17.

45. Head of the international relations department, interview, Budapest, January 1997.

46. Bartlomiej Kaminski and Michelle Riboud, *Foreign Involvement in Restructuring*, 2003, 11.

47. Gyorgy Takacs in "Privatisation: Trade Union Policy and Strategies," report for ILO Conference for Russian Trade Unions, Moscow, February 1995, 29.

48. Neumann, 1997. See similar comments in the Russian case by Tarasenko, 2001.

49. Andras Tóth, "The Role of Multi-Employer Collective Agreements in Regulating Terms and Conditions of Employment in Hungary," 1997: 329–56.

50. Frege and Tóth, 1999, 131.

51. Tóth, 2000, 308.

52. Neumann, 1999.

53. Neumann, 1999, 17.

54. Greskovits and Bohle, 2001, 21.

55. Kaminski and Riboud, 2003, 7.

56. From report of MSZOSZ, "Multinational Companies in Central and Eastern Europe: New Possibilities and Challenges for Trade Unions," presented at ILO Conference, Prague, December 1995. The largest investors in Hungary through the 1990s were Audi, IBM, Phillips, GM-Opel, General Electric, Zollnek Electric, and Ford, all of which, save GE, were greenfield projects.

57. Greskovits and Bohle, 2001, 20.

58. Tóth, 2000, 305.

59. OECD, *OECD Reviews of Foreign Direct Investment*, 2000.

60. Good overviews include Makó and Novoszáth, 1995; and David Bangert and József Poór, "Foreign Involvement in the Hungarian Economy," 1993: 817–40.

61. Kaminski and Riboud, 2003, 29.

62. MSZOSZ, "Multinational Companies,"1995.

63. Bangert and Poór, 1993, 837.

64. Makó and Novoszáth, 1995, 255–56.

65. Tóth, 1999.

66. Ladó, 1994, 27

67. Makó and Novoszáth, 1995; and Tóth, 1999.

68. Interview with Arpad, 1997.

69. Tóth, 1999.

70. Meardi, 2000, 195.

71. See Tóth, "Invention of Works Councils," 1997; and MSZOSZ, 1995.

72. Thirkell et al., 1998, 141–45.

73. Tóth, 1994, 31–35, develops this case at length. The circumstances that facilitated the emergence of the union, aside from the proclivities of management, included the strategic role of the union, the workers' high degree of qualification that makes replacement difficult, and the relatively low cost of wages in the total costs of the enterprise.

74. Makó and Novoszáth, 1995, 273.

75. Karoly Lorant, "The Impact of IMF Structural Adjustment Policies," 1999, also at www.developmentgap.org.

76. Stone, 2002.

77. Attila Agh, "Europeanization of Policy-Making in East Central Europe," 1999: 839–54.

78. Statement of MSZOSZ, "Evaluation," 2000.

79. Statement of István Gaskó, "The Day They Broke," 1999.

80. EU statement, quoted in Gaskó, 1999.

81. Emilio Gabaglio in "Management Turns Back on Talks with Rail Unions," at liga.telnet.hu/strike2.htm#management.

82. MSZOSZ, "Evaluation," 2000.

83. The Socialists came to power in the 2002 elections and have delivered wage increases to state sector workers and eliminated taxes on the minimum wage portion of earnings. Worker-friendly though this may be, it could produce larger problems in the economy, especially on competitiveness issue, as some MNCs (e.g., IBM, Phillips) have already closed some plants and moved to locales with cheaper labor. These developments, coming after most research for the Hungarian case was conducted, warrant further examination but cannot be covered here.

Chapter 7: Organized Labor in Ukraine

1. *Post-Postup* (Kyiv-L'viv), September 29–October 5, 1993, 3.

2. For a general review of democratic shortcomings in the country, see Kubicek, "The Limits of Electoral Democracy in Ukraine," 2001: 117–39.

3. Taras Kuzio, *Ukraine*, 1998.

4. Kubicek, *Unbroken Ties*, 2000.

5. Official figures supplied by the FPU organizational and membership department.

6. Figures in *Profspilkovki visti* (Kyiv, FPU paper), May 18, 2001, 2.

7. ILO (Kyiv office), "Dopolnitel'naia informatsiia k baze dannykh Konfederatsii Svobodnykh profsoiuzov Ukrainy," mimeo., 2001.

8. Yurii Pivavarov of the Solidarnost' Union informed me (interview, Donetsk, June 30, 1994) his union of small enterprise workers, Solidarity, had two million members, whereas all others estimated his membership at no more than ten thousand. Simon, 2000, 150, notes that VOST (All-Ukrainian Association of Workers' Solidarity) claimed two million members in 1992, although in 1994 VOST officials told me membership was a mere eight thousand.

9. Data come from figures reported by the Confederation of Ukrainian Free Trade Unions.

10. Semen Karikov, interview, Kyiv, July 24, 1994.

11. Viktor Stepanov, interview, Kyiv, July 4, 2001. At the time of the interview, he was ten days into a hunger strike in front of the parliament building, to win rights for his union.

12. *Aspekt* (Kyiv, newspaper of NPGU), July 2001, 6; and remarks of Volnyets at the IV Congress of the NPGU, Kyiv, July 2001.

13. Viacheslav Brodovsky, deputy chairman of the Volyn branch of the Capital-Regions Union, interview, Kyiv, July 2001.

14. ILO and State Committee on Statistics of Ukraine, "Personal Social and Economic Safety," 2001, 49–50. The survey sampled 8,200 residents of the country. A 1997 survey of 1,810 Ukrainians by Democratic Initiatives found that 88 percent of respondents claimed no membership in any type of association, even when trade unions were on the list of available choices. See data at www.dif.com.ua.

15. ILO, "Personal, Social and Economic Safety," 2001, 50–53.

16. Ihor Kharchenko, interview, Kyiv, June 8, 1994.

17. Mark Tarnawsky, head of the Free Union Institute (since closed), Kyiv, interview, May 19, 1994.

18. Konstanin Fesenko, former leader of the Coal Workers' Union, interview, Kyiv, May 24, 1994; and Ludmila Pereligina, chairman of the Cultural Workers' Union, interview, Kyiv, June 7, 1994.

19. *Mist* (Kyiv, former paper of the VPU), July 11, 1994, 13.

20. *Profsplikova hazeta* (Kyiv, former FPU paper), May 25, 1994, 3.

21. *Profspilkovi visti*, April 6, 2001, 1.

22. Bohdan Andrushkiv, head of the Ternopil Region FPU Unions, in *Profspilkovi visti*, April 6, 2001, 2.

23. Interview with Leonid Sachkov, head of the Union of Education and Science Workers, Kyiv, July 6, 2001.

24. Petr Shvets, "Narushiteli konstitutsii—kotvetu," *Profsoiuzy* (Moscow), no. 5, 2000, 17.

25. *Profspilkovi vedomosti*, 1995.

26. Mikhail Volnyets of the NPGU is its head, and its headquarters is in the NPGU office.

27. Brudovsky, 2001; and Viktor Dykovsky, head of the Independent Union of Kyiv Metro Drivers, interview, Kyiv, July 8, 2001.

28. Nikola Mitrov, head of the NPGU at Dobropoleugol (Donetsk region), interview, Kyiv, July 8, 2001.

29. Volnyets, presentation at IV Congress of the NPGU, Kyiv, July 2001.

30. Miners in Volyn rallied, calling for presidential rule in the country, and held meetings under the slogan "We Stand for Ukrainian Statehood." Meanwhile, miners in Luhansk in eastern Ukraine appealed directly to the Russian parliament for help. See Borisov, *Zabastovki*, 2001, 164.

31. For more details on Ukrainian regionalism, see Kubicek, "Regional Polarisation in Ukraine," 2000: 273–94.

32. The greatest cooperation has been in the coal mining sector, but even there it has been quite sporadic, and in 2001 Volnyets of the NPGU had little positive to say about his FPU rivals, accusing them of being in league with local authorities and doing little to protect workers.

33. A June 2001 survey by Democratic Initiatives found only 11 percent reporting satisfaction with the general direction of the country, and 68 percent thought Ukraine was headed in the wrong direction. These figures have been roughly the same since independence. See www.dif.com.ua.

34. For more on this period, see Roman Solchanyk, ed., *Ukraine*, 1992; and Taras Kuzio and Andrew Wilson, *Ukraine*, 1994.

35. Kubicek, *Unbroken Ties*, 2000.

36. V. V. Postolatij, "Sotsial'ne partnerstvo," 2000, 230.

37. Yurii Krivenko, head of the L'viv region Auto Transport and Road Workers, in *Profspilkovi visti*, April 6, 2001, 2.

38. Sachkov, 2001; and Pereligina, 1994. Yaroslav Kendzior, chairman of the L'viv FPU Unions, did produce a split in the organization by openly joining forces with Rukh, the national-democratic party whose primary constituencies are in western Ukraine.

39. Mykola Dvirnyi, FPU adviser to Stoian on political questions, interview, Kyiv, July 11, 2001.

40. Sachkov, interview, 2001.

41. Seven union leaders won majoritarian seats in 1998 elections. For more on unions and electoral activity, see D. Balan, "Uchast' Federatsiyi profesiykykh spilok Ukrayiny u vyborchykh kampaniiakh, 1994 ta 1998 rokiv," 2000, 26–40.

42. In its makeup, this body is perhaps the most pluralist in the region, as almost all of the non-FPU unions (VOST, NPGU, the railroad workers, the Academy of Science workers, the Solidarity unions) are included. Three independent unions that are closely allied to the FPU—those of internal affairs, military, and railroads —are also on this committee.

43. For a critical view of social partnership in Ukraine, see *Postolatij*, 2000, 227–30; and articles by V. I. Zhukov, I. M. Novak, and I. M. Dubrovs'kyj in *Suchasnyi prof-spilkobyi rukh v Ukrayiny*, 2000.

44. Kubicek, *Unbroken Ties*, 2000, 100–103.

45. Oleksandr Stoian, "Zakony prinimaiutsia i," 2000, 5–6.

46. Data from reports in *Profspilkovi visti*, March 23, 2001; April 13, 2001; May 18, 2001; and June 8, 2001.

47. G. Osovyj, "Profspilkovyj rukh v Ukraini," 2001, 3.

48. Serhei Donkriuk, FPU specialist on defense of socioeconomic questions, interview, Kyiv, July 23, 2001.

49. Evgen Golovakha, "Suchasna politychna sytuatsiia I perspektyva derzhavno-politychnoho ekonomichnoho rozvytku Ukrainy," 1993, 5.

50. More complete accounts are available in Borisov, *Zabastovki*, 2001, chapter 4; and Simon, 2000, chapter 6.

51. Kubicek, *Unbroken Ties*, 2000, 112–13.

52. Karikov, 1994; and statement by Mril' in *Mist*, May 16, 1994, 4.

53. Paul Kubicek, "What Happened to the Nationalists in Ukraine," 1999: 29–45.

54. Brudovsky, 2001.

55. Mitrov, 2001.

56. *Aspekt*, April 2001, 3.

57. *Profspilkovki visti*, March 16, 2001, 2.

58. Nina Karpachova, presentation at ILO Conference, Moscow.

59. Richard Frydman et al., *The Privatization Process in Russia, Ukraine, and the Baltic States*, 1993, 123.

60. Volodymyr Cherniak, "Privatizatsiia ili kollektivizatsiia?" 1994, 3.

61. EBRD, *Transition Report 2000*, 2000.

62. Cited in Trevor Buck et al., "Employee Welfare, Firm Governance and Performance in Ukraine," 2001.

63. Frydman et al., 1993, 122.

64. Ludmila Yakovleva, vice president of the Ukrainian Union of Industrialists and Entrepreneurs, interview, Kyiv, June 22, 1994.

65. Inna Styrnyk, "Profspilky ta pryvatizatsiia," 2000, 184.

66. Styrnyk, 184–85.

67. Styrnyk, interview, Kyiv, July 24, 2001.

68. Vasyl Kostrytsya, ILO representative in Kyiv (formerly president of the Union of Workers of Cooperatives and Other Forms of Non-State Property), interview, July 5, 2001.

69. Serhei Ukrainets, representative of the Union of Seafarers in Kyiv, interview, July 12, 2001.

70. Styrnyk, interview, 2001.

71. Vasil Yan'shyn, chairman of the Construction Workers Union, interview, Kyiv, July 9, 2001.

72. Vasyl Levchenko, vice chairman of the Union of Machine and Instrument Building Workers, interview, Kyiv, July 13, 2001. He estimates that this is the case in over half of the enterprises in his sector.

73. Sachkov, interview, Kyiv, July 6, 2001.

74. Styrnyk, interview, 2001.

75. Vasil Dudnyk, head of the Union of Automobile and Agricultural Machinery Workers, interview, Kyiv, July 9, 2001.

76. Oleksandr Chernysh, head of the Defense Workers Union, interview, Kyiv, July 9, 2001.

77. Bohdan Prokopenko, head of the L'viv Region Textile and Light Industry Workers, interview, L'viv, July 23, 2001; and Anatolii Taranchuk, chairman of the Union of Metal Treatment Workers, interview, Kyiv, July 11, 2001.

78. Dudnyk, 2001.

79. Svetlana Rodina, secretary for socioeconomic questions for the Unions of Agro-Industrial Workers, interview, Kyiv, July 4, 2001.

80. Oleksandr Popel, president of the Oil and Gas Workers' Union, interview, Kyiv, July 6, 2001.

81. Yan'shyn, 2001.

82. Cited in report of Volodymyr Bondarenko, president of the Union of Workers in Innovative and Small Business, presented to III Congress of the Union, 2000.

83. Vladimir Bondarenko, interview, Kyiv, July 10, 2001.

84. Volnyets, remarks at IV Congress of NPGU, Kyiv, July 26, 2001.

85. Yan'shyn, 2001.

86. Stepanov, 2001.

87. *Profspilkovki visti*, March 9, 2001, 7.

88. Yarema Zhugayvich, president of the Workers in Aviation Industry, interview, Kyiv, July 11, 2001. Figures are from his compilation, made in February 2001.

89. Buck et al., 2001.

90. Yan'shyn, 2001.

91. Ihor Lutsyshyn, head of the L'viv regional FPU, in *Profspilkovi visti*, April 20, 2001, 2.

92. EBRD, *Transition Report 2001*, 2001.

93. Buck et al., "Exporting Activity in Transitional Economies," 2000: 44–66.

94. Data on Ukraine from *Kyiv Post*, June 29, 2001. Other countries' figures from EBRD, *Transition Report 2000*, 2000.

95. The one exception in terms of international financial institutions has been the coal sector, viewed as generally doomed by the IMF and World Bank, which have urged closure of many mines, on safety and profitability grounds. Some representatives of miners do grumble about this influence but insist that the larger part of the problem is corruption by the government and mine owners which prevents restructuring funds from saving mines and jobs.

96. Kostrytsya, 2001.

97. Dudnyk, 2001.

98. Popel, 2001.

99. Yan'shyn, 2001.

100. Stepan Matviykiv, head of the L'viv Region Auto and Agricultural Machinery Workers Unions, interview, L'viv; and Lutsyshyn, interview, L'viv, both on July 23, 2001.

101. Rodina, 2001; and Volodymyr Chepur, president of the Union of Agro-Industrial Workers, interview, Kyiv, July 27, 2001.

102. Dudnyk, 2001; and Chepur, 2001.

103. Most of this information comes from Brodovsky, 2001, who works at the plant and actively participates in the alternative union movement.

104. Matviykiv, 2001.

105. Many of these joint ventures are part of a larger enterprise, and thus their unions are part of the branch union of the larger enterprise and fall within the FPU structure.

106. Interview and on-site tour with Anatolii Mykhailenko, president of the Union of Joint Ventures Workers, Kyiv, July 12, 2001.

Chapter 8: Conclusion

1. Quoted in Davis, 2001, 103.
2. Andrzej Mokrzyszewski, "Zaufanie pracownikow do zwiazkow zawodowych," reported by CBOS, August 2001, online.
3. Boris Golovkin, vice chairman of the FNPR Nizhniy Novgorod Regional Branch, interview, Nizhniy Novgorod, June 8, 2001.
4. As we saw in the Russian and Ukrainian cases, any such "Union of Workers in Small Business" should be regarded as a union of employers interested in furthering the small business sector.
5. Stone, 2002.
6. Garrett, 1998; and Peter Lange and Lyle Scruggs, "Where Have All the Members Gone?" 1998.
7. Mandel, 1996, 59.
8. Anders Aslund, "Lessons of the First Four Years of Systematic Change in Eastern Europe," 1994: 22–38.
9. Ost, "Labor Weakness," 2001, 47–48.
10. Quoted in Grzegorz Kolodko, *Post-Communist Transition*, 2000, 54.
11. In particular, see Stephan Haggard and Robert Kaufman, *The Political Economy of Democratic Transitions*, 1995; and Geddes, 1995.
12. Peregudov, 1999.
13. Linz and Stepan, 1996, 5.
14. Data are drawn from the sourcebook for this study: Loek Halman, *The European Values Study*, 2001.
15. See Richard Rose, "A Decade of New Russia Barometer Surveys," 2002; and periodic report "Politychny portret Ukrainy," by Democratic Initiatives, available at www.dif.com.ua.
16. All data are taken from Anna Grudniewicz and Michal Wenzel, "Rozumienie, Akceptacja i Ocena Funkcjonowania Polskiej Demokratacji," CBOS Report, 2001, available online at www.cbos.org.pl. The representative samples included 1,052 respondents.
17. Kolarska-Bobinska, 1994, 147.
18. Ost and Crowley, "The Surprise," 2001, 9.
19. Greskovits, 1998.
20. I do not include in this discussion Russia and Ukraine, where incumbent executives have won, but often using questionable tactics.
21. This is not to say that the weaknesses of unions in Western states have been without negative effects. An example is the increasing inequality in the United States and Britain as a result of deunionization.
22. See Przeworski et al., "What Makes Democracies Endure?" 1997.
23. One day, of course, the situation may improve in these states, but those who had pinned their hopes on the 2002 parliamentary elections in Ukraine, in which the "party of power" ended up with the most seats, would be disappointed. Viktor Yushchenko, head of the largest "democratic" force, lamented, "Democracy is the loser. That is the main defeat of these elections." See *New York Times*, April 2, 2002.
24. Colin Crouch, "Conclusion," 1990, 359.
25. Meardi, 2000.

26. In particular see Ost, 2000; and my earlier work, Kubicek, 2000, that examined corporatist structures in a number of countries.

27. Colin Crouch, "National Wage Determination and European Monetary Union," 2000.

28. Ost, 2002.

29. Neumann, 1997.

30. See Turner, 1991; Thelen, 1994; and Wolfgang Streeck, "Neo-Corporatist Industrial Relations and the Economic Crisis in West Germany,"1984.

31. Ost, 2002, 47.

32. Interview, Budapest, January 1997.

33. Kubicek, 1999, 98.

34. For a critique of the civil society program and discourse, see Peter Kopecky and Edward Barnfield, "Charting the Decline of Civil Society," 1999.

35. Andrzej Matla, coordinator of the International Department, interview, Gdansk, July 8, 2002.

36. Neumann, 1997.

37. This point was brought home very explicitly during a roundtable with Solidarity officials at the Volkswagen plant in Poznan, July 5, 2002; and also mentioned with respect to the auto industry in Poland by Matla, 2002.

38. Borisov, *Zabastovki*, 2001.

39. Gardawski, *Rzeczpospolita*, March 20, 2002.

40. Ost, "Labor Weakness," 2001, 48.

41. Meardi, 2000, 2.

42. For more on this point, see Laba, 1991; and Goodwyn, 1991.

43. Anecdote told to author by Matla, 2002. For more on the nostalgia of workers in Poland, see Meardi, 2000.

BIBLIOGRAPHY

10 *Let GMPR Budushchee Profsoiuza—za molodezh'iu*. Moscow: Federation of Independent Russian Trade Unions, 2001.

Addison, John, and W. Stanley Siebert. "Recent Developments in Social Policy in the New European Union." *Industrial and Labor Relations Review* 48:1 (October 1994): 5–27.

Agh, Attila. "Europeanization of Policy-Making in East Central Europe: The Hungarian Approach to EU Accession." *Journal of European Public Policy* 6:5 (1999): 839–54.

Aro, Pekka, and Paula Repo. *Trade Union Experiences in Collective Bargaining in Central Europe*. Budapest: International Labor Organization, 1997.

Ash, Timothy Garton. *The Magic Lantern*. New York: Random House, 1990.

Ashwin, Sarah. "Russia's Official Trade Unions: Renewal or Redundancy?" *Industrial Relations Journal* 26 (September 1995): 192–203.

———. *Russian Workers: The Anatomy of Patience*. Manchester: Manchester University Press, 1999.

Aslund, Anders. *How Russia Became a Market Economy*. Washington, DC: Brookings Institution, 1995.

———. "Lessons of the First Four Years of Systematic Change in Eastern Europe." *Journal of Comparative Economics* 19:1 (1994): 22–38.

Baglioni, Giovanni, and Colin Crouch, eds. *European Industrial Relations: The Challenge of Flexibility*. London: Sage, 1990.

Balan, D. "Uchast' Federatsiyi profesiykykh spilok Ukrayiny u vyborchykh kampaniiakh 1994 ta 1998 rokiv." In *Suchasnyi profspilkobyi rukh v Ukrayiny*. Kyiv: Academy of Labor and Social Relations, 2000.

Balcerowicz, Leszek. "Understanding Post-Communist Transitions." *Journal of Democracy* 5:4 (1994): 75–89.

Bamber, Greg, and Valentin Peschanski. "Transforming Industrial Relations in Russia: A Case of Convergence with Industrialized Market Economies?" *Industrial Relations Journal* 27 (March 1996): 74–88.

Bangert, David, and József Poór. "Foreign Involvement in the Hungarian Economy: Its Impact on Human Resource Management." *The International Journal of Human Resource Management* 4:4 (December 1993): 817–40.

Bartlett, David, and Anna Seleny. "The Political Enforcement of Liberalism: Bargaining, Institutions, and Auto Multinationals in Hungary." *International Studies Quarterly* 42:3 (1998): 319–38.

Bartosz, Julian. "Polish Trade Unions: Caught Up in the Political Battle." *Labor Focus on Eastern Europe* (1996): 38–58.

Bedi, Arjun, and Andrzej Cieslik. "Foreign Direct Investment and Host Country Regional Export Performance: Evidence from Poland." Warsaw: University of Warsaw, Faculty of Economics, Discussion Paper #52, 2000.

Berman, Sheri. "Civil Society and the Collapse of the Weimar Republic." *World Politics* 49:3 (April 1997): 401–29.

Bermeo, Nancy. "Civil Society after Democracy: Some Conclusions." In *Civil Society before Democracy: Lessons from Nineteenth Century Europe*, edited by Nancy Bermeo and Philip Nord. Lanham, MD: Rowman and Littlefield, 2000.

Bielasiak, Jack. "Workers and Mass Participation in 'Socialist Democracy.'" In *Blue Collar Workers in Eastern Europe*, edited by Jan Triska and Charles Gati. London: George Allen and Unwin, 1981.

Biziukov, Petr. "Al'ternativnye profsoiuzy na puti osvoeniia sotsial'novo prostranstva." *Sotsiologicheskie issledovanie* 5 (2001): 34–36.

Blanchflower, David, and Richard Freeman. "Attitudinal Legacies of Communist Labor Relations." *Industrial and Labor Relations* Review 50:3 (April 1997): 438–59.

Blasi, Joseph, Maya Kroumova, and Douglas Kruse. *Kremlin Capitalism: Privatizing the Russian Economy*. Ithaca: Cornell University Press, 1997.

Blejer, Mario, and Fabrizio Coricelli, eds. *The Making of Economic Reform in Eastern Europe*. Aldershot, U.K.: Edward Elgar, 1995.

Borisov, Vadim. "Sotsial'noe partnerstvo v Rossii: spetsifika ili podmena poniatii." *Sotsiologicheskie issledovanie* 5 (2001): 56–66.

———. *Zabastovki v ugol'oi promyshlenosti*. Moscow: Centre for Comparative Labor Research, 2001.

Borisov, Vadim, Simon Clarke, and Peter Fairbrother. "Does Trade Unionism Have a Future in Russia?" *Industrial Relations Journal* 25:1 (1994): 15–25.

Bruszt, Laszlo. "Workers, Managers, and State Bureaucrats and the Economic Transformation in Hungary." In *Paradoxes of Transition*, edited by Jody Jensen and Ferenc Miszlivetz. Szombathely: Savaria University Press, 1993.

Buck, Trevor, Igor Filatotchev, Natalya Demina, and Mike Wright. "Exporting Activity in Transitional Economies: An Enterprise-Level Study." *Journal of Development Studies* 37 (2000): 44–66.

Buck, Trevor, Mike Wright, Igor Filatotchev, and Natalya Demina. "Employee Welfare, Firm Governance and Performance in Ukraine." Presented to ILO Conference "Confronting Socio-Economic Insecurity in Ukraine." Kyiv, 31 May–1 June 2001.

Bunce, Valerie. "Paper Curtains and Paper Tigers." *Slavic Review* 54:4 (Winter 1995): 979–87.

———. "Should Transitologists Be Grounded?" *Slavic Review* 54:1 (Spring 1995): 111–27.

Bunce, Valerie, and John Echols. "Soviet Politics in the Brezhnev Era: Pluralism or Corporatism?" In *Soviet Politics in the Brezhnev Era*, edited by Donald Kelley. New York: Praeger, 1980.

Cameron, David. "Social Democracy, Corporatism, Labor Quiescence and the Representation of Economic Interests in Advanced Capitalist Society." In *Order and Conflict in Contemporary Capitalism*, edited by John Goldthorpe. Oxford: Oxford University Press, 1984.

Carothers, Thomas. *Aiding Democracy Abroad*. Washington, DC: Carnegie Endowment for International Peace, 1999.

Cerny, Philip. "Paradoxes of the Competition State: The Dynamics of Political Globalization." *Government and Opposition* 32:2 (1997): 251–74.

Chetvernina, T., P. Smirnov, and N. Dunaeva. "Mesto profsoiuza na predpriiatii." *Voprosy ekonomiki* 6 (June 1995): 83–89.

Christensen, Paul T. *Russia's Workers in Transition: Labor, Management, and the State under Gorbachev and Yeltsin.* De Kalb: Northern Illinois University Press, 1999.

Clarke, Gerald. "NGOs and Politics in the Developing World." *Political Studies* 46:1 (March 1998): 36–52.

Clarke, Simon. "Russian Trade Unions in the 1999 Duma Election." *Journal of Communist Studies and Transition Politics* 17:2 (June 2001): 43–69.

Clarke, Simon, Peter Fairbrother, and Vadim Borisov. *The Workers' Movement in Russia.* Aldershot, U.K.: Edward Elgar, 1995.

Clarke, Simon, Peter Fairbrother, Michael Burawoy, and Pavel Krotov. *What about the Workers?: Workers and the Transition to Capitalism in Russia.* London: Verso, 1993.

Cohen, Stephen. *Failed Crusade: America and the Tragedy of Post-Communist Russia.* New York: Norton, 2000.

Collier, David, and Ruth B. Collier. *Shaping the Political Arena: Critical Junctures, the Labor Movement, and Regime Dynamics in Latin America.* Princeton: Princeton University Press, 1991.

Connor, Walter D. *The Accidental Proletariat: Workers, Politics, and Crisis in Gorbachev's Russia.* Princeton: Princeton University Press, 1991.

———. *Tattered Banners: Labor, Conflict, and Corporatism in Postcommunist Russia.* Boulder: Westview, 1996.

Conquest, Robert. *Industrial Workers in the U.S.S.R.* New York: Praeger, 1967.

Cook, Linda. *Labor and Liberalization: Trade Unions in the New Russia.* New York: Twentieth Century Fund Press, 1997.

———. "Russia's Labor Relations: Consolidation or Disintegration?" In *Russia's Future: Consolidation or Disintegration?* edited by Douglas Blum. Boulder: Westview, 1994.

———. *The Soviet Social Contract and Why It Failed: Welfare Policy and Workers' Politics from Brezhnev to Yeltsin.* Cambridge: Harvard University Press, 1993.

Cooke, Philip, Robert Wilson, and Krzysztov Bialon. "Inward Investment and Economic Development in Poland." *European Planning Studies* 5:5 (October 1997): 691–98.

Cox, Terry, and Laszlo Vas. "Hungary: The Politics of Unions and Employers' Associations." Paper presented to the Annual Meeting of the American Political Science Association, Boston, September 1998.

Crouch, Colin. *Industrial Relations and European State Traditions.* Oxford: Oxford University Press, 1993.

———. "National Wage Determination and European Monetary Union." In *After the Euro: Shaping Institutions for Governance in the Wake of European Monetary Union,* edited by Colin Crouch. Oxford: Oxford University Press, 2000.

Crowley, Stephen. *Hot Coal, Cold Steel: Russian and Ukrainian Workers from the End of the Soviet Union to the Post-Communist Transformations.* Ann Arbor: University of Michigan Press, 1997.

Crowley, Stephen, and David Ost, eds. *Workers after Workers' States.* Lanham, MD: Rowman and Littlefield, 2001.

Dahl, Robert. *Polyarchy.* New Haven: Yale University Press, 1971.

Davis, Joe C. "The Splintering of the Hungarian Labor Movement." *East European Quarterly* 29:3 (September 1995): 371–88.

Davis, Sue. *Trade Unions in Russia and Ukraine, 1985–1995*. New York: Palgrave, 2001.

de Weydenthal, Jan B. "Poland: Workers and Politics." In *Blue Collar Workers in Eastern Europe*, edited by Jan Triska and Charles Gati. London: George Allen and Unwin, 1981.

Di Palma, Guiseppe. *To Craft Democracies: An Essay on Democratic Transitions*. Berkeley: University of California Press, 1990.

Diamond, Larry. "Is the Third Wave Over?" *Journal of Democracy* 7:3 (April 1996): 20–37.

Djilas, Milan. *The New Class*. New York: Harcourt Brace, 1957.

Drezner, Daniel. "Globalization and Policy Convergence." *International Studies Review* 3:1 (Spring 2001): 53–78.

EBRD. *EBRD Transition Report 1995*. London: European Bank for Reconstruction and Development, 1995.

———. *EBRD Transition Report 2000*. London: European Bank for Reconstruction and Development, 2000.

———. *EBRD Transition Report 2001*. London: European Bank for Reconstruction and Development, 2001.

Egorov, V. "Privatisation and Labour Relations in the Countries of Central and Eastern Europe." *Industrial Relations Journal* 27:1 (1996): 89–100.

Ekiert, Grzegorz, and Jan Kubik. *Rebellious Civil Society: Popular Protest and Democratic Consolidation in Poland, 1989–1993*. Ann Arbor: University of Michigan Press, 1999.

Elster, Jon. *The Cement of Society*. Cambridge: Cambridge University Press, 1989.

Elster, Jon, Claus Offe, and U. K. Preuss. *Institutional Design in Post-Communist Democracies: Rebuilding the Ship at Sea*. Cambridge: Cambridge University Press, 1998.

Ernst, Maurice, Michael Alexeev, and Paul Marer. *Transforming the Core: Restructuring Industrial Enterprises in Russia and Central Europe*. Boulder: Westview, 1995.

Estrin, Saul. *Privatization in Central and Eastern Europe*. London: Longman, 1994.

Filtzer, Donald. *Soviet Workers and De-Stalinization*. Cambridge: Cambridge University Press, 1992.

Fine, Cory. "Public Sector Unionism and Strikes in Developing Countries: The Case of Hungary." *Journal of Collective Negotiations in the Public Sector* 28:1 (1999): 1–15.

Fischer, Paul. *Foreign Direct Investment in Russia*. New York: St. Martin's, 2000.

Fish, M. Steven. *Democracy from Scratch*. Princeton: Princeton University Press, 1995.

Freeland, Chrystia. *Sale of the Century: Russia's Wild Ride from Communism to Capitalism*. New York: Crown Business, 2000.

Freeman, Richard. "Are Your Wages Set in Beijing?" *Journal of Economic Perspectives* 9:3 (Summer 1995): 15–32.

Frege, Carola, and Andras Tóth. "Institutions Matter: Union Solidarity in Hungary and East Germany." *British Journal of Industrial Relations* 37:1 (March 1999): 117–40.

Friedgut, Theodore, and Lewis Siegelbaum. "Perestroika from Below: The Soviet Miners' Strike and Its Aftermath." *New Left Review* 181 (1990): 5–32.

Friedman, Thomas. *The Lexus and the Olive Tree*. New York: Farrar, Strauss, and Giroux, 1999.

Frydman, Richard, Andrzej Rapaczynski, and John Earle. *The Privatization Process in Russia, Ukraine, and the Baltic States.* Budapest: Central European University Press, 1993.

Gaciarz, Barbara, and Wlodzimierz Panków. *Przeksztalcenia przedsiebiorstw przemyslowych: strategie, aktorzy, efety.* Warsaw: Higher School of Enterprise and Administration, 1997.

Gardawski, Juliusz. "Forms and Structure of Ownership." In *Direct Privatization: Investors, Managers, Employees,* edited by Barbara Morocz. Warsaw: Institute of Political Studies, 1999.

———. *Poland's Industrial Workers on the Return to Democracy and Market Economy.* Warsaw: Friedrich Ebert Foundation, 1996.

———. "Zasieg zwiazkow zawodowych w wybranych dzialach przemyslu i sekcjach uslug publicznych." In *Rozpad Bastionu? Zwiazki zawodowe w gospodarce prywatyzowanej,* edited by Juliusz Gardawski et al. Warsaw: Institute of Public Affairs, 1999.

———. *Zwiazki zawodowe na rozdrozu.* Warsaw: Institute of Public Affairs, 2001.

Garnett, Geoffrey. *Partisan Politics in the Global Economy.* Cambridge: Cambridge University Press, 1998.

Geddes, Barbara. "Challenging the Conventional Wisdom." In *Economic Reform and Democracy,* edited by Larry Diamond and Marc Plattner. Baltimore: Johns Hopkins University Press, 1995.

———. "What Do We Know about Democratization after Twenty Years?" *Annual Review of Political Science* 2 (1999): 115–44.

Gellner, Ernest. *Conditions of Liberty: Civil Society and Its Rivals.* New York: Allen Lane, 1994.

Golden, Miriam. "The Dynamics of Trade Unionism and National Economic Performance." *American Political Science Review* 87:2 (June 1993): 439–54.

Golden, Miriam, Michael Wallerstein, and Peter Lange. "Unions, Employers' Associations and Wage-Setting Institutions in North and Central Europe, 1950–1992." *Industrial and Labor Relations Review* 50:3 (1997): 379–401.

Golovakha, Evgen. "Suchasna politychna sytuatsiia I perspektyva derzhavnopolitychnoho ekonomichnoho rozvytku Ukrainy." *Politychny portret Ukrainy* 4 (December 1993): 1–6.

Gomulka, Stanislaw. "The IMF-Supported Programs of Poland and Russia, 1990–1994: Principles, Errors, and Results." *Journal of Comparative Economics* 20 (June 1995): 316–46.

Goodwyn, Lawrence. *Breaking the Barrier: The Rise of Solidarity in Poland.* Oxford: Oxford University Press, 1991.

Gordon, Leonid. "Massovoe rasprostranenie skrytykh zarabotkov." *VARIA* (2000): 3–63.

Gordon, Leonid, et al. *Kpytoy plast.* Moscow: Reformugol, 1999.

Gould-Davies, Nigel, and Ngarie Woods. "Russia and the IMF." *International Affairs* 75:1 (1999): 1–22.

Gradev, Grigor. "Bulgarian Trade Unions in Transition: The Taming of the Hedgehog." In *Workers after Workers' States,* edited by Stephen Crowley and David Ost. Lanham, MD: Rowman and Littlefield, 2001.

Graham, Carol. "Safety Nets and Market Transitions: What Poland Can Learn from Latin America." *Brookings Review* (Winter 1994): 36–40.

Greskovits, Bela. *The Political Economy of Protest and Patience: East European and Latin American Transformations Compared.* Budapest: Central European University Press, 1998.

Greskovits, Bela, and Dorothee Bohle. "Development Paths on Europe's Periphery: Hungary's and Poland's Return to Europe Compared." *Polish Sociological Review* 133:1 (2001): 3–27.

Haggard, Stephan, and Robert Kaufman. *The Political Economy of Democratic Transitions.* Princeton: Princeton University Press, 1995.

Hall, John A., ed. *Civil Society: Theory, History, Comparison.* Cambridge: Polity Press, 1995.

Halman, Loek. *The European Values Study: A Third Wave.* Tilburg, Netherlands: Tilburg University, 2001.

Hanson, Stephen, and Jeffrey Kopstein. "The Weimar/Russia Comparision." *Post-Soviet Affairs* 13:3 (1997): 252–83.

Havel, Vaclav, et al. *Power of the Powerless.* Armonk, NY: M. E. Sharpe, 1990.

Hedlund, Stefan. "Russia and the IMF: A Sordid Tale of Moral Hazard." *Demokratizatsiya* 9:1 (Winter 2001): 104–43.

Herod, Andrew. "Theorising Trade Unions in Transition." In *Theorising Transition: The Political Economy of Post-Communist Transformations,* edited by John Pickles and Adrian Smith. London: Routledge, 1998.

Héthy, Lajos. "Anatomy of a Tripartite Experiment: Attempted Social and Economic Agreement in Hungary." *International Labour Review* 134:3 (1995): 361–76.

———. "Negotiated Social Peace? An Attempt to Reach a Social and Economic Agreement in Hungary." In *Parliaments and Organized Interests: Second Steps,* edited by Attila Agh and Gabriella Ilonszki. Budapest: Hungarian Centre for Democracy Studies, 1996.

Hewett, Ed. *Reforming the Soviet Economy: Equality versus Efficiency.* Washington, DC: Brookings Institution, 1988.

Higley, John, and Robert Gunther, eds. *Elites and Democratic Consolidation in Latin America and Southern Europe.* Cambridge: Cambridge University Press, 1992.

Hirsch, Barry, and John Addison. *Analysis of Unions: New Approaches and Evidence.* London: Allen and Unwin, 1986.

Hirst, Paul, and Graham Thompson. *Globalization in Question.* Cambridge: Polity, 1999.

Holmes, Leslie. *Postcommunism: An Introduction.* Durham, NC: Duke University Press, 1997.

Hough, Jerry. "Policy-Making and the Worker." In *Industrial Labor in the USSR,* edited by Arcadius Kahan and Blair Ruble. New York: Pergamon Press, 1979.

Huntington, Samuel. *Political Order in Changing Societies.* New Haven: Yale University Press, 1968.

ILO. *Key Indicators of the Labour Market, 1999.* Geneva: International Labour Organization, 1999.

———. *World Employment Report, 1996–1997.* Geneva: International Labour Organization, 1997.

———. *Yearbook of Labor Statistics, 1999–2000.* Geneva: International Labour Organization, 2000.

ILO and State Committee on Statistics of Ukraine. "Personal Social and Economic

Safety: Measurement Problems and Solutions." Geneva and Kyiv: International Labour Organization, 2001.

ILO-CEET. "Dealing with Multinationals: A Handbook for Trade Unions in Central and Eastern Europe." Budapest: International Labour Organization Central and East European Team, 1996.

―――. "Report on ILO Seminar on Collective Bargaining in Central and Eastern Europe." Budapest: International Labour Organization Central and East European Team, 1996.

Inglot, Tomasz. "Between High Politics and Civil Society: Polish Trade Unions in the Process of Democratization after 1989." *Perspectives on Political Science* 27:3 (Summer 1998): 148–54.

Jackiewicz, Irena. "Solidairity in a Double Role: Political Representation and Pressure Group, 1991–1994." In *Parliaments and Organized Interests: Second Steps,* edited by Attila Agh and Gabriella Ilonszki. Budapest: Hungarian Centre for Democracy Studies, 1996.

Javeline, Debra. *Protest and the Politics of Blame: The Russian Response to Unpaid Wages.* Ann Arbor: University of Michigan Press, 2003.

Jowitt, Ken. *New World Disorder.* Berkeley: University of California Press, 1992.

Kaminski, Bartlomiej, and Michelle Ribound. *Foreign Involvement in Restructuring: Evidence from Hungary.* Washington, DC: World Bank Technical Paper No. 453, 2003.

Kapstein, Ethan. "Workers and the World Economy." *Foreign Affairs* 75:3 (May–June 1996): 16–37.

Karelina, Marina. "Tendentsii izmeneniia chislennocti professional'nykh soiuzov." *Sotsiologicheskie issledovanie* 5 (2001): 40–48.

Karklins, Rasma. "Explaining Regime Change in the Soviet Union." *Europe-Asia Studies* 46:1 (January 1994): 29–45.

Karl, Terry Lynn. "Dilemmas of Democratization in Latin America." *Comparative Politics* 23:1 (October 1990): 1–23.

Katzenstein, Peter. *Small States in World Markets.* Ithaca: Cornell University Press, 1985.

Kideckel, David. "Winning the Battles, Losing the War: Contradictions of Romanian Labor in the Post-Communist Transformation." In *Workers after Workers' States,* edited by Stephen Crowley and David Ost. Lanham, MD: Rowman and Littlefield, 2001.

King, Charles. "Post-Postcommunism: Transition, Comparison, and the End of 'Eastern Europe,'" *World Politics* 53:1 (October 2000): 143–72.

Klement, Karin. "Predposylki kollektubhykh aktsii protests ha predpriiatiiakh." *Sotsualogicheskie issledovaniia* 9 (1996): 64–76.

Kloc, Kazimierz. "Polish Labor in Transition." *Telos* 92 (1992): 139–48.

Kolakowski, Leszek. "The Intelligentsia." In *Poland: The Genesis of a Revolution,* edited by Abraham Brumberg. New York: Random House, 1983.

Kolarska-Bobinska, Lena. *Aspirations, Values and Interests: Poland, 1989–1994.* Warsaw: IFIS Publishers, 1994.

Kolodko, Grzegorz. *Post-Communist Transition.* Rochester: University of Rochester Press, 2000.

Konrad, George. *Antipolitics.* New York: Harcourt Brace, 1984.

Kopecky, Peter, and Edward Barnfield. "Charting the Decline of Civil Society." In *Democracy without Borders: Transnationalization and Conditionality in New Democracies,* edited by Jean Grugel. London: Routledge, 1999.

Kopecky, Peter, and Cas Mudde. "What Has Eastern Europe Taught Us about the Democratization Literature (and Vice Versa)?" *European Journal of Political Research* 37:4 (2000): 517–39.

Kovaleva, Natalia. "Konflikty, profsoiuzy, sotsial'naia zashchita: otsenki rabotnikov i rukovoditelei predpriiatii." *Monitoring obshchestbennovo mneniia* 5:31 (September–October 1997): 26–32.

Kowalik, Tadeusz. "From 'Self-Governing Republic' to Capitalism: Polish Workers and Intellectuals." In *Europe: Central and East,* edited by Marguerite Mendell and Klaus Nielsen. Montreal: Black Rose Books, 1995.

Kramer, Mark. "Polish Workers and the Post-Communist Transition." *Communist and Post-Communist Studies* 28:1 (March 1995): 71–114.

Kubicek, Paul. "Delegative Democracy in Russia and Ukraine." *Communist and Post-Communist Studies* (December 1994): 443–61.

———. "The Limits of Electoral Democracy in Ukraine." *Democratization* 8:2 (Summer 2001): 117–39.

———. "Organized Labor in Postcommunist States: Will the Western Sun Set on It, Too?" *Comparative Politics* 32:1 (October 1999): 83–102.

———. "Regional Polarisation in Ukraine: Public Opinion, Voting and Legislative Behaviour." *Europe-Asia Studies* 52:2 (March 2000): 273–94.

———. *Unbroken Ties: The State, Interest Associations, and Corporatism in Post-Soviet Ukraine.* Ann Arbor: University of Michigan Press, 2000.

———. "What Happened to the Nationalists in Ukraine." *Nationalism and Ethnic Politics* 5:1 (Spring 1999): 29–45.

Kubik, Jan. "Between the State and Networks of 'Cousins': The Role of Civil Society and Noncivil Associations in the Democratization of Poland." In *Civil Society before Democracy: Lessons from Nineteenth-Century Europe,* edited by Nancy Bermeo and Philip Nord. Lanham, MD: Rowman and Littlefield, 2000.

Kusmierz, Magdalena. "Unions versus Union: Challenges of Poland's Integration and Opportunities for Polish Labor Movement." Graduate School of Social Research at Institute of Philosophy and Sociology, Polish Academy of Sciences, unpublished manuscript, 2001.

Kuzio, Taras. *Ukraine: State and Nation Building.* London: Routledge, 1998.

Kuzio, Taras, and Andrew Wilson. *Ukraine: Perestroika to Independence.* New York: St. Martin's, 1994.

Laba, Roman. *The Roots of Solidarity.* Princeton: Princeton University Press, 1991.

Ladó, Maria. "Continuity and Changes in Tripartism in Hungary." In *Parliaments and Organized Interests: Second Steps,* edited by Attila Agh and Gabriella Ilonszki. Budapest: Hungarian Centre for Democracy Studies, 1996.

———. "Workers' and Employers' Interests—As They Are Represented in the Changing Industrial Relations in Hungary." Budapest: Institute for Labor Research, 1994.

Laki, Mihaly. "Opportunities for Workers' Participation in Privatization in Hungary: The Case of the Eger Flour Mill." *Europe-Asia Studies* 47:2 (February 1995): 317–35.

Lane, David. *Soviet Labour and the Ethic of Communism: Full Employment and the Labour Process in the USSR.* Boulder: Westview, 1987.

Lange, Peter, and Lyle Scruggs. "Globalization and National Labor Market Institutions." *Journal of Politics* 64:1 (2002): 126–53.

———. "Where Have All the Members Gone? Union Density in the Era of Globalization." Working Paper 1.63, Center for German and European Studies, University of California, Berkeley, 1998.

Lee, Eddy. "Globalization and Labour Standards: A Review of Issues." *International Labour Review* 136:2 (Summer 1997): 173–89.

Levi, Margaret. "Social and Unsocial Capital: A Review Essay of Robert Putnam's *Making Democracy Work.*" *Politics and Society* 24:1 (March 1996): 45–55.

Levitsky, Steven, and Lucan Way. "Between a Shock and a Hard Place: The Dynamics of Labor–Backed Adjustment in Poland and Argentina." *Comparative Politics* 30:2 (January 1998): 171–92.

Lewis, Paul G., ed. *Democracy and Civil Society in Eastern Europe.* New York: St. Martin's, 1992.

Linz, Juan, and Alfred Stepan. *Problems of Democratic Transition and Consolidation.* Baltimore: Johns Hopkins University Press, 1996.

Lohr, Eric. "Arkadii Volsky's Political Base." *Europe-Asia Studies* 45:5 (1993): 811–29.

Lorant, Karoly. "The Impact of IMF Structural Adjustment Policies: The Case of Hungary." In *The All-Too-Visible Hand: A Five-Country Look at the Long and Destructive Reach of the IMF.* Washington, DC: Development Gap, 1999.

Lukács, János. "Privatization and Employee Ownership in Hungary." *The Journal of Employee Ownership Law and Finance* 7:4 (1995): 133–44.

Madison, James. "Federalist X." In *The Federalist Papers*, edited by Isaac Kramnick. New York: Penguin, 1987 [first published 1788].

Makó, Csaba, and Péter Novoszáth. "Employment Relations in Multinational Companies: The Hungarian Case." In *Industrial Transformation in Europe*, edited by Eckhard Dittrich et al. London: Sage, 1995.

Maksimov, B. I. "Klasovyi konflikt na Vyborgskom TBK: nabliudeniia i analiz." *Sotsiologicheskie issledovanie* 1 (2001): 35–47.

Mandel, David. *Perestroika and the Soviet People.* Montreal: Black Rose Books, 1991.

———. *Rabotyagi: Perestroika and After Viewed from Below.* New York: Monthly Review Press, 1994.

McFaul, Michael, and Tova Perlmutter, eds. *Privatization, Conversion, and Enterprise Reform in Russia.* Boulder: Westview, 1995.

Meardi, Guglielmo. *Trade Union Activists, East and West.* Aldershot, U.K.: Gower, 2000.

Michnik, Adam. *Letters from Prison and Other Essays.* Berkeley: University of California Press, 1989.

Mishler, William, and Richard Rose. "Trust, Distrust, and Skepticism: Popular Evaluations of Civil and Political Institutions in Post-Communist Societies." *Journal of Politics* 59 (1997): 418–51.

Mitchell, Neil. "Theoretical and Empirical Issues in the Comparative Measurement of Union Power and Corporatism." *British Journal of Political Science* 26:3 (July 1996): 419–28.

Mizguireva, Tatiana. "Between Voice and Exit: National Response to the Crisis of Wage Arrears, Russia, 1992–2000." *Polish Sociological Review* 1331:1 (2001): 77–98.

Moody, Kim. *Workers in a Lean World*. London: Verso, 1997.

Mrost, Andrii. "Praktika raboty mezhdunarodnykh profsoiuznykh organizatsii i TNK." In *Profsoiuzy Moskvy v usloviiakh globalizatsii ekonomiki*. Moscow: Moscow Federation of Unions, 1999.

Naumov, V., and S. Tatarnikova. *Motivatsiia profsoiuznovo chlenestva*. Moscow: Moscow Federation of Trade Unions, 1996.

Nelson, Daniel. "Romania: Participatory Dynamics in 'Developed Socialism.'" In *Blue Collar Workers in Eastern Europe*, edited by Jan Triska and Charles Gati. London: George Allen and Unwin, 1981.

Neumann, Laszlo. "Circumventing Trade Unions in Hungary: Old and New Channels of Wage Bargaining." *European Journal of Industrial Relations* 3:2 (July 1997): 183–202.

———. "Privatisation As a Challenge for Hungarian Trade Unions." Paper presented to the Trade Unions and Industrial Relations in Central-Eastern Europe seminar, Berlin, March 1999.

Nott, Stephen. "The Shifting Position of Hungarian Trade Unions midst Social and Economic Reforms." *Soviet Studies* 39:1 (January 1987): 63–87.

O'Donnell, Guillermo. "On the State, Democratization, and Some Conceptual Problems: A Latin American View with Glances at Some Postcommunist Countries." *World Development* 21:8 (1993): 1355–69.

OECD. *OECD Economic Surveys, 2000–2001: Poland*. Paris: Organization for Economic Cooperation and Development, 2001.

———. *OECD Reviews of Foreign Direct Investment: Hungary*. Paris: Organization for Economic Cooperation and Development, 2000.

Offe, Claus. "Capitalism by Democratic Design? Democratic Theory Facing the Triple Transition in East Central Europe." *Social Research* 58:4 (Winter 1991): 865–902.

Orenstein, Mitchell. "The Czech Tripartite Council and Its Contribution to Social Peace." In *Parliaments and Organized Interests: Second Steps*, edited by Attila Agh and Gabriella Ilonszki. Budapest: Hungarian Centre for Democracy Studies, 1996.

Osa, Maryjane. "Contention and Democracy: Labor Protest in Poland, 1989–1993." *Communist and Post-Communist Studies* 31:1 (March 1998): 29–42.

Ost, David. "Illusory Corporatism in Eastern Europe: Neoliberal Tripartism and Postcommunist Class Identities." *Politics and Society* 28:4 (December 2000): 503–30.

———. "Labor Weakness Is No Condition for Success." *Polish Sociological Review*, 133:1 (2001): 45–49.

———. "Polish Labor before and after Solidarity." *International Labor and Working-Class History* 50 (Fall 1996): 29–43.

———. "The Politics of Interest in Post-Communist Europe." *Theory and Society* 22:4 (1993): 453–85.

———. *Solidarity and the Politics of Anti-Politics*. Philadelphia: Temple University Press, 1990.

———. "The Weakness of Strong Social Movements: Models of Unionism in the East European Context." *European Journal of Industrial Relations* 8:1 (March 2002): 33–53.

———. "The Weakness of Symbolic Strength: Labor and Union Identity in Poland,

1989–2000." In *Workers after Workers' States,* edited by Stephen Crowley and David Ost. Lanham, MD: Rowman and Littlefield, 2001.

Ost, David, and Stephen Crowley. "Making Sense of Labor Weakness in Postcommunism." In *Workers after Workers' States,* edited by Stephen Crowley and David Ost. Lanham, MD: Rowman and Littlefield, 2001.

———. "The Surprise of Labor Weakness in Postcommunist Society." In *Workers after Workers' States,* edited by Stephen Crowley and David Ost. Lanham, MD: Rowman and Littlefield, 2001.

Ost, David, and Marc Weinstein. "Unionists against Unions: Toward Hierarchical Management in Post-Communist Poland." *East European Politics and Societies* 13:1 (Winter 1999): 1–33.

Panków, Irena. "The Main Actors on the Political Scene in Poland." In *Parliaments and Organized Interests: Second Steps,* edited by Attila Agh and Gabriella Ilonszki. Budapest: Hungarian Centre for Democracy Studies, 1996.

Panków, Wlodzimierz. "Funkcje zwiazkow zwodowych w zakladach pracy." In *Rozpad Bastionu? Zwiazki zawodowe w gospodarce prywatyzowanej,* edited by Juliusz Gardawski et al. Warsaw: Institute of Public Affairs, 1999.

Panków, Wlodzimierz, and Barbara Gaciarz. "Industrial Relations in Poland: From Social Partnership to Enlightened Paternalism?" manuscript, no date.

Pataki, Judith. "Trade Unions' Role in Victory of Former Communists in Hungary." *RFE-RL Report* 3:26 (July 1994): 1–3.

Peetz, David. *Unions in a Contrary World: The Future of the Australian Trade Union Movement.* Cambridge: Cambridge University Press, 1998.

Peregudov, Sergei P. *Gruppy interecov i Rossiiskoe gosudarstvo.* Moscow: Editorial URSS, 1999.

Politychny portret Ukrainy 20. Kyiv: Democratic Initiatives, 1998.

Pollert, Anna. "Labor and Trade Unions in the Czech Republic, 1989–1999." In *Workers after Workers' States,* edited by Stephen Crowley and David Ost. Lanham, MD: Rowman and Littlefield, 2001.

———. "Trade Unionism in the Czech Republic." *Labor Focus on Eastern Europe* 55 (Autumn 1996): 6–37.

Pontusson, Jonas. "Explaining the Decline of European Social Democracy: The Role of Structural Economic Change." *World Politics* 47:4 (July 1995): 495–533.

Postolatij, V. V. "Sotsial'ne partnerstvo—pomylky, uroky, perspektyvy." *Suchasnyi profspilkobyi rukh v Ukrayiny.* Kyiv: Academy of Labor and Social Relations, 2000.

Pravda, Alex. "Political Attitudes and Activity." In *Blue Collar Workers in Eastern Europe,* edited by Jan Triska and Charles Gati. London: George Allen and Unwin, 1981.

Przeworski, Adam. *Democracy and the Market.* Cambridge: Cambridge University Press, 1991.

Przeworski, Adam, Michael Alvarez, José Antonio Cheibub, and Fernando Limongi. "What Makes Democracies Endure?" In *Consolidating the Third Wave Democracies,* edited by Larry Diamond. Baltimore: Johns Hopkins University Press, 1997.

Putnam, Robert. *Making Democracy Work.* Princeton: Princeton University Press, 1993.

Rainnie, Al, and Jane Hardy. "Desperately Seeking Capitalism: Solidarity and Polish Industrial Relations in the 1990s." *Industrial Relations Journal* 26:4 (1995): 267–79.

Rapacki, Ryszard. "Privatization in Poland: Performance, Problems, and Prospects." *Comparative Economic Studies* 37:3 (Fall 1995): 57–75.

Rau, Zbigniew, ed. *The Reemergence of Civil Society in Eastern Europe and the Soviet Union.* Boulder: Westview, 1991.

Rifkin, Jeremy. *The End of Work.* New York: Touchstone, 1994.

Rock, Charles. "Employment and Privatization in Bulgaria's Reform." Geneva: International Labour Organization, 1994.

Rodrik, Dani. *Has Globalization Gone Too Far?* Washington, DC: Institute for International Economics, 1997.

Rose, Richard. "A Decade of New Russia Barometer Surveys." Studies in Public Policy Paper No. 360, Centre for the Study of Public Policy, University of Strathclyde, 2002.

————. "A Divided Europe." *Journal of Democracy* 12:1 (2001): 93–106.

Rose, Richard, Stephen White, and Ian MacAllister. *How Russia Votes.* Chatnam, NJ: Chatnam House, 1997.

Ross, George, and Andrew Martin. "European Unions Face the Millennium." In *The Brave New World of European Labor,* edited by Andrew Martin and George Ross. New York: Berghahn Books, 1999.

Rothstein, Bo. "Labor Market Institutions and Working-Class Strength." In *Structuring Politics,* edited by Sven Steinmo et al. Cambridge: Cambridge University Press, 1992.

Ruble, Blair. *The Applicability of Corporatist Models to the Study of Soviet Politics.* Pittsburgh: Carl Beck Papers, 1983.

————. *Soviet Trade Unions: Their Development in the 1970s.* Cambridge: Cambridge University Press, 1981.

Rueschemeyer, Dietrich, Evelyne Huber, and John D. Stephens. *Capitalist Development and Democracy.* Chicago: University of Chicago Press, 1992.

Rupets, V. G. *Profsoiuzy i problemy demokratii v Rossii.* Moscow: Institute for Prospects and Problems of the Country, 1997.

Sachs, Jeffrey. *Poland's Jump to the Market Economy.* Cambridge: MIT Press, 1993.

Sakwa, Richard. *Postcommunism.* Philadelphia: Open University Press, 1999.

Schedler, A. "What Is Democratic Consolidation?" *Journal of Democracy* 9 (1998): 91–107.

Schliwa, R. "Enterprise Privatization and Employee Buy-Outs in Poland: An Analysis of the Process." International Labour Organization Working Paper IPPRED-2, 1996, updated 2000, available from ILO website at www.ilo.org/public/english/employment/ent/papers/ippred2.htm.

Schmitter, Philippe. "The Consolidation of Democracy and Representation of Social Groups." *American Behavioral Scientist* 35:3–4 (1992): 422–49.

————. "Corporatism Is Dead! Long Live Corporatism!" *Government and Opposition* 24:1 (1989): 54–73.

————. "Still the Century of Corporatism?" *Review of Politics* 36:1 (1974): 85–131.

Schmitter, Philippe, and Terry Lynn Karl. "The Conceptual Travels of Transitologists and Consolidologists: How Far East Should They Attempt to Go?" *Slavic Review* 53:1 (Spring 1994): 173–85.

————. "From an Iron Curtain to a Paper Curtain: Grounding Transitologists or Students of Postcommunism?" *Slavic Review* 54:4 (Winter 1995): 965–78.

Schmitter, Philippe, Guillermo O'Donnell, and Laurence Whitehead, eds. *Transitions from Authoritarian Rule*. Baltimore: Johns Hopkins University Press, 1986.

Schulten, T. "European Works Councils: Prospects for a New System of European Industrial Relations." *European Journal of Industrial Relations* 2:3 (1996): 303–24.

Schumpeter, Joseph A. *Capitalism, Socialism, and Democracy*. London: Allen and Unwin, 1976.

Seligman, Adam. *The Idea of Civil Society*. New York: Free Press, 1992.

Sewerynski, Michal. "Trade Unions in the Post-Communist Countries: Regulations, Problems, and Prospects." *Comparative Labor Law Journal* 16 (Winter 1995): 177–230.

Shmakov, Mikhail. "Profsoiuzy Rossii na poroge XXI veka." Moscow: Profizdat, 2000.

Silvia, Stephen. "The Social Charter of the European Community: A Defeat for European Labor." *Industrial and Labor Relations Review* 44:4 (July 1991): 626–43.

Simon, Rick. *Labour and Political Transformation in Russia and Ukraine*. London: Ashgate, 2000.

Solchanyk, Roman, ed. *Ukraine: From Chernobyl' to Sovereignty*. New York: St. Martin's, 1992.

Staniszkis, Jadwiga. *Poland's Self-Limiting Revolution*. Princeton: Princeton University Press, 1984.

Stark, David. "Recombinant Property in East European Capitalism." *American Journal of Sociology* 101:4 (1996): 993–1027.

Stark, David, and Laszlo Bruszt. *Postsocialist Pathways: Transforming Politics and Property in East Central Europe*. Cambridge: Cambridge University Press, 1998.

Stein, Jonathan. "Neocorporatism in Slovakia: Formalizing Labor Weakness in a (Re)democratizing State." In *Workers after Workers' States,* edited by Stephen Crowley and David Ost. Lanham, MD: Rowman and Littlefield, 2001.

Stone, Randall. *Lending Credibility: The International Monetary Fund and the Post-Communist Transition*. Princeton: Princeton University Press, 2002.

Strange, Susan. *The Retreat of the State: The Diffusion of Power in the World Economy*. Cambridge: Cambridge University Press, 1996.

Streeck, Wolfgang. "Neo-Corporatist Industrial Relations and the Economic Crisis in West Germany." In *Order and Conflict in Contemporary Capitalism,* edited by John Goldthorpe. Oxford: Oxford University Press, 1984.

Styrnyk, Inna. "Profspilky ta pryvatizatsiia." In *Suchasnyi profspilkobyi rukh v Ukrayiny*. Kyiv: Academy of Labor and Social Relations, 2000.

Suhij, Ivan, and Vladimir Lepekhin. "Evolution of Interest Representation and Development of Labour Relations in Russia." Working Paper, Moscow, Institute for Political Technologies, 1994.

Teague, Elizabeth. "Pluralism versus Corporatism: Government, Labor, and Business in the Russian Federation." In *In Search of Pluralism: Soviet and Post-Soviet Politics,* edited by Carol Saivetz and Anthony Jones. Boulder: Westview, 1994.

Thelen, Kathleen. "Beyond Corporatism: Toward a New Framework for the Study of Labor in Advanced Capitalism." *Comparative Politics* 27:1 (October 1994): 107–24.

———. "West European Labor in Transition: Sweden and Germany Compared." *World Politics* 46:1 (October 1993): 23–49.

Thirkell, J. E. M., K. Petrov, and S. A. Vickerstaff. *The Transformation of Labour Re-*

lations: Restructuring and Privatization in Eastern Europe and Russia. Oxford: Oxford University Press, 1998.

Thomas, Henk. "The Erosion of Trade Unions." In *Globalization and Third World Trade Unions: The Challenge of Rapid Economic Change,* edited by Henk Thomas. London: Zed Books, 1995.

Tilly, Charles. "Globalization Hurts Organized Labor." *International Labour and Working Class History* 47 (1995): 1–23.

Timko, Carol. "The 1992–93 Strike Wave and the Disorganization of Worker Interests in Poland." Paper presented at the 1996 Annual Meeting of the American Political Science Association, San Francisco, 1996.

Tiongson, Erwin. "Poland and IMF Conditionality Programs: 1990–1995." *East European Quarterly* 31 (March 1997): 55–68.

Tismaneanu, Vladimir. *Fantasies of Salvation.* Princeton: Princeton University Press, 1998.

———. *Reinventing Politics.* New York: Free Press, 1992.

Tocqueville, Alexis de. *Democracy in America.* New York: Alfred Knopf, 1951 [first published 1835].

Tóth, Andras. "Attempts to Reform a Workers' Movement without Mass Participation." In *Trade Unions in Europe,* edited by Jeremy Waddington and Reiner Hoffmann. Brussels: European Trade Union Institute, 2000.

———. "Building Union Organization at Autotransplants in Hungary." In *Globalization and Patterns of Labour Resistance,* edited by Jeremy Waddington. London: Mansell, 1999.

———. "The Failure of Social-Democratic Industrial Relations Model in Hungary." In *Workers after Workers' States,* edited by Stephen Crowley and David Ost. Lanham, MD: Rowman and Littlefield, 2001.

———. "Invention of Works Councils in Hungary." *European Journal of Industrial Relations* 3:2 (July 1997): 161–82.

———. *Labor Movements and Transition in Hungary from Socialism to Democracy.* Budapest: Central European University, 1994.

———. "The Role of Multi-Employer Collective Agreements in Regulating Terms and Conditions of Employment in Hungary." *Transfer* 3 (1997): 329–56.

Triska, Jan, and Charles Gati. *Blue Collar Workers in Eastern Europe.* London: George Allen and Unwin, 1981.

Turner, Lowell. *Democracy at Work: Changing World Markets and the Future of Labor Unions.* Ithaca: Cornell University Press, 1991.

Ulman, Lloyd, Barry Eichengreen, and William Dickens, eds. *Labor and an Integrated Europe.* Washington, DC: Brookings, 1993.

Valenzuela, Samuel. "Labor Movements in Transitions to Democracy: A Framework for Analysis." *Comparative Politics* 21:4 (July 1989): 445–72.

Waddington, Jeremy. "Situating Labour within the Globalization Debate." In *Globalization and Patterns of Labour Resistance,* edited by Jeremy Waddington. London: Mansell, 1999.

Wallerstein, Michael. "Union Growth in Advanced Industrial Democracies." *American Political Science Review* 83 (1989): 481–501.

Wedel, Janine. Collision and Collusion: The Strange Case of Western Aid to Eastern Europe, 1990–1997. New York: Palgrave Macmillan, 1998.

Weinstein, Marc. "From Co-Governance to Ungovernability: The Reconfiguration of Polish Industrial Relations, 1989–1993." In *The Comparative Political Economy of Industrial Relations,* edited by Kirsten Weaver and Lowell Turner. Madison, WI: Industrial Relations Research Association, 1995.

———. "Solidarity's Abandonment of Worker Councils: Redefining Employee Stakeholder Rights in Post-Socialist Poland." *British Journal of Industrial Relations* 38:1 (March 2000): 49–73.

Western, Bruce. *Between Class and Market: Postwar Unionization in the Capitalist Democracies.* Princeton: Princeton University Press, 1997.

Winter, Mary, Earl Morris, and Krystyna Gutkowska. "Polish Workers during Economic Transformation: Stability and Change, 1984–1994." *International Labour Review* 137:1 (1998): 61–80.

Zaslavsky, Viktor. *The Neo-Stalinist State: Class, Ethnicity, and Consensus in Soviet Society.* Armonk, NY: M. E. Sharpe, 1982.

INDEX